EVIL CORP

Allstate Insurance, Shadow Networks, and the Corruption of a Major American City.

First Edition

DENISE McVEA

AURIS PRESS
San Antonio
©2023

EVIL CORP

ALLSTATE INSURANCE, SHADOW NETWORKS, AND THE CORRUPTION OF A MAJOR AMERICAN CITY.

Copyright © 2023 by Denise McVea

ALL RIGHTS RESERVED. No part of this publication may be reproduced, distributed, or transmitted in any form or by any means, including photocopying, recording, or other electronic or mechanical methods without the prior written permission of the publisher except in the case of brief quotations embodied in critical reviews and certain other noncommercial uses permitted by law.

LIBRARY OF CONGRESS CONTROL NUMBER: 2021921703

FIRST EDITION

MCVEA, DENISE

Evil Corp: Allstate Insurance, Shadow Networks, and the Corruption of a Major American City. – Includes bibliographical references and index.

ISBN:
978-1-948955-36-2 (Hardcover)
978-1-948955-35-5 (Paperback)

Any illustrations, graphics and reproductions in this book are credited as they appear and are in the public domain or constitute fair use due to their brevity. Cover design copyrighted by Auris Project, Inc. Auris Press logos are trademarks or registered trademarks of the Auris Project, Inc.

For permission requests, write to Auris Press at publishing@aurisproject.org.

Evil Corp: Allstate Insurance, Shadow Networks, and the Corruption of a Major American City. True Crime. By Denise McVea. Auris Press, San Antonio, Texas. Copyright © 2023.

Auris Press is an enterprise of the Auris Project, Inc., a federally recognized 501c3 non-profit organization whose mission is to enhance marginalized communities' access to key rights and development information. All rights reserved.

EVIL CORP

CONTENTS

EVIL CORP	**III**
CONTENTS	**V**
PROLOGUE	**XIII**
THE SECURITY GUARD	XIII
THE MURDERER/ESCAPEE	XIV
THE DA	XIV
THE MAYORAL CANDIDATE	XV
THE FBI WIRETAPS	XVI
THE GENTRIFICATION JUGGERNAUT	XVII
INTRODUCTION	**XVIII**
THE WORST INSURANCE COMPANY IN AMERICA	XX
MUNICIPALITY AS CRIMINAL ENTERPRISE	XXIII
VENAL WHORES AND DOWNTRODDEN LOSERS	XXIII
1 | INTERSECTION	**1**
THE WRECK ON HILDEBRAND AND BLANCO	1
THE DIAGNOSIS	3
ALLSTATE'S GOOD HANDS	5
THE RESEARCH	7
2 | CREATION	**11**
THE BIRTH OF ALLSTATE INSURANCE COMPANY	11
THE SCIENTOLOGY SEMINAR	14
THE MCKINSEY ENGAGEMENT	18
ZERO SUM AND FAIR GAME	21
ALLSTATE V. CUSTOMERS	22
3 | ORIGIN	**24**
THE RUNAWAY WRITER	24
SAN ANTONIO DE BEJAR	35
4 | REGULARS	**38**

How to get rid of poor folks	38
The hallway hearings	41
"Keep your voice down."	43

5 | CIRCLING — 45

Bad neighborhood	45
From crack house to information center	46

6 | GLOVES — 49

McVea Deposition, *McVea v. Keller*	49
Accord and Satisfaction	53
The Unauthorized Practice of Law Committee	54

7 | ORCHESTRATION — 57

False arrest No. 1	57
"I am the police."	60
The FBI, part I: fidelity, bravery, integrity.	66

8 | IMPLEMENTATION — 69

The NASA engineer	69
McVea v. Keller, the trial	72
The Appeal	76

9 | MALICE — 78

False Arrest No. 2	78
How to get away with burglary	80
The search	84
The third burglary	86

10 | FAKERY — 90

The notary fraud	90
Kissler v. McVea and Ethics Follies	92
The forgery report	94
Dear Judge	97

11 | ERRORS — 99

False arrest No. 3	99
The billboard attorney	104

12 | COLLUSION — 107

The informant	107

THE KILLING OF MICHAEL OLIVER OTTEN	109
MCGINTY TRIES TO DROP A DIME	111
ALLSTATE'S KITCHEN SINK	114
THE TAX COLLECTOR	115
DARK TINTED WINDOWS	118

13 | KANGAROO — 119

DETECTIVE VAL GARCIA	119
MCVEA V. SWAN	119
THE SURVEILLANCE CAMERA	125

1 | OPPRESSION — 129

THE STATE OF TEXAS V. DENISE MCVEA	129
THE STATE ANNOUNCES READY	131
"LIKE MONKEYS ON A FENCE."	132
HOW TO GET AWAY WITH RAILROADING	136
A SUDDEN TRIP TO MEXICO	138
THE UNAVAILABLE "VICTIM"	140

15 | SHADOWS — 142

OPERATION SNOW WHITE	142
ALLSTATE AS PUPIL	147
THE "CHURCH" AT 315 S. OLIVE.	150
THE VAN	151

16 | IMPUNITY — 155

"WE GET A LOT OF THOSE PEOPLE IN HERE."	155
THE TEXAS CIVIL RIGHTS PROJECT	157
THE SUNSET COMMISSION	161
THE FBI, PART II: A STRUGGLING AGENCY	161
THE DESIRE TERRORIST	165

17 | DYSTOPIA — 168

THE GASLIGHTING OF AMERICA	168
COCKROACHES, GOONS, & ZEROS	170
CRIME FIGHTING, SAN ANTONIO STYLE	171
THE MAYOR'S POLICE FORUM	173
BURYING THE NUT AT THE *EXPRESS-NEWS*	175
THE ACTIVIST LAWYER	178

18 | SPECTACLE — 180

DEBATES, RESOLUTIONS, AND FRAUD	180
THE NAUGHTY TABLE	183
THE QUITCLAIM DEEDS AND WOODY WILSON	190
THE DISTRICT 2 TOWN HALL	191

19 | AUTHENTICITY — 193

THE DESCENDENT	193
A HARD "NO" ON JURY DUTY	195
THE URGENT CASE OF THE SERVICE DOG	199
WHAT'S GOING ON AT THE U.S. POST OFFICE?	201

20 | ATTENDANCE — 204

THE NEXT DA AND THE RESTAURATEUR	204
STAFF ATTORNEY'S OFFICE PART II	206
CATCHING COCKROACHES	210

21 | IMMUNITY — 216

THE GHOST OF BOBBY JOE PHILLIPS	216
THE FBI, PART III: A NEW REALITY	219
UNDER COLOR OF LAW	223

22 | REVELATION — 227

A NEW ERA	227
MY LAST TRIP TO THE FBI	228
THE KILLING OF KIRSTEN KLOPPE	229

23 | BIRDSEYE — 236

THE CITY ATTACKS 1006 WYOMING	236
A TALE OF TWO CITIES	241

CONCLUSION — 243

THE ZERO SUM GAME	243
ALLSTATE STRATEGIZES ITS SURVIVAL	245
MCKINSEY STILL CALLS THE SHOTS	249

PERP WALK — 252

OFFICER CHRISTIAN VALADEZ	252
ATTORNEY ELLIOT CAPPUCCIO	252
JUDGE MICHAEL MERY	253
JUDGE JOHN PRIMOMO	254
KRISTINA COMBS	255

NOTARY OFELIA LISA HERNANDEZ	255
ATTORNEY MARTIN PHIPPS	255
SGT. VAL GARCIA	257
JUDGE SCOTT ROBERTS	257
FORMER DISTRICT ATTORNEY NICO LAHOOD	257
EPILOGUE	**260**
THE SAN ANTONIO BARBECUE MURDER	260
ABOUT THE AUTHOR	**265**
INDEX	**267**
NOTES	**277**

*In memory
of
Monica Martin*

PROLOGUE

IT ALL SEEMED TO HAPPEN IN rapid succession.

There seemed to be something not quite right in San Antonio, a concerning series of strange occurrences with our police, local government, and courts that were not being fully explained.

The security guard

There was that summer night in 2018 when a Statewide Patrol security guard shot a man in front of his 11-year-old son. Nicholas Bosch was swimming in his apartment complex pool after hours when the guard ordered him out. Bosch complied, but somehow ended up shot dead just steps away from his apartment. Authorities offered several conflicting versions of events before officially resting on an account favorable to the guard. The final, official report stated that an argument between Bosch and the guard ensued and Bosch became "aggressive." The baby-faced security guard pepper sprayed and then shot Bosch three times in order to "defend himself." Bosch's son was not hurt in the incident, the sheriff's office added.

But family and neighbors told a different story. The boy did get pepper sprayed, they said, and had told relatives that his father was trying to protect him during the fight. Local TV news cameras captured local law enforcement officers consoling the killer. To date, neither the police nor the local news media have identified the guard by name. A man whose only crime was swimming at night was dead, and the people of San Antonio don't know the name of his killer.

The murderer/escapee

Then there was the baffling capital murder case of Luis Antonio Arroyo. On January 21, 2016, Arroyo, a purported drug trafficker, walked past several witnesses and began shooting and stabbing three drug acquaintances in the apartment complex where he lived.

The lone surviving victim, Tandylyn Jackson, called 911 as the assailant began murdering. While on the phone with police dispatch, Jackson called Arroyo by name and begged him to stop. He didn't. Jackson's daughter and childhood friend died. Jackson was stabbed.

Still, Arroyo's own defense attorneys stared at each other in shock and disbelief when the sequestered jury announced it could not agree to convict him. Despite the phone call. Despite the witnesses.

The judge declared a mistrial.

Arroyo would go on trial again, but not before managing a bold escape with two other killers from the Bexar County jail. The three inmates enjoyed 40 minutes of freedom before being recaptured while eating lunch at a Sonic fast food restaurant. There were other jailbreaks, and it started to look like escaping from the Bexar County jail was a very real possibility for an inmate with the right connections. Arroyo got 99 years for the escape attempt, but his second trial for the apartment murders ended in a full acquittal.

His lawyers couldn't believe their luck.

The DA

Then there was the election of Joe Gonzales as district attorney in 2018. The billboard defense attorney trounced incumbent DA Nico LaHood in the Democratic primaries and then handily beat the Republican nominee, a dignified attorney whose very name sounded like old money and unearned privileges.[1] Despite his record of representing pugilists and pedophiles, Gonzales' shadowy campaign apparatus cleverly painted Joe as a civil rights attorney. That strategy was so successful it led the progressive billionaire philanthropist George Soros to contribute nearly $1 million to his campaign.

Upon taking office, however, Joe quickly quashed his hastily built image of a civil rights champion when he appointed as his second-in-command the less-than-honorable lawyer Philip Kazen. Prior to being handed the deputy district attorney post by his old pal, Kazen was best known for his role in the unjust conviction of one of the now-famous San Antonio Four. Kazen had used junk medical "evidence," bizarre and easily discredited accusations, the unconvincing testimony of a spurned heterosexual man, and inflammatory appeals to jurors' collective homophobia to help hound four innocent lesbians into prison for nearly 15 years.[2]

Kazen's arguments during trial were a textbook example of how to inflame prejudice in a jury to garner a false conviction. Now, thanks to Joe Gonzales, he was the second most powerful government lawyer in Bexar County. He hardly managed an apology to his victim for arguably one of the biggest civil rights outrages in contemporary San Antonio history.

A few months into Joe Gonzales's tenure as district attorney, a 16-year-old girl killed her rival in a fight over a boy. Police arrested the killer but the district attorney soon dropped charges. Was it murder or self-defense? According to news reports, both girls flooded social media with threats and challenges. The killer, in fact, had starred in a video where she fist-fought another girl while at school.[3] On the day of the killing, the victim had shown up with a friend to confront her enemy. When the confrontation occurred, the accused pulled a knife and stabbed both her adversaries, killing one. Media reports – and the killer's own social media accounts – established that she had been a mutual combatant and a full participant in the physical confrontation that occurred. Her two adversaries, however, were reportedly unarmed.

Still, the DA's office under Joe Gonzales dropped the murder charges against the stabber. In media reports, the district attorney's office seemed to team up with the girl's defense attorney, excusing the murder based on unnamed, contradictory testimony that was not in evidence. Television news reports would later show the defendant, hands handcuffed in front of her, sauntering into the courtroom to hear that all charges against her had been dropped.

One young San Antonio woman had been stabbed to death, but there would be no evidence presented at trial and no public accounting for a homicide involving mutual combatants where one was armed and the other was not.

The mayoral candidate

Then there was the shady case of mayoral candidate Greg Brockhouse. One night in 2009, according to a police report, Brockhouse got drunk, held his wife down, and then tried to punch her. It was not the first time the former city council member had been accused of domestic violence. But later, sometime before Brockhouse announced his 2019 candidacy for mayor, an unnamed Bexar County judge ordered the police report hidden.

It was an unlawful order, but it allowed Brockhouse to pretend the incident never happened. And he did, for a time.

Someone in the police department, presumably irked by a local judge's attempt to deceive San Antonians, leaked the report to the *San Antonio Express-News*, the city's lone daily print newspaper. A firestorm ensued. Activists and journalists demanded Brockhouse explain himself. Brockhouse, furious and defiant, hemmed and hawed, huffed and puffed. The report was fake, he lied.

It was not a good look. When the report could no longer be denied, Brockhouse's wife stood before cameras and blamed the whole mess on *her* postpartum depression. But the damage had been done. Brockhouse, a mercurial former city councilmember with murky ties to the police and firefighters unions, lost the mayoral race by a few percentage points.

Later, the candidate who at first claimed there was no report would start a campaign to find out who in the San Antonio Police Department leaked it. He enlisted the help of his crony, SAPD police union president Michael Helle, whose connections to shadowy but deep-pocketed supporters have long bedeviled the city council. Helle began hassling SAPD internal affairs detectives, demanding they help Brockhouse locate the culprit who leaked the report. Internal affairs investigators balked, and police brass told both Helle and Brockhouse to take a hike. So did the voters. Brockhouse ran for mayor again a few years later, and lost a second time, this time by a much larger margin. San Antonians had made up their minds: they could not trust Greg Brockhouse.

The identity of the alleged SAPD whistleblower who leaked the hidden report remained a mystery. And the judge who unlawfully ordered the record hidden in the first place?

He remained a mystery, too.

The FBI wiretaps

Then there was the revelation that a federal task force was investigating public corruption in the Bexar County Courthouse. In early 2014, the U.S. Federal Bureau of Investigation sent hundreds of letters to lawyers, judges, administrators and others in the courthouse. The letters stated federal authorities had tapped their phones for three months in late 2013. Courthouse regulars were spooked.

The feds soon arrested a criminal defense lawyer and judge for a bribery scheme that entailed the judge issuing favorable court rulings to the lawyer in exchange for mechanic work on his aging Mercedes Benz sedan.

Upon conviction, the judge, Angus McGinty, and the lawyer, Alberto "Al" Acevedo, were stripped of their law licenses and toted off to prison to serve light sentences. During trial, McGinty raised a feeble defense that caused federal prosecutors to mock him mercilessly. Federal law, they pointed out sarcastically, does not provide for an "everybody's doing it" defense.

But the FBI, beset by a series of public scandals, political attacks, and internal struggles, went eerily silent.

The gentrification juggernaut

Then there was the rapid-fire gentrification of San Antonio's historically neglected inner city. Code enforcement inspectors began ordering a record number of folks to vacate their aging homes for the sole purpose of demolishing them, often without any due process. Swarms of investors and brokers quickly scooped up the properties. Almost magically, the swarm of outsiders was able to claim title to hundreds of old houses on the Eastside and Westside, experiencing none of the title transfer problems that title companies and lenders historically imposed on legitimate heirs of color.

At the same time, the two areas, historically black, brown, and poor, experienced a significant uptick in arson.

THE LOCAL NEWS OUTLETS REPORTED these troubling occurrences with the intensity of a metronome. City officials avoided addressing the cascade of odd events in public. Behind closed doors, however, there emerged in San Antonio a certain baffled insecurity, a niggling sense of growing alarm. Dangerous things were happening in city and county government that no one was explaining to San Antonians. Our protective institutions simply were not protecting many of us, while some folks seemed to be getting away with murder. It was as if some unseen malevolent force was nudging, poking, prodding, testing the seams of our social fabric – and finding them satisfyingly frayed.

It's time, I thought.

I can finally start talking about Allstate.

INTRODUCTION

Embezzlement: the fraudulent taking of personal property by someone to whom it was entrusted.[4]

THESE ARE THE FACTS:

IN the early 1990's, Allstate Insurance Company, known nationwide for its "You're in Good Hands" slogan, hired the McKinsey & Co. consulting firm to help the insurance company make better profits. Meeting with Allstate executives, McKinsey consultants drew up a daring game plan.

In the simplest of terms, the consultants showed Allstate how to embezzle money from its massive portfolio of 16 million customers by shaving off money from payouts on all claims filed.

To do this, McKinsey helped Allstate create mechanisms that methodically paid a lesser amount than the claims were worth. These systems had fancy names. There was the Colossus, a computer evaluation system used against motorists, and IntegriClaim, a similar system used against homeowners. Both systems accomplished the same task: produce, as a matter of course, lowball offers to settle its policyholders' insurance claims. If a claim was worth $15,000, let's say, Allstate might pay $5,000 or less, no exceptions. Make lowball offers on virtually every claim, McKinsey essentially advised, and watch the profits roll in!

Allstate executives loved the idea. They ran with it, and it worked. That single adjustment helped Allstate enjoy a windfall in profits. New Mexico attorney David Berardinelli crunched the numbers in his eye opening book, *From Good Hands to Boxing Gloves; The Dark Side of Insurance*.

The insurer's income increased more than 3000 percent.[5]

Thus began a decades-long campaign by one of America's largest insurers to do whatever it took to unlawfully keep as much of its customers' money as regulators and the courts would allow.

That turned out to be quite a lot.

Billions.

The only real snag, as McKinsey saw it, came from the policyholders themselves. The consultants suspected that not every customer would cooperate. Recognizing that people generally expect to get what they pay for – in this case a fair financial settlement to help recover from accidents and other insurable misfortunes – McKinsey helped Allstate adopt a policy that would reward customers who did not resist the theft and punish customers who complained. That policy needed to permeate the entire company, and executives would have to make sure everyone in the hierarchy stuck to it. It did and they did.

They called it the "Good Hands/Boxing Gloves" program.

In theory, it was surprisingly simple: if claimants accepted the theft, Allstate would treat them with "good hands," just like all the actors in Allstate TV commercials said they would. The agent would be nice, the adjustor supportive, and the (smaller) check cut right on time.

If, on the other hand, a customer balked, Allstate would use "boxing gloves." The conspirators devised surefire tactics to deal with resistant everyday Americans who would not lie down, a policy they dubbed: "delay, deny, defend." This, too, was a simple proposition: all Allstate had to do was make the claims process so nasty and unmanageable that the complaining customer would eventually give in and accept the lowball offer.

To frustrate policyholders, Allstate purposely delayed its claims process. It often denied valid claims or offered a lower amount than what the claim was worth. "In some cases," CNN reported, "Allstate proposed settlement amounts as small as $50, asking claimants to 'take it or leave it.' Insurance companies often make it so expensive and time-consuming to go to court to get full settlement amounts that it would not be worth the victims' time."[6]

It ruthlessly defended claims in court that it should have paid. It rewarded agents who routinely lied to customers, giving prizes to agents who kept payouts low.

This also worked like a charm. Allstate's payouts on its claims steadily dwindled from 79 percent in 1996 to just 58 percent by 2006.[7]

According to Jon Haber, CEO of the American Association for Justice, "Allstate ducks, bobs and weaves to avoid paying claims to increase its profits."

The insurance company had a name for that, too: the zero sum game. No compromise, all in, Allstate wins, customer loses, every time, no mercy.

Allstate deployed its army of private investigators and lawyers across the nation to squash troublesome customers in court, making it an unsound business practice for most small law firms to take on lawsuits against the insurer. Many Allstate customers, unable to get a lawyer, filed suit themselves. (In court parlance, these determined souls are "pro se litigants".) Allstate lawyers thrashed them.

Profits continued to roll in.

Executive compensation exploded.

The worst insurance company in America

Still, the mindless greed gripping Allstate executives blinded them to an important and inescapable fact: people don't like thieves.

Soon, evidence of Allstate's tarnished brand began surfacing all over the place. Numerous polls showed that Allstate customers were just not satisfied with the insurer. Although most journalists continued to give the company a pass, disgusted consumers flocked to support websites like http://www.allstateinsurancesucks.com. Complaints flooded state insurance departments. Regulators in some states began investigations. Crowds booed Allstate agents marching in parades. And for several years in a row, Allstate topped the Trial Lawyers Association's "Worst Insurance Companies in America" list.

Despite all of that, Allstate executives were committed to McKinsey's scheme, willing to do "whatever it takes." The company was losing customers and face but it was still making big money using the tactics that were destroying its reputation. Consumers might vilify Allstate at kitchen tables across America, especially in the homes of minorities and the poor, but the company still had legislators, journalists, and the courts. Yes, the company's anti-consumer tactics might incur the occasional fine from some regulators and judges, but those sanctions were like dropping pennies into the sea compared to the boatloads of money the scheme was hauling in.

Still, the company *was* losing customers. To preserve profits, Allstate Insurance Company found other ways to keep its customers' money.

The company created "complex and confusing" pricing schemes to keep its unlucky customers guessing as to exactly what they were paying for. This scheme made comparison shopping virtually impossible. Allstate also carefully chose language in its policies that would "hollow out" the protections it offered. For instance, Allstate – and other insurers – would use language that would cause a consumer to lose wind coverage if flood losses occurred, even if the wind losses came before the floods.

Allstate customers, relying on the assurances of Allstate agents, would often first learn they didn't have the expected coverage at precisely the moment they needed it.

"Consumers often think they are buying insurance, only to find they've bought a list of exclusions," J. Robert Hunter, director of insurance for the

Consumer Federation of America testified before the Senate judiciary committee. "Nowhere was this more apparent than after Hurricane Katrina."⁸

After Hurricane Katrina devastated the Gulf Coast in 2005, Allstate began dropping coverage for policyholders living in coastal areas.

Allstate often abandoned its remaining coastal customers to unclear government disaster programs on claims it should have paid. "We don't know who we're fighting," said Allstate customer Chuck Gill after the historic 2016 Louisiana floods. "We don't know if we're fighting FEMA, or we don't know if we're fighting Allstate...."

If customers seemed to get the short end of Allstate's zero sum stick, so did its agents. Allstate often made abrupt policy changes that ensured its agents would pay more of the company's expenses.

At every turn, it seemed, Allstate kept money that should have gone to someone else.

Despite all those efforts – or, indeed, because of them – Allstate's growth in the insurance market stalled. By 2021, it had dropped to fourth place in auto insurance, behind State Farm, Geico, and Progressive.

So, what does all of this have to do with San Antonio, Texas?

These are the allegations, based on certain facts:

With its reputation fraying, customers fleeing, market share dwindling and shareholders complaining, Allstate executives continued to "think outside the box." The Boxing Gloves program had been extremely lucrative, but it had also caused some debilitating, potentially fatal problems for the company. Yes, the insurer had helped weaken consumer protection laws and scared off hordes of lawyers from representing desperate consumers. But more could be done.

Under McKinsey's direction and blessed with its vast stores of ill-gotten resources, Allstate would set about refining a last ditch program that would ensure it could continue to post incredible profits – whether consumers liked it or not.

The new program had several objectives but two were most crucial. It would:

- Block consumers' access to fair courts, and
- Normalize and make routine this new consumer alienation.

(Sure, the scope of this alleged plan is staggering, but people tend to think anything is possible when they are sitting on mountains of other people's money.)

For this pilot program to work, the courts needed to reject consumers and their complaints against insurers *as a rule*. And, the press and other watchdogs would have to remain silent about the court's rejection. This, of course, would allow Allstate to continue a modified version of the Boxing Gloves program and still sell new policies.

The company mobilized its army of agents, adjustors, advisors, lawyers, contractors, private investigators, and private intelligence firms to carve out a place in the American landscape where neither the rules nor the law would stand in the way of its profits. Allstate executives, for reasons that will become obvious, began shifting attention, resources, and personnel to Texas.

Texas, well known for its conservative, pro-business, anti-regulation, good-old-boy approach to corporate misdeeds, would be the ideal place for Allstate and this new, necessary stage of its zero sum game. San Antonio had a long history of social inequities and often losing battles against corruption, nepotism, and graft. It would serve nicely as the location for Allstate's inventive, last ditch pilot program. The Bexar County Courthouse and other local government agencies – and the people who managed them – were central to the plan. If all went well, consumers would simply have nowhere to turn in a faceoff with Allstate.

By the time an inattentive motorist t-boned my car at a San Antonio intersection in 2009, Allstate's zero sum game program in San Antonio was well in play. At the time, I was a poor independent journalist and civil rights advocate settling back into her hometown of San Antonio after 10 years living in Mexico. When I began insisting on a fair settlement for my injuries, I unknowingly activated Allstate's infamous Boxing Gloves program. Representing myself, I sued Allstate for breach of contract.

Soon, private investigators began following me. At the writing of this book, twelve years after the wreck on Hildebrand and Blanco, Allstate operatives are still actively stalking me in addition to committing numerous other crimes. I didn't know it back in 2010, but I had become inescapably enmeshed in a critical stage of Allstate's zero sum game in San Antonio.

I fought back, first in court and then, literally, in the streets of San Antonio. Allstate's lawyers, arrogant and dismissive, at first thought I would be easily disposed of, another poor activist in over her head. And I was certainly that. But the company had missed something key: I was also a trained investigative journalist and an expert in public records. I knew where to look for documents they were accustomed to burying in government archives. I began collecting city and county records to explain what I was witnessing.

Municipality as criminal enterprise

It wasn't long before I had an amazing story to tell. It was a story about public corruption, official misconduct, abuse of power, obstruction of justice, and organized crime in Bexar County, Texas. And it wasn't just my word against theirs.

The records provided clear evidence of abusive, unlawful, and often criminal actions taken by local judges, cops, lawyers, politicians, and city and county administrators against local residents. In a few cases, the records revealed connections between corrupt officials and street level criminals preying openly on San Antonians. And disturbingly, the records revealed how government oversight agencies meant to protect citizens from criminal actors and corrupt officials had stopped functioning in San Antonio almost entirely. And always in the distance watching everything unfold was Allstate.

Belatedly, it dawned on Allstate's local collaborators that some of their conduct could come back to haunt them if exposed. Long before the Harvey Weinstein story exposed corporate use of private intelligence firms to cover up misdeeds, I was exposed to those very same tactics controlled by Allstate. But despite a constant barrage of abusive and criminal tactics heaped on me, I kept hanging around, kept asking questions, kept taking notes. I became a thorn, and then a threat, and then a massive problem for Allstate and the local people doing its bidding. Eventually, I became the central target of a widespread cover-up.

I documented that, too.

Over time, it all made sense. I had against all odds cracked the case. Covert operatives in Allstate's zero sum game were masterfully exploiting - and expanding - preexisting white-collar criminal networks already operating in San Antonio. I couldn't believe my luck.

Good and bad.

Venal whores and downtrodden losers

In part, this book is about the burgeoning class of corrupt citizens willing to help villains prey on vulnerable communities. This book will discuss who they are, what positions of power some of them occupy, what places of trust they hold in our communities, and what they are willing to do for actors like Allstate.

"What do you need?" covert operatives prowling San Antonio streets reportedly asked their recruits. "What can we do for you?"

I learned the names and faces of many of the people who answered those questions. I was able to track many participants to all sorts of illegal schemes: title fraud, drug trafficking, money laundering, abuse of power, judicial misconduct, consumer fraud, and other crimes. I learned a lot. And the more I learned the more vicious Allstate's response.

This was a harrowing, stressful, disheartening era. Yes, it was nightmarish, but as an investigative journalist and human rights activist, I couldn't help but see that I had been handed a rare opportunity to expose at least some of the hidden powers undermining American society. By the time I started writing the book in earnest, I had gotten a very good look. I saw firsthand how hidden criminal networks turned people against their own communities, institutions, and employers, often funded by money stolen from those very communities.

Allstate collaborators spanned the socio-economic spectrum, from judges to the petty con. But the most valuable assets, I would learn, were middle managers. Installed in both public and private organizations, managers act as gatekeepers. Hardly anyone had more power to disenfranchise more citizens than corrupted employees who had been promoted to a middle management position. They have the ability to modify the official record, recruit, hire, corrupt, and manage underlings, undermine and deceive leadership, reject applications and complaints, promote personalities who would do anything for cash, and hijack resources from the companies and agencies for which they nominally work.

But knowing the story and telling the story are two very distinct things. The constant attacks from Allstate conspirators began to take a toll. By 2017, Allstate and corrupt local authorities had falsely arrested me three times, maliciously prosecuted me twice, facilitated physical assaults against me, and robbed me of nearly a quarter million dollars in assets. SAPD cops facilitated constant attacks on me, my home, and my family. Thanks to constant hacking, my phones and the phones of my friends and family members had become GPS trackers and microphones. Judges provided legal cover for criminal acts meant to silence me. (In one bizarre contrast, police arrested and jailed me for allegedly having a garage sale without a permit but only ticketed and released a habitual violent offender who assaulted me with a tree branch near my home.)

It took a toll. Eventually, I couldn't explain what was happening to me without experiencing a panic attack. Allstate had bet the bank on their operatives' ability to heap on me so many traumas that folks would dismiss any accusation I might lodge as the delusional rant of a hopelessly paranoid woman.

Indeed, during the height of the oppression, many SAPD police officers and co-conspirators flooded court and police records with repeated suggestions that I was not only delusional, but violently psychotic as well. By the time the Black Lives Matter movement began exposing the system of lies used by police and local officials to cover up criminal and often deadly police misconduct, corrupt SAPD officers had spent years flooding police records with falsehoods and strategic omissions. By wrecking my credibility, conspirators could plot a course of plausible deniability.[9]

That gambit failed.

I went back to my investigative journalism roots, concentrating on gathering and securing evidence. I began making my own, legal recordings, and those files directly contradicted the narrative Allstate and its collaborators were working to construct. I dedicated thousands of hours to retrieving, organizing, duplicating and securing records and other evidence. I wrote dozens of public information act requests (many were ignored), dug up fraudulent documents that Allstate conspirators buried in clerk's offices, and hired forensic experts that exposed the extent to which the public record was being tainted. Much to my attackers' dismay, I learned how to track down the identities of key Allstate operatives and documented them breaking the law with impunity.

As I learned more, I began devising my own tactics to deny Allstate access to my data. Over time, I learned enough about cyber security to secure and encrypt my network and devices from constant cyberattacks. I began reconnecting securely with people online. I learned to recognize phishing attacks. I used forensic tools to recover hundreds of gigabytes of data I thought lost forever. I obsessively backed up and duplicated my data. I learned how to go "ghost" on the internet, evading the potent social engineering, denial of service, and man-in-the-middle attacks meant to keep me isolated.

There was never any doubt that I would lose my fender bender case against Allstate. And that is the irony of the entire saga. The initial objectives had been met, but the corporation's arrogant, overconfident proxies had left so much harmful evidence lying around that the company would end up having to spend millions to silence me.

That effort also failed.

Allstate is not responsible for every outrage you read in this book. However, the fact remains that Allstate Insurance Company is much more than your average irresponsible corporation.

It is, according to all available evidence, the personification of Evil Corp.

1 | INTERSECTION

The Wreck on Hildebrand and Blanco

IT WASN'T EVEN MY OWN car I was driving. It belonged to my girlfriend, a sporty little black 1999 Nissan that she loved. I had borrowed it because my truck was in the shop.

The wreck that changed everything happened like this:

It was January 21, 2009. I was driving West on Hildebrand making a left turn south onto Blanco. It was a typical San Antonio intersection: a Valero gas station on one corner, a Bill Miller's barbeque restaurant on another and a few small businesses on the other two. There was foot traffic, too, and a bus stop.

It was a bright and sunny day.

As I was making the turn, I saw him. He was a thin, middle-aged man in an old, faded Pinto driving north on Blanco. Then he suddenly decided to go west on Hildebrand. I first noticed him while I was mid-turn when he pulled from behind a northbound car to zip into the left turn lane. Something at the Valero on his left immediately caught his interest. He stared at it. He didn't slow down to rubberneck but barreled straight towards me.

"Sir," I said to his profile. "Sir!"

Then he hit me. I felt my body torque and my head hit the driver's side door. I was wearing a seatbelt but I must have briefly passed out because the next thing I remember, the man who was in the Pinto was now standing outside my door, beating on the driver side window, yelling urgently. "Get up! Get up!"

It took me a minute, but the fog slowly lifted. I got out of the car. I was shaken, wobbly, weak. The man was saying something. He was agitated and acting guilty. My head started clearing up. "You came out of nowhere," he was repeating. "Where did you come from?"

"I was right in front of you," I managed.

We were still in the middle of the road. I looked down and saw a gash of crushed and jagged metal in the driver side door where he had struck me. It was a bad hit.

An ambulance appeared, then a cop car. The man was talking animatedly to the cop, being very persuasive. The cop was nodding in sympathy. I heard him say it again: I had come out of nowhere.

When the cop came to talk to me, I told him that the man was looking to his left when he struck me. He did not write that down. He asked me to move the car out of the middle of the street. I pulled it into the gas station. At some point, a paramedic walked me to the ambulance. I remember stepping up and inside, but don't remember what examination, if any, he performed. He asked me if I needed transport. I told him no, that my home, an old Victorian we were renting on Mulberry Street in Beacon Hill, was just a few blocks away. Tedi's car, although surely totaled, was still running. I could drive home.

The cop approached. He took my contact information and Allstate insurance card and gave me the other driver's information. The driver's name was James Keller. He was 50 years old and a hospice nurse. He also had Allstate insurance.

I got home, took some ibuprofen, and went to bed. My sister Rene came to check on me.

"You look like shit," she said. "You should go to the emergency room."

"I'm just a little sore," I said, "I'll be okay."

"You won't be saying that tomorrow," she said.

She was right.

The next morning, I could not move my neck. My head hurt. My body felt like it had been in a wreck. My left arm was numb, then throbbing, then numb again. I remember being very worried. Something felt serious. I felt like I had some sort of spinal injury. Tedi, my girlfriend, rummaged in the medicine cabinet for some old painkillers and found some codeine. "Here take this," she instructed. A few minutes later, I did feel much better.

"You need to go to the hospital," Tedi said. "I'll take you."

"I'm sorry about your car," I said.

"Let's just get you looked at."

In the car, I apologized again. "This sucks," I said.

"Don't worry," she said.

She explained that her mother, an insurance agent, had been insuring the Nissan through Allstate for years. "Mom keeps good insurance. She makes sure to include medical coverage."

I made a lame joke. "Oh, so, I'm in good hands?" I asked, invoking Allstate's ubiquitous advertising slogan.

She played along. "You are in good hands."

I had no reason to disbelieve her.

The diagnosis

The first thing you notice in the emergency room after a bad wreck is how hard and unyielding the chairs are. I tried to get comfortable, shifting here, there. Fox News blasted on the wall-mounted television screen, adding to my distress. When the nurse called me into the examination room, I explained that my left arm was in pain, my neck was sore, and that I had a headache. The doctor examined me. He placed my throbbing arm in a brace, prescribed painkillers, and gave me a referral to an orthopedic surgeon. He told me that I had several contusions from the impact. I also may have injured my cervix, he said. That was probably the cause of my headaches. He explained to me that while I may be feeling poorly now, I could expect the symptoms to get much worse.

Several days later, I sat in the expansive and well-appointed waiting room of the San Antonio Orthopaedic Group waiting to see one of the group's neck specialists, Dr. Frank Kuwamura. The waiting room teemed with assorted broken people using all sorts of supports: wheelchairs, braces, slings, crutches. I waited for four hours before getting x-rays of my neck and arm. Fox News blared on these television monitors too, further demoralizing me. Finally I found myself in an examination room. Dr. Kuwamura popped in, a slim, earnest orthopedic surgeon in his late 30s. Energetic and efficient, he spoke with a trace of a vague accent. He told me that he had looked over my x-rays. That was the first time I learned that I had spinal compression in my cervix, the portion of the spine located in the neck. I didn't have a lot of cartilage between the spinal disks in my neck, he informed me. That cartilage, he informed me, had been absent before the accident. Folks in the insurance industry call that a preexisting condition.

Dr. Kuwamura explained that I didn't know I had a problem with my cervix because the condition had been asymptomatic. The wreck, he explained, aggravated the condition. I asked him if my cervix problem is why I passed out. He said the impact, the neck snapping, would have been enough to cause me to black out temporarily. The continued headaches, though, were most likely a symptom of the cervix injury.

The good news, he said, was that there were no broken bones in my arm. It should start to feel better within a few weeks. The spinal injury, however, was another story. These types of injuries, he explained, were famously slow to heal. It could take months, perhaps years, for me to recover fully, he said. He referred me to a physical therapist.

I asked him to write a report that I could submit to my insurance company.

"No problem," he said.

As he typed, we chatted about this and that. After hearing a few offhand comments about his business manager and accountant, contemplating the dozens of patients cycling through the orthopedic group's waiting room, and remembering the hours-long wait to be seen, I left the clinic with the distinct impression that I had just met a young man who was well on his way to becoming a millionaire.

As Kuwamura predicted, the neck injury was slow to heal. Neck pain nagged me from the moment I woke up until the moment I took to bed. Often, the pain would wake me up in the middle of the night. I saw Dr. Kuwamura a couple of times in search of relief; he eventually referred me to a pain management surgeon, Dr. Ellen Duncan. Dr. Duncan specialized in epidurals. I began getting steroid shots between the disks in my upper neck and they mightily relieved the pain for three to six months. Then the pain would start up again and I would have to make an appointment with Dr. Duncan.

During all of this, I called Allstate to make a medical claim. At first, things went smoothly. Teresa, who held the policy on the wrecked Nissan, was herself an insurance agent who knew the ends and outs of claims. She explained the policy in detail. The policy had two products, she explained, one for medical expenses and one for personal injury. The policy limit for the medical was $5000. The other was up to $10,000. She called that PIP and MedPay.

Soon I was getting calls from several Allstate insurance agents, but none seemed to know what the policy was worth and how I was going to get my mounting medical bills paid. It wasn't long before it became impossible to know which agent was representing me and which agent was representing James Keller, the motorist who struck me. One day, an Allstate agent would request medical bills; the next day, another Allstate agent would ask for the same bills. Then an adjuster would call, asking for the same documents I had already twice submitted. Then a manager would call asking for the same thing.

This organized chaos went on for several months. Suffering from headaches and unrelenting neck pain, I became increasingly annoyed and frustrated. I would consult with Teresa Butolph, who had been selling insurance for more than 15 years. A retiring woman, she couldn't explain the vagaries and prevarications that were defining my insurance claim with Allstate.

I began doing internet research on how to negotiate with insurance companies. That was the first time I heard about Allstate's tactic of delaying payment on a claim in order to wear down a claimant to the point where he would accept a lowball offer. When I told the agents I knew what they were doing, they laughed.

I could tell that my increasing annoyance and frustration satisfied the Allstate employees, so I asked them what it would take to get them out of my life.

They offered a payout of $2600 and payment of all my medical bills.

I immediately saw that as a problem. How was Allstate proposing to pay for future medical bills?

"Send us the bills that you already have," the agent told me, "and we will set up a direct payment with your care providers. They will send bills directly to us and we will pay them. You don't have to worry about them."

That didn't sound right, but I knew little about insurance practices. In my earlier wreck, the other insurance company had me sign a settlement contract where I waived any future claims when it sent me a check. I determined to read Allstate's settlement agreement very carefully to make sure I didn't waive any future medical payments.

When the $2600 Allstate check came in the mail, no settlement contract accompanied it.

Oh, I thought, the agent must have been telling the truth.

Allstate's Good Hands

When the medical bills started coming back unpaid, I called Allstate. The Allstate customer service representative told me that, according to Allstate records, the company had settled the claim for $2600. That check didn't include medical bills, I told her. According to her records, she corrected me, it did. I balked; that was not what the agent had told me. Thus began another round of useless phone calls and wasted conversations.

"Sue me," said Teresa, the Allstate policyholder for the car I was driving during the accident. "At least you can get the $5000 from MedPay. I've been paying on that policy for years."

When I called to ask about the MedPay policy, Allstate agents said they didn't know anything about that.

I began doing research on the internet, and, encouragingly, found the Texas Deceptive Trade Practices Act on the Texas Attorney General website.

"The primary tool the Office of the Attorney General uses to protect Texas consumers is the Deceptive Trade Practices Act (DTPA)," the AG website explained. "This law lists many practices that are false, deceptive, or misleading." The AG site explained that if a consumer sued a misbehaving company and won under the deceptive trade practices act, he could win three times the amount of judgment.

One section of the law contained a laundry list of 25 practices that under the law are deceptive and illegal. Through its vile Boxing Gloves program, Allstate had violated nearly all of them.

With a law like that on the books, I thought, I had a solid case against Allstate.

I began calling personal injury lawyers in San Antonio. I couldn't say what most of their offices looked like because I never made it past the initial phone call. Immediately upon taking the call, the lawyer would begin asking a series of questions about the policy. "That's not a very big policy," said the first and second lawyer. The policy, they told me, was not big enough to make me whole *and* pay my lawyer. They declined to represent me. It just wasn't worth their time. When I called the third lawyer, I tried to preempt his financial calculations by immediately invoking the Texas Deceptive Trade Practices Act. Quickly, I embarked on a rapid-fire discussion of all the ways Allstate was violating it.

My speech gained me no traction at all. Still, the lawyer was sympathetic. "Here's what you are facing," he told me. "Allstate will bury your lawyers in paper work; they will drag out the case for years. That's why you can't find anyone to represent you. They make it impossible for a lawyer to make a living and still take these kinds of cases. I'm sorry, but the only way you are going to be able to sue Allstate is if you sue them yourself."

Sue them myself.

That's how it all started.

Sue Allstate myself. That wasn't a terrible idea. I had acted as a lawyer myself before in court, with varying degrees of success. Once, a slumlord sued me for libel. I won that case. Another time, I sued a Texas historian and some librarians for libel. I lost that case. So I knew what it took to go to court without a lawyer. It was a stressful, solitary endeavor, I knew, and very time-consuming. But I also knew that even when I didn't win in court, I was able to get information from my opponents through the court's discovery process that, it turns out, is sometimes the only way on earth to get it.[10] Being an investigative journalist at my core, I could count those losses as partial wins. I got some good info through the court's discovery process.

A germ of an idea began forming in my head. Maybe I should sue them. I could take what I learn about court processes and rules and put it in a guide book for pro se litigants. It was certainly a growing market.

I started doing research on the internet about Allstate, insurance law, and people who represented themselves.

It was a wakeup call.

The research

By the time I turned off my computer in the rented house on Mulberry Street in 2009, I knew that the American judicial system was failing. Allstate, it would later become clear, knew it, too.

Allstate had earned a reputation for being the worst insurance company in the United States. According to the American Association for Justice, a nonprofit advocacy and lobbying group that includes many consumer lawyers, outlined in stark terms Allstate's crimes against American consumers. I read consumer watchdog websites with growing alarm.

The more I read, the more I understood the system I was about to enter.

My experiences, it turned out, were not unique. The Allstate agents running me in circles were not rogue actors running amok. They were dedicated employees faithfully following rules set by Allstate executives. Seeing Allstate's amazing profits, State Farm and other insurers reportedly copied at least some of Allstate's tactics. Several insurance companies, emboldened by weak or nonexistent consumer protection enforcement, were avidly selling insurance policies that they had no intention of honoring. Allstate remained at the head of the pack.

Allstate customers flocked to consumer complaint sites to voice their outrage. "We have been with Allstate for over 40 years," complained one Maryland policyholder. "My roof sustained wind damage, along with four other homes on my street. Allstate was the only insurance company that would not pay and we had the most damage! USAA, State Farm, they all treated their policyholders respectfully. When I finally spoke with someone from Allstate, I was greeted with sarcasm and a total lack of knowledge. I have worked with the public for many years, and I would never have treated a loyal policyholder as I was treated. Shame on Allstate! I will be changing insurance companies as loyalty means nothing to Allstate."[11]

Unbeknownst to the homeowner, she was one of millions. Allstate chugged on with its lucrative zero sum game against its own customers.

But how could the courts let this happen? I began typing search terms in Google: civil courts, self-representation in Texas, consumer law, courtroom procedure.

That research was also a wake-up call.

American courts, I learned, were similar to American newspapers. They were both running unsustainable enterprises. The minimum wage for Americans at the time was around $12 an hour. Lawyers charged $100 to $200 an hour. The economics of law as practiced in America guaranteed that most civil plaintiffs just would not be able to afford a lawyer. But it wasn't just about the money.

Despite the costly price tag, many lawyers couldn't be trusted. In Texas, virtually nothing existed to stop lawyers who abused or defrauded their clients. Take, for instance, the State Bar of Texas. A quasi-governmental association, the state bar was the sole agency responsible for oversight of lawyers. But the bar is highly incestuous. Run by its own members, the bar, by design, fails miserably at protecting citizens from lawyers.

If a complaint against a crooked lawyer made the nightly news, the chance the state bar would investigate substantially improved. In fact, media coverage seemed to be the state bar's primary test to determine if it would investigate lawyer misconduct. The Texas Judicial Commission, responsible for oversight of judges, took the same tack. If a news organization reported judicial misconduct, the commission would investigate.

But crooked lawyers and judges knew that just a tiny fraction of legal misconduct made the news.

The state bar had a simple process for handling the thousands of complaints it received. The agency would send out a form letter acknowledging receipt of the complaint. A few weeks later, the agency would announce that the investigation – usually conducted by local investigators and panels of lawyers where the wrongdoing occurred – found no misconduct. The complainant would be reminded that state bar proceedings were confidential and the case would be closed.

The judicial commission managed complaints against judges essentially the same way: a cursory investigation by pals of the offenders, routine absolution, everything confidential.

These policies emboldened corrupt and misbehaving judges and lawyers and severely damaged public perception of both.

Over time, the lawyer brand became thoroughly debased, fraught with exploitation and mistrust. Despite the "one who represents himself has a fool for a client" axiom, citizens became convinced that their chances in court were better without an attorney. The courts use Latin terms to describe these litigants: pro se, or propia persona, "one who represents himself."

As it turned out, more than half of Americans suing in civil court in 2009 were going to court without a lawyer. In some jurisdictions, a whopping 85 percent of civil plaintiffs represented themselves.[12] The courts reacted to this flood of aggrieved but unrepresented citizens with impatience, frustration, and in many cases, unbridled hostility.

I felt a surging sense of respect and admiration for the thousands of faceless Americans trying on their own to get a measure of justice from the very judicial system that refused to protect them. In Bexar County, the reception was unapologetically antagonistic. Somewhere along the line, many judges and lawyers in Bexar County had come to view Americans expecting to have free and informed access to the judicial system without a lawyer as a nuisance.

Poor, unrepresented citizens were a pain, yes, but as luck would have it, these citizens were also powerless. Judges in Bexar County – *as a policy* – routinely oppressed poor people coming to court without a lawyer.

The question wasn't *why* they treated citizens this way. The question was: what's to stop them? The answer was obvious:

Nothing, really.

It looked like Allstate had at its disposal at least one foolproof tool in its quest to keep its customers' money: the American court system.

I had made up my mind. I would sue Allstate. I would not stop, I determined naively, until the company had paid the full measure of my legitimate claim.

Even if I didn't win, the exercise could be valuable. I could use the lawsuit to learn the civil legal process and write a guidebook on how people without lawyers could navigate the courtroom. The book would detail every stage of the pretrial process I encountered and explain what I learned about it. I envisioned the book as an educational tool for all people seeking justice in the American civil courts as their own advocate. I would title the book *Pro Se Nation*.

When I informed my friends and family that I had decided to sue Allstate *pro se* and write a guidebook about my experiences, looks of weary resignation crossed their faces. I knew my reputation. It seemed that every couple of years I would announce that I had decided to fight some impossibly powerful entity engaged in some unjust activity against the powerless. There was the Immigration and Naturalization Service in Portland, Oregon, the Urban Rehabilitation Standards Board in Dallas and the white male historian cabal across Texas, among others. All of these projects turned into knockout, drag-out fights, and my loved ones watched helplessly as they each took a measurable toll on me.

Still, I was proud of the outcomes. As a poor black woman daring to challenge the entrenched, well-funded white male power structure, I had learned that even the most powerful adversary had inherent weaknesses. I knew that my opponents would think that I could be easily disposed of and that assumption would make them careless. When you're careless, you make mistakes. When you're arrogant, you go all in when you should probably hedge your bets.

I hold to what I called the "alley cat" method of resistance: win or lose, everyone limps away bloodied. When you belong to a disadvantaged, discounted class, leaving marks on your more powerful opponents can be very rewarding, a victory unto itself. It was a given: my richer, more powerful opponents were certain to underestimate me and I, for one, was grateful for that bias. It was the only real advantage I had.

I made a pledge to myself: I would stick with it, no matter what Allstate threw my way. I mean, they couldn't kill me, right?

I had always been that way, a fierce advocate for my class, someone incapable of walking away from injustice once witnessed and who lacked the fear gene that kept sensible folks in my circumstances away from such ill-advised, lopsided fights.

"Here's your problem, Nisey," my sister Jacquie once told me with a sigh, "You don't pick your fights. You let your fights pick you."

2 | CREATION

The Birth of Allstate Insurance Company

IN THE SPRING OF 1730, Philadelphia's Fishbourne Wharf caught fire. A fierce and fast-moving blaze, it quickly became too much for the city's single fire engine. At the time, fire engines were primitive contraptions that consisted of a wooden cart with a hand pump that connected to a water barrel and a hose.

The fire quickly consumed several homes and businesses and threatened to burn down the whole city before it was finally doused.[13] Afterwards, shaken city officials began thinking earnestly about ways to prevent and quickly put out fires. They started investing in more engines, ladders, and buckets.

The fire also troubled Benjamin Franklin, the American inventor and statesman. At that time the young editor of the local *Gazette* newspaper, Franklin began writing columns about fire prevention. In his columns, he harped on residents to be more careful with the coals they used to heat their homes. Some say Franklin created the nation's first fire brigade.

He also created the Philadelphia Contributionship, the first organization in the American colonies to provide fire insurance. Each member of the group agreed to pay a certain amount annually into a till to insure against fire. If any of the members' properties caught fire, they could count on funds in the till to help recover. Citizens saw the value in such protection. The Philadelphia Contributionship issued 143 policies. None of the members' property caught fire, and so the group eventually disbanded.

Still, Franklin continued to promote insurance as a surefire way for Americans to protect their assets. Insurance policies, he contended, could offer protections for crops, death, widows, and even orphans.

More than 100 years later, Gilbert J. Loomis of Dayton, Ohio bought the first automotive liability insurance policy. The policy protected Loomis if his car damaged property or injured or killed someone. From there, the insurance industry slowly began to take shape. By 1902, Americans could also buy fire and theft insurance for their automobiles. Before long, insurance companies began combining property, liability and fire coverage for cars and homes in a single policy.

Insurance policies have evolved since the Philadelphia Contributionship, but the basic principles behind the policies are essentially the same. Simply put, insurance protects consumers from financial losses in case of unforeseen misfortunes.

It also turned out to be a proven, sustainable, lucrative business. Today, the U.S. insurance industry collects more than $1 trillion dollars a year and controls more than $3 trillion in assets. Only two countries in the world, the U.S. and Japan, report more in gross domestic product.[14]

Insurance companies, however, are different from other corporations and businesses in crucial ways. Because they have a protective role in the lives of ordinary citizens, they must follow stricter ethics rules and standards than other corporations.

Theoretically.

ALLSTATE FIRST ENTERED THE AMERICAN CONSCIOUSNESS as a tire brand created by Sears Roebuck & Company in 1925. To stir up interest, the American retailer held a national contest, inviting consumers to give the new tire brand a name. It was a wildly successful marketing campaign: more than ten million submissions flooded the company from across the nation.

The winning submission was "Allstate." The company adopted the trademark the following year. The tires went on to sell handily in both the Sears catalog and retail stores. Company chairman Robert E. Wood was thrilled with Allstate Tires' success.

The idea for Allstate Insurance Company came on a commuter train five years later. Wood and his neighbor Carl L. Odell were playing bridge in their seats to pass the time when Odell, an ambitious insurance broker, shared what he thought was a great idea.

What did the Sears chairman think, Odell asked, about Sears selling auto insurance through the mail? The idea intrigued Wood. The automobile was fast becoming a mainstay of American life. The Depression wouldn't last forever and an automobile insurance company could help Sears offer more services to the public, thereby improving the company's bottom line. Sears had been mass mailing its catalogue for nearly 40 years. Adding car insurance to the company's direct mail system would not be reinventing the proverbial wheel. Woods thought it could work, but he needed to be sure. He commissioned an exhaustive study on insurance issues. When the report came back, he liked what he saw. He proposed the idea to the Sears board of directors. The board quickly approved financing for the newfangled insurance company to the tune of $700,000.

Odell's big idea that day on the train paid him professional dividends. The board named him the new company's first vice president and secretary.

Sears executives decided to name the new insurance company after their signature tire brand. Sears launched Allstate Insurance Company on April 17, 1931, offering auto insurance through the Sears catalog and direct mail.

A month later, William Lehnertz, a tool and die maker from Aurora, IL, became Allstate's first policyholder when he paid $41.60 for a 12-month policy to insure his 1930 Studebaker. Other car owners followed suit. That same year, Allstate paid its first claim on the spot when it reimbursed the cost of replacing a car door handle that thieves had jimmied off and stolen.

By year's end, Allstate had 4,217 policies in force, a premium volume of $118,323 and 20 employees. Richard Roskam became Allstate's first agent when he set up a card table in the Sears exhibit at the 1933 Chicago World's Fair. Fairgoers swamped him with applications. A year later, Allstate opened its first sales location in a Chicago Sears store. By 1937, Allstate had hired its first full-time salaried claims adjuster. Two years later, it revolutionized the insurance industry by charging consumers depending on their age and how much they drove their car.

From that auspicious start, Allstate grew rapidly. For decades, it remained an innovative leader in the insurance industry. It was the first company to offer better insurance rates to safe drivers. Other insurance companies began adopting Allstate's innovations. Now an industry leader, Allstate began looking at expanding its offerings to include life, health and commercial insurance.

By 1949, Allstate had moved its headquarters to Chicago's affluent North Side. A year later, a general sales manager created the company's enduring "You're In Good Hands with Allstate" slogan.

The rapidly growing company also needed a logo. Allstate managers started an in-house contest, ginning up participation by telling employees that whoever could come up with the best logo would win a cash prize. Allstate employee Theodore Conterio won the contest with an attractive sketch of a pair of hands cradling a car. That drawing would serve as the foundation for Allstate's ubiquitous "Good Hands" logo now recognized by millions of people worldwide. Conterio won $50.

In 1952, Allstate began to offer personal liability insurance. Around the same time, Allstate opened its first drive-in claims office. In 1953, the company started selling insurance to Canadians. By the end of the 1960s, Allstate had added fire, homeowners, life, workers compensation, marine, and other insurance policies to its offerings.

For a time the brand included other products: fire extinguishers, car batteries, motor scooters, and even, very briefly, a car named the Allstate. But by 1977, Allstate concentrated on selling its most popular and lucrative product: insurance.

The company continued to grow, aided in part by new state laws that required motorists to buy liability insurance.

In the 1960s, the company helped convince the government to make seat belt use mandatory. In 1963, Allstate hit a major milestone, managing more than $1 billion in insurance policies. In the 1970s and 1980s, Allstate led the call for air bags.

Agents began migrating out of Sears's stores and into neighborhood offices in the early 1980s. The company soon boasted 31 regional offices, 219 claim offices, 687 inspection stations, and 2,720 sales and service centers.

In 1990, Allstate launched its Neighborhood Exclusive Agent Program, which turned employees into independent contractors who would manage their own insurance businesses for Allstate. This move, too, was groundbreaking: it placed more of the administrative burden on the agents, which helped preserve Allstate's robust profit margins. It also set the stage for more schemes that would change the very nature and purpose of the company.

In 1993, Sears began to sell off and distribute its shares of Allstate. The burgeoning insurer, now a behemoth, went public. By 1995, Sears had sold or distributed all of its ownership shares of Allstate.

Allstate executives, freed from a declining Sears and leading a trillion dollar industry, began searching in earnest for strategies that would increase its already staggering riches. What they found would change everything.

First, they found Scientology.

Then they found McKinsey & Associates.

The Scientology seminar

Allstate has for more than 30 years denied it engages in unethical or criminal activities as an integral part of its business practices, but the record tells another story.

References to Allstate resorting to unethical intimidation tactics goes back to at least the early 1990s, almost immediately after it teamed up with

Scientologists. In 1988, Allstate hired management consultant Donald Pearson. By many accounts a dynamic, charismatic personality, Pearson quickly gained national influence within Allstate's expanding workforce, conducting productivity seminars across the country. In the span of about four years, more than 3,500 Allstate employees across the country attended Pearson's seminars.

Almost immediately, though, some employees felt discomfited by not just the seminar's message, but the source of the message. Seminar handouts and worksheets made frequent references to the controversial Church of Scientology. Attendees soon learned that Pearson was a devout Scientologist teaching management precepts developed by Scientology's late founder, science fiction writer L. Ron Hubbard.

International Executive Technology Inc., the management consultant firm Pearson represented, sits on a list of what critics describe as Scientology front companies.[15]

IET's most controversial seminar principle: profits over ethics.

According to *The Wall Street Journal*, the big takeaway from Pearson's trainings was that Allstate needed to reward employees who consistently brought in money and punish those who didn't.[16] Productivity was king. Ethics were not nearly as important as results. Hubbard called this philosophy "management by statistics".[17]

Under this philosophy, employees who were not bringing in big profits were showing "down" statistics. They needed to be hounded mercilessly or gotten rid of. Employees who brought in big profits were showing "up" statistics. They were not to be questioned, corrected, or disciplined in any way.

"We reward production and up statistics and penalize nonproduction and down statistics," Hubbard once said. "Always."[18]

Hubbard founded Scientology in 1954. A wildly eccentric (some say "insane") and prolific science fiction writer, Hubbard merged many concepts he created for his science fiction books into church doctrine. Somehow, it resonated. Scientologists hold many much-maligned beliefs, including the conviction that humans are immortal souls called "Thetans" who must undergo "auditing" to erase trauma particles called "engrams" that have accumulated on their bodies over trillions of years.

Based initially in California, the Church of Scientology is often criticized for its recruiting methods, unconventional belief system, and aggressive - sometimes criminal - treatment of critics.

The federal government recognized the church as tax-exempt in 1957 but revoked the designation ten years later.[19] Even though the church could be considered a religion, the IRS determined, numerous Scientology organizations had been operating as for-profit entities personally benefitting L. Ron Hubbard and his associates.[20]

Often described as a brutish cult, the insular group has recently garnered increased public scrutiny. A growing chorus of former members (most famously, the strong-willed actor Leah Remini) charges that the church engages in mind control, physical and mental abuse, extortion, and forced labor. Her television show, "Leah Remini: Scientology and the Aftermath," deftly exposed the church's shocking use of surveillance, invasion of privacy, stalking, harassment, and other abuses and crimes to silence or punish detractors.[21]

Despite mounting evidence, Scientology forcefully denies charges of improper or illegal behavior. Yet Hubbard himself frequently boasted that the church doctrine, Dianetics, had at its core the science of controlling others.

"Dianetics is important politically," Hubbard once wrote. "It indicates ways of controling [sic] people or de-controling [sic] them and of handling groups which is good technology.... Dianetics could become an ideology if anyone let it."[22]

In addition to being a powerful religious movement, the Church of Scientology had also grown into a massive corporate enterprise.

"In Scientology," wrote sociologist Hugh B. Urban, "we find elements of the secret society and the financial corporation combined very successfully into one powerful organization."

In the 1960s and 70s, the organization was in protracted conflict with a host of entities, including the federal government and the psychiatric community. Chief among their enemies was the Internal Revenue Service, which had revoked the church's tax-exempt status in 1967.

It was during this time that Hubbard adopted a principle known as "Fair Game." Someone who is declared "fair game" is an individual who has been identified as a major threat to the organization. Those people or entities are designated "suppressive". A suppressive person can be harassed, threatened, or punished using any means possible. In an October 18, 1966 policy letter, Hubbard instructed that victims considered "fair game" could be "deprived of property or injured by any means by any Scientologist without any discipline of Scientologists. (They) may be tricked, sued...lied to, or destroyed."[23]

Ethics as proposed by Scientology was determined by not what was good, but by what was good for the organization. If it was good for Scientology, then it was ethical. If it was against Scientology, it was unethical and needed to be stopped "by any means." Officially, the Fair Game program was canceled in the 1960s, but unofficially, evidence shows that fair game practices continue unabated and are a principal tactic used by Scientologists today.

In the Pearson seminars, Allstate managers were encouraged to coddle employees who produced so-called "up" statistics. It rang an eerie similarity to Fair Game tactics so popular in Hubbard's ethical worldview.

"Never even discipline someone with an up statistic," Allstate seminar materials advised. "Never accept an ethics report on one – just stamp it 'Sorry, up statistic' and send it back."

History shows that Allstate corporate executives found much to like about Scientology's ruthless approach to business success. After all, even at that time, Scientology was a mind-bogglingly successful organization worth hundreds of millions of dollars. And it had gotten that way through sheer and utter ruthlessness.

Allstate, according to former employees, took Pearson's recommendations to heart, hounding and harassing employees considered unproductive.

"It was like a big fraternal system," said ex-Texas manager Bill Adams. "I mean, you either played the game their way by their rules or you got dealt a bad hand - or you got eliminated from the game. It's just the way it worked."

During Pearson's four-year tenure as Allstate's chief trainer, numerous employees accused Allstate of wrongfully firing them. Many sued. Soon, reporters from major newspapers started paying attention.

In 1995, *The Wall Street Journal* wrote an article about Scientology's "profits over ethics" principle. Citing training materials, the newspaper drew a connection between mounting complaints of unethical corporate behavior and the principles that Allstate managers learned in Pearson's productivity seminars. Pearson, an unapologetic devotee of L. Ron Hubbard's teachings, complained that detractors were taking the lessons out of context. For its part, the Church of Scientology pushed back against the mounting criticism levied at its training seminars. Hubbard's management approach was a proven method for increasing productivity, the group insisted, and the negative news reports were the results of complaints from "a few disgruntled employees of a huge corporation."[24]

At first, Allstate took a similar stance. Executives dismissed the complaints, saying some agents just could not hack Allstate's new "entrepreneurial" approach to selling insurance. But scrutiny spurred by mounting complaints intensified. Under growing public pressure, Allstate decided that Scientology "profits over ethics" management principles were "unacceptable."

"We dropped the ball," company spokesman Al Orendorff told *The Wall Street Journal*. "We should have managed that part of it better and didn't."

The company officially discontinued the workshops in 1993, the same year the Church of Scientology claimed victory over the Internal Revenue Service.

Despite publicly cutting ties with IET and Pearson, Allstate executives could not bring themselves to issue a full-throated condemnation of the Scientology ideas taught. While some of the training was problematic, Allstate executives told reporters, parts of it *were* valuable. Allstate soon erased the names associated with Scientology from the training course, but many of the materials in the original training manuals remained.

Tactics taught openly in the seminars continued, critics alleged. Allstate also began engaging in unsavory practices that had less to do with productivity and more to do with suppressing dissent, say former employees.[25] It also began a brazen campaign to raid its own employees' pension funds, lawyers say.

Despite denials from Allstate, Scientology reportedly had a profound effect on Allstate's culture and ideals. Officially, it taught the insurance company to focus almost entirely on the bottom line, and to remove any obstacles that threatened it. Unofficially, it appears to have influenced how Allstate executives confronted criticism and dissent. Scientology training materials introduced a fundamental maxim that may have profoundly inspired Allstate as it went in search of more profits.

"A person is as successful as he is able to adjust the environment to him," the Scientology maxim goes, "not the other way around."

The McKinsey engagement

About the same time Allstate was succumbing to pressure to end public ties with Scientology, Allstate corporate executives reached out to management consulting firm McKinsey & Company. Established in Chicago in 1926, McKinsey had by the early 1990s developed into one of the most influential – and controversial – business consulting firms in the world. It has advised huge corporations like General Motors, American Express, Nike, and AT&T.

McKinsey had a lot in common with Scientology. Like Scientology, its influence had spread globally over time. It controlled massive wealth and information. It also had at its core the conviction that people who did not show 100 percent loyalty to the cause should be excised.

Founder James O. McKinsey was an accounting professor. His successor, Marvin Bower, was a lawyer. In the early 1940s, Bower made several structural changes to the firm that seemed eerily similar to the Scientology precepts hawked by IET decades later. Under Bower, the firm established an "up or out" policy: At employee reviews, McKinsey consultants learn whether they are promoted or fired.

McKinsey grew rapidly in the 1940s and 50s, expanding into Europe and opening offices in Melbourne, Amsterdam, London and Paris. In 1994, the firm elected Rajat Gupta as the first non-American to be elected as the firm's managing director. Gupta expanded the firm further, opening offices in numerous international cities, including Bangkok, Moscow, and Beijing.

Over time, McKinsey's tentacles reached around the world. Referred to by employees as "the firm," McKinsey grew from a Chicago staff of 88 in 1951 to a worldwide staff of more than 27,000 by 2020. A consulting powerhouse with 127 offices around the globe and annual revenue of more than $10 billion, McKinsey had cachet.

Ivy League graduates flock to the firm, knowing that a stint as a McKinsey consultant virtually assures a highly profitable business career and entry into the halls of power. The firm often leaves McKinsey consultants with clients as managing employees. In fact, many CEOs and senior executives at Fortune 500 companies had first worked for McKinsey. As such, the consulting firm has access to a network of powerful alumni who control trillions of dollars.

McKinsey consultants diligently insert themselves into communities, seeking affiliations with boards, churches, foundations, and other community institutions. To gain access to non-profit organizations and local government agencies, the firm sometimes offers its services free of charge.

The company has also advised numerous government agencies, including the Federal Bureau of Investigation, the Central Intelligence Agency, and the Department of Defense.

Not coincidentally, these connections helped McKinsey add to its "knowledge management" databases. That's another thing McKinsey has in common with the Church of Scientology. Like Scientology, McKinsey over the years has acquired a massive intelligence apparatus that rival those of government spy agencies. Now that McKinsey has successfully infiltrated the U.S. intelligence community through government contracts, it is possible that the firm's apparatus now exceeds government capabilities.

Like Scientology, McKinsey's secrecy is well known. It uses nondisclosure agreements to shield its activities. When things go awry within a company it advises, McKinsey quickly cites confidentiality agreements as a way to avoid discussing failures. Blanket confidentiality allows it to operate largely in the shadows, a fact highlighted by the recent presidential campaign of former South Bend, Indiana mayor Pete Buttigieg.

Buttigieg, a former McKinsey consultant who at one time spoke glowingly of the firm, suffered a significant blow to his presidential campaign when he had to ask McKinsey for permission to talk about his time there. Like all McKinsey employees, Buttigieg had signed a confidentiality agreement as a condition of employment. The irony was not lost on McKinsey critics or voters. Pete Buttigieg, after all, was seeking to lead what at the time was the most powerful country in the world. It was unsettling to see that he could not speak freely about his qualifications without McKinsey's permission.

Over time, however, McKinsey began losing its ability to hide its failures and transgressions behind non-disclosure agreements. Yes, it had advised some of the world's most successful corporations, but it was also behind some of the most devastating catastrophes the business world had ever seen. The list of McKinsey-advised corporate disasters is long and growing. Valeant, the Canadian pharmaceutical company, lost 73 percent of its stock value under the leadership of Michael Pearson, a 23-year veteran of McKinsey. McKinsey consultants were also involved in the ruinous merger between Time Warner and America Online.

Most famously, Enron, the tragic Houston-based energy and trading company, imploded spectacularly in 2001 under the leadership of former McKinsey partner Jeffrey Skilling while being advised by McKinsey. As CEO of Enron, Skilling led the company's illicit bid to hide its debts behind fake companies McKinsey helped create. When the hidden debt load became too much, the company suddenly collapsed. One day the corporation was hailed as a miracle energy corporation, the next its employees stood shell-shocked on the street.

Several Enron executives headed for prison. Skilling served more than 12 years in prison after his convictions on several felony charges, including insider trading and securities fraud.

Skilling is not the only McKinsey protégé indicted for unethical behavior that turned criminal. In 2008, managing director Rajat Gupta was convicted of insider trading. In 2018, McKinsey partner Navdeep Arora was sentenced to two years in prison for charging more than half a million dollars in bogus consulting fees to State Farm.[26]

The firm has also worked for totalitarian regimes and earned a reputation for giving advice that would fail the most basic ethics test. Recently, McKinsey was at the center of a massive corruption scandal in South Africa, where it overcharged millions of dollars for six months of dubious work on a failing utility.

And during the Trump administration, activists accused McKinsey consultants of being behind some of the harshest policies aimed at undocumented immigrants along the U.S. southern border. McKinsey reportedly advised the government to focus on cutting costs on food, medical care, and even supervision of immigrants captured and detained.[27]

The consulting firm also won a million dollar contract to consult with the FBI, advising on ways the bureau could restructure its budget.

That consultation also had mixed reviews.

"They were receiving a generous consulting fee," a veteran intelligence official told *Politico*, "but did not appear from my vantage to bring any particular expertise to the task."[28]

Perhaps most troubling, American intelligence officers say that a controversial government consulting contract with McKinsey in 2015 damaged the United States' intelligence network. The national intelligence network includes agencies like the CIA, National Security Agency and Office of the Director of National Intelligence.

The federal contract left McKinsey with a $10 million payday, but left the U.S. spy network clumsy: American intelligence after McKinsey was now reportedly slower and less agile when responding to threats.

American spies began accusing McKinsey of weakening the nation's crucial spy apparatus at a time of exponential threats.[29]

Still, McKinsey's sheen had barely dulled. Despite its many failures and lapses, it continued to rake in multi-million dollar contracts from both the private and public sectors. The American government, particularly the Justice Department, seemed not to see any potential conflicts of interests, despite criminal activity documented from within the firm and the damage the company had done to its own capabilities.

To add insult to injury, McKinsey & Company earned $100 million advising the Trump administration's disastrous government response to the coronavirus.[30]

McKinsey's collaboration with Allstate turned out to be a natural extension of the Scientology/Allstate partnership. Like the Church of Scientology, McKinsey approached business problems with a fanatical eye on the bottom line, and it believed in 100 percent loyalty from its adherents. It also placed an almost mythical premium on information control. If Allstate executives had wanted to continue down the path started by Scientology without the reputational damage of being publically associated with the church, it had found an ideal substitute in McKinsey.

Zero Sum and Fair Game

McKinsey offered Allstate its "zero sum game" approach to profits.

A popular game theory among McKinsey consultants, a zero sum game involves a limited amount of resources. In a zero sum game, one player wins exactly what the other players lose. Poker is a perfect example of a zero sum game: the amount of money on the table doesn't change, but how much of the money one player wins from the others determines success. It is normally applied in business, where companies seek to gain market advantages over their competitors.

What makes McKinsey's advice to Allstate so remarkable – and repugnant – is that in this game, one player is Allstate and the other player is the unsuspecting Allstate customer. Allstate began using its claims process as a "zero sum economic game," keeping much of the money owed the customer for itself.

A McKinsey PowerPoint slide shamelessly advised that where "Allstate gains...others must lose."[31] That advice would shape the company for the next 20-odd years and it was, at the very least, highly unethical.

For Allstate, McKinsey's zero sum game took Scientology's Fair Game policies to a new level. Indeed, much of the Church of Scientology's immense wealth had come from bait and switch practices that charged devotees for higher access to censored doctrine.[32] If you wanted to reach higher spiritual awareness in Scientology, you had to pay for it, and pay big. If you fought back, the church was ruthless.

"The church censors critics and controls information through an aggressive litigation campaign that is well resourced to outlast the financial means of their competition."[33] (Ironically, Scientology's financial advantage was a direct result of its tax-exempt status.)

Under McKinsey's zero sum game, Allstate would "bait" its customers by selling insurance protection it did not intend to provide. And, like Scientologists, Allstate would pay millions to predatory lawyers to exhaust and outlast its victims.

Allstate v. customers

Allstate put its zero sum game to work across the United States, leading the industry in customer complaints.

In Maryland, regulators fined the company $18.6 million for raising premiums and changing policies behind its customers' backs. In Louisiana, Allstate had twice as many complaints from customers for denying claims after Hurricane Katrina. In California, the company received more than 600 complaints from homeowners insured by Allstate after wildfires destroyed more than 2000 homes and killed 15 near San Diego. In Florida, Allstate allegedly began dropping homeowners who did not also have auto insurance.[34]

Inundated with complaints and confronted with a litany of Allstate misdeeds across the country, the National Association of Insurance Commissioners finally began investigating Allstate for unfair settlements regarding bodily injury claims in over 45 states. After an investigation, regulators forced Allstate to pay a $10 million regulatory settlement, a pittance. The Texas Department of Insurance fined the insurer a more substantial penalty – $70 million – for routinely overcharging homeowners across the state. Allstate easily paid that, too. That was something else Allstate executives learned. They could break just about any law and when the law finally caught up to them, if indeed it ever did, their profitable zero sum game allowed them to settle any punishment without admitting guilt. They would simply pay the fines and go about business as usual.

The lessons Allstate learned from the church and the consulting firm shaped its culture and its future, for better or worse. The three corporations shared fundamental ideals, and those ideals made all three some of the most lucrative, expansive, powerful, and controversial companies in the history of the United States.

First, they agreed that the bottom line should trump almost any other consideration. Second, they shared the belief that information and secrecy equaled power. Third, they displayed a lasting commitment to rooting out and punishing dissent. Lastly, all three corporations exhibited a profound conviction that one could gain so much wealth and power he could place himself and his interests above the law. In many ways, all three organizations became untouchable.

When I sued Allstate in San Antonio in 2010, I didn't know any of that.

3 | ORIGIN

The runaway writer

THE FIRST THING YOU NEED to know about me is that I am a product of trauma, compliments of the United States government.

One of my earliest memories is of my mother and five siblings waiting breathlessly in the small living room of our Coleman Street duplex, waiting for my father to come home from war.

He arrived in uniform directly from Vietnam, a tall, handsome, well-built young black man in jungle fatigues and spit-shined black army boots. He scooped all six of us up and held us tight as my mother cried. We whooped, giggled, and hugged his neck. That was one of my first memories and it is as indelible today as it ever was. Other memory fragments remain. I remember riding my father's back as he galloped through the house as my youngest brother clomped around in my father's army boots trying mightily to catch the rest of us. I remember the many times my father and mother danced to big band music played on reel-to-reel tape as my siblings and I sat on the floor in the doorway watching in delight. I remember a warm house with loud voices, bellowing laughter, and spontaneous dance. My mother often said we were poor in money and rich in love and we knew that to be true.

I also remember my father, a decorated army sergeant, being absent as he served two overseas tours as a medic in Vietnam and Korea. My mother struggled to care for her six children mostly alone. When my Aunt Theresa died unexpectedly from a brain aneurism, three more children lived in the house. During my father's tour in Korea, my mother moved us from our claptrap duplex on the outskirts of Fort Sam Houston army base to a much larger four-bedroom, two-bath ranch house in Eastwood Village. It was a middle class neighborhood on the city's Eastside with tidy lawns and solid houses. It was racially diverse, still in the middle of the phenomenon Americans call white flight. Soon, it became predominantly black, but remained diverse. By the time I reached adulthood, Eastwood Village was predominantly Hispanic but still diverse. A lot of white folks, it turned out, didn't have a problem with black folks or Mexicans and so they stayed when other white folks fled. We grew up with them, were close personal friends with a lot of them and retain some of those friendships today. As a young journalist, I marveled at their invisibility in the U.S. news media.

The house on Elbel Lane had a family room, garage, a covered patio, and a fenced-in backyard with a wooden playhouse and a peach tree. It fit our family like a glove. Nine children crowded into three bedrooms on the northeast side of the house while my mother and father could have a measure of quiet and privacy on the southwest side, separated from our din by a kitchen, the family room and two hallways. We loved the new house.

When my father returned from overseas the second time, he was not the same. The house was bigger, but so where all of his children, loud, lumbering bodies stealing space, air, and quiet. He did his best, I suppose, but mostly he depended on my mother to rear us. I spent my time lost in books that were probably too old for me. From first to eighth grade, I spent most of my afternoons at Monica Martin's house. My best friend, she belonged to a family of liberal Texas Catholics who lived across the street from St. Patrick's. After school, we would skip across Mason Street and spend the afternoon playing until my mother picked me up on her way home from work.

My father had a short fuse. He would sometimes rage. An innocent remark, a childish grimace, indeed, the very presence of some of us could set him off. I once asked him at dinner if he had ever had to kill anyone during the war. He exploded, slamming his hand on the table and yelling that I talked too much. I grew to be afraid of our handsome, proud father.

After graduating eighth grade, my best friend and I headed in different directions. Monica went off to a private Catholic high school and I went off to the public high school in my district: Sam Houston, arguably one of the most difficult high schools in the San Antonio Independent School District. The house on Elbel Lane was increasingly chaotic and dysfunctional, but I could no longer seek daily refuge at the Martins. I began to dread the moment my father came home from work at Fort Sam Houston. During our teen years, some of us made sure to be out of the house by the time my father came home from work, and we stayed away until dinner. I don't recall him ever having a problem with that.

At the same time, television news channels were reporting that American postal workers, many Vietnam veterans, were spontaneously shooting down their coworkers and families in repeated mass shootings. *Going postal,* Americans called it. I began to worry that our father might one day kill us. I became adept at reading infinitesimal clues – micro-expressions, slight shifts in tonal action, at times even trivial changes in the room's air pressure – to determine whether or not my father was about to explode.

I left home a few months after my seventeenth birthday. I had dropped out of Sam Houston High School at 16, passed the general equivalency exam, and started classes at San Antonio Community College. I was taking college classes, but my father made it clear that all he saw was a high school dropout.

I remember the day I left. My father, holding a telephone bill from Southwestern Bell, falsely accused me of making a long distance phone call. Tell the truth, I told myself, and everything will be fine. Summoning all of my personal strength and courage, I firmly denied the accusation. He assessed me with a hard look.

"You're arrogant," he said.

Knowing that I suffered from low self-esteem, I thought he was paying me a compliment. I took the word "arrogant" to mean "confident."

"Thank you," I said artlessly.

He slapped me across the face.

That was the first time my father had ever slapped me, and before I could think, I protested.

"Don't you hit me, goddamn it," I blurted, disastrously.

A clamoring row ensued. I fled backwards out of the house, cursing my father as my siblings poured out of their hiding places to keep his hands from re-encircling my neck. I stayed with my cousin Vanessa a few days before emptying out my modest bank account and catching a Greyhound bus to Miami.

The day the bus trundled into Miami, I looked out the bus window and saw the city in flames. It was May, 1980. Burning buildings, smoldering cars, downed power lines. I had escaped an abusive household in Texas and landed on a race riot in Florida. Four Dade County police officers had just been acquitted of brutally murdering Arthur McDuffie, a 33-year-old insurance salesman and U.S. Marine. Up to a dozen officers had beaten McDuffie to death during a traffic stop and then tried to stage the crime scene to make it look like an accident. When a Dade County jury acquitted the officers, on May 18, 1980, riots broke out in the black neighborhoods of Overtown and Liberty City. They continued for weeks.

I spent a few lonely years in Miami struggling to make ends meet, at one point sharing a one-room garage apartment with my step-cousin Rodney Nesmith just off the notorious 79th Avenue strip. Hookers, pimps, and drug dealers were amused and intrigued by this odd, proper-talking little Texan with the maroon satchel. They treated me gently as I waited daily on the bus stop for the 45-minute ride to work as a telephone interviewer for Rife Market Research. "Red," they called me, because the strong Miami sun and the chlorine from the neighborhood swimming pool had lightened my hair.

I soon earned enough money to get an apartment along the Miami River. My roommate, Portia Ogbu, was a bona fide Nigerian princess who had enjoyed some fleeting success as a singer in San Francisco. I shared the apartment with Portia and her boyfriend Fox, a dreadlocked bass guitar player who spent his nights walking the neighborhoods of Miami in search of premier marijuana. He spent his days pilfering the can foods I had begun hiding under my bed.

I didn't speak to my father for two years. Occasionally, I would call home. Sometimes my mother would answer the phone. Sometimes a sibling would answer. If my father answered, I coldly requested to speak to someone else. He would quietly comply. And while the fleeing of my home was a traumatic life experience for me, I later learned that there was never any discussion about my hasty departure among members of my family. Life went on.

Many years after our eventual reconciliation, a large tumor began to grow on the back of my father's neck. The doctors at Brooke Army Medical Center at Fort Sam removed it. A biopsy revealed that it was benign. A few years later, a malignant version rose up in the same spot.

The Pentagon eventually admitted that the tumor was a result of First Sergeant Robert C. McVea's exposure to Agent Orange while serving as a combat medic during the Vietnam War. The Pentagon had dropped tons of the chemical defoliant on its troops in a desperate attempt to destroy the Vietnam jungles so that it could at last see its clever, elusive enemy and finally win the war. By 2015, more than 300,000 American Vietnam veterans had died from exposure to Agent Orange – nearly five times the number killed in combat.[35]

The United States government, through its disastrous war in Vietnam, managed to not just traumatize my father but kill him as well. He was a good, hardworking man, and I loved and admired him despite the many conflicts between us.

Years later, a psychotherapist began treating me for childhood-onset post-traumatic stress disorder and generalized anxiety disorder. He asked me how I felt directly after my father died from what Army doctors diagnosed as metastasized malignant lymphoma of an unknown source.

"Heartbroken," I told him.

"What else?" he asked mildly.

It was a complex question in search of a simple answer and I was shocked at the word that instantly came to mind.

"Relieved," I said.

After a few years of living hand to mouth in Miami, I returned to San Antonio. Back home, I knocked about waiting tables, sharing rent with roommates, and writing short stories.

I had identified as a writer since my sixth grade teacher at St. Patrick's, Mrs. Cathy Venezia, handed me back an essay I had written and told me that I had talent. A voracious reader, I devoured the works of iconic American authors who insisted on living the unconventional writer's life. Their life stories inspired me: writers like James Baldwin, Zora Neal Hurston, John Steinbeck, Jean-Paul Sartre, Vladimir Nabokov, and Anaïs Nin. Those lives seemed planets away from San Antonio and often read like fiction. Their biographies teemed with adventure and excitement, tragedy and conflict, freedom and nonconformity. They were my heroes and I wanted to be like them. More than anything, I wanted to live the writer's life. But my life in South Texas seemed aimless, unproductive.

If only, I thought, but the wish lacked specificity.

I would write short stories, send them to publishers, and wait. Most would not bother to respond. One day, I received a typewritten rejection letter from a major Madison Avenue publishing house. I was thrilled. New York publishers *did* exist, I thought. The writing world was real!

Time passed in a whirl of adolescent pointlessness, and before I knew it, I had slipped into my early 20s with just a handful of published works. My financial take from writing added up to less than $200.

Eventually, I would find myself sitting in a bar after work with my friend Lisa Rossi. Lisa had also been a runaway. She was a thin, slight girl with wistful eyes, a solemn expression, and long, wispy light brown hair. We sat around drinking beer and regaling the table with stories of the near escapes that defined our runaway adventures. We both understood that it was remarkable that either of us was still alive.

Lisa once told the story of how she and a fellow runaway were hitchhiking on a Texas highway one night when a trucker stopped, pulled a gun, and chased the girls into the nearby woods. He hunted the quietly weeping girls for what seemed like hours, she recalled, before finally giving up and driving away.

I once told the story of how I was sitting at a bus stop in Overtown, Miami's once thriving black cultural center turned infamous slum, waiting for the transfer bus to take me to my minimum wage job as a market research interviewer across town.

I had been in Miami for several months. I had just bought a sandwich and I was contemplating whether I wanted to eat it now or save it for later when an addict spotted me from across the street. There were two other women on the bus stop but I was the only one sitting on the bench. When the junkie started across the street, his eyes focused exclusively on me. I belatedly realized that there were certain places in America where you could not sit down in public. This bus bench in Miami was one of them. The two standing women shifted their bodies. They both turned in opposite directions but their individual movements contributed to the same effect: both of their backs were now facing me and I was suddenly very much alone.

"Hey, little sister!" the junkie said jovially and plopped down next to me. The women started walking down the street in opposite directions. The man was dressed casually and cleanly with a relatively well-groomed short beard and neck-length dreadlocks. He smiled at me but his eyes gave him away: dead, callous, predatory.

I knew that I was in trouble. I tried to appear calm and friendly. I smiled at the man. "Hello," I piped. I was holding my maroon faux leather satchel in one hand and my wrapped sandwich in the other. He grinned.

"You look like my brother," I lied, apropos of nothing visible.

"Is that right?" he asked, his toothy grin widening.

He perused me briefly. Dead eyes.

"What you got there?" he asked, his eyes focused on my satchel.

"A sandwich," I answered, pretending.

"Can I have it?"

Only a slight hesitation.

"Sure," I said and handed the sandwich over.

He took it and threw it on the ground. Cars zoomed by.

"Why did you do that?" I asked angrily. The sandwich had spilled out of the plastic wrap, mingling on the ground with sandy dirt, bottle caps, and cigarette butts. It was unsalvageable.

"I'm sorry about this," he muttered and, reaching behind, shifted toward me.

The city bus arrived. I hastily skipped on and paid my fare. The bus's door closed behind me. Through the bus windows, I watched the diminishing frame of the frustrated addict, frozen on the bus stop like a zombie.

One night, sitting in the same rustic bar, Lisa said eleven words that changed my life forever. She had met a woman the week before, she told me, who turned out to be a lawyer. A lawyer! I had never met a lawyer in my life. Then she said something that struck me like a thunderbolt.

"It's too bad," she said idly, "that we didn't do anything with our lives."

The next day, I visited San Antonio Community College. *I'm going to get a college degree*, I told myself. I intended to start classes as soon as possible, but ran into a problem. I had enrolled in community college after earning my GED but had dropped all of my classes when I fled my parents' home during the awful fight with my father. The college had placed me on academic suspension. I would need to ask permission to enroll. I applied for a provisional enrollment and SAC allowed me to enroll on a conditional basis.

It turned out that I enjoyed college immensely. At Sam Houston, inarguably one of San Antonio's most unruly high schools, academics had been weak. The chaotic social environment, the fights, the bullying and the constant class disruptions had contributed to my decision to drop out. San Antonio College was different. The setting was mature and intellectual. Everybody there wanted to learn. It was diverse; people of all races and ages sat in the classrooms. Some of San Antonio's finest minds taught there. Perhaps because of this, the school had done a great job of attracting students from other countries, adding to the mosaic of cultures that enhanced the rich campus atmosphere.

My first semester, I took nine semester hours and made the dean's list. My confidence grew, and I continued taking classes part time for a few years while waiting tables. Soon, I realized it was time to start thinking about transferring to a four-year university.

Two things happened that set my university and career choices.

First, I came across an old hardcover book written by Oriana Fallaci in the Moody Library. Fallaci, a hard-drinking, chain-smoking Italian journalist, had interviewed some of the world's most powerful people. The book, *Interview with History*, was riveting. Oriana Fallaci was fearless. She was famous for asking world leaders hard questions and didn't hesitate to call them liars. She inspired me. I decided I wanted to be an investigative journalist.

Second, I came across an Associated Press article about a study that scrutinized who teachers focused on most in class, divided by race and gender. The study concluded that teachers in the U.S taught to white men first, then black men, and then to white women. *Then* they taught black women. I decided to attend Texas Woman's University, at that time the only state college reserved for female students. I wanted to even the odds.

I majored in journalism. On the weekends, I drove 30 miles from Denton to Dallas's West End to wait tables at Dick's Last Resort. Undereducated in math and clumsy in the science lab, I was thrilled to learn I could minor in Spanish. Mary Sparks, a wholesome Midwesterner with a doctorate in journalism headed TWU's journalism school. In the late 1980s, Dr. Sparks was passionate about racially integrating American newsrooms and she had developed relationships with editors across the country. TWU's journalism school was small, but it gave a solid foundation in journalism. I joined the school newspaper, the *Daily Lasso*, spending long nights with about seven other young women cutting and pasting articles onto broadsheets that we sent off to the printer.

I covered courts for TWU's *Lasso* newspaper. I got my first taste of Texas justice when as a J school reporter I attended the Denton trial of a young black man convicted of stealing a T-top from a sports car. During the penalty portion of his trial, his parents, well-dressed and soft-spoken, testified that their son was a good person who had gotten involved with drugs and had begun stealing to support his habit. They testified that they would do whatever it took to get him the help he needed. They begged the court for mercy.

But Texas was a three-times-you're-out state, and this was his third conviction. The judge, following state guidelines, sentenced him to 60 years in prison. My jaw dropped. That was twice as much as Texas judge Jack Hampton in nearby Midlothian had given to Richard Lee Bednarski, a white 18-year old who had shot and killed two harmless, unarmed gay men in a park. The Denton judge, a former Denton County assistant prosecutor and adjunct law professor at TWU, looked embarrassed.

Upon the recommendation of Dr. Sparks, the journalism dean, editors at *The Dallas Morning News* hired me as a part time paid intern. Two or three nights a week, I manned the city desk, wrote obituaries, and helped an investigative team input information into a database. In my first big Metro story for the *The Dallas Morning News*, I wrote a story about how Dallas police officers made hundreds of prostitution arrests each year, but rarely made cases against pimps. My senior year, I won a coveted paid summer internship with *The Oregonian*, the largest daily newspaper in the Pacific Northwest. That summer, a teenager home alone shot and killed an intruder trying to squeeze through a doggy door. Editors assigned me to cover the incident and it became my first front page story.

When I entered the newsroom in the early 1990s, newspapers were just starting to racially integrate, more than 30 years after the civil rights movement. The American Association of Newspaper Editors had at last made integrating the newsroom a national goal, but the hiring of even a few minority writers could reliably trigger consternation and resentment among many white journalists. The newsroom's response to integration looked nothing like the violent, deranged hostility that defined the white resistance to racial integration in the South. Instead, it was muted, covert. Many white journalists inexplicably saw the trickling thread of incoming journalists of color as threats and treated them with a host of micro-aggressions. Newsrooms across the U.S. teemed with racial tensions.

Meanwhile, the white, college educated editors, impervious to any suggestion that their privilege made them naïve to the larger diverse world, failed to provide content relevant to non-white, working class readers. Stories became repetitive, unrevealing. In Portland, critics of *The Oregonian* derisively referred to the paper as the "BOR-e-gonian".

Working for modern-day corporate newspapers was a poor choice for a writer inspired by muckrakers and civil rights champions like Ida B. Wells and Oriana Fallaci. My time as a staff writer for corporate newspapers lasted six years.

The thrill of writing stories to the front page eventually subsided. Stories go through a series of edits before publication. The best editors are careful and perceptive, with a strong eye for detail and nuance. Many of the editors I wrote for were of this ilk, steady professionals determined to make the story I had submitted clearer and more meaningful to the reader. Others were more determined to fit the story to their limited worldview. Very quickly, a reporter learns that the story the newspaper publishes might look very different from the story she submitted, even though it had her name, her byline, attached.

At the same time, newspapers were losing their way. Stumbling under massive overheads, publishers and managing editors began pandering to advertisers. Soon, recognizing their dollars were crucial to newspaper survival, advertisers became increasingly opinionated about how newspapers covered their interests. As a result, publishers began to frown on investigative journalism. It tended to upset wealthy folks who had the means to sue for libel or withhold crucial advertising funds. News articles that might anger powerful companies or individuals received heavy, censuring edits. A newspaper story important to the safety and security of a vulnerable community might simply vanish on its way to the page. Management timidity hurt the quality of the newspaper's editorial content, bored readers, and frustrated the reporting staff.

I had the privilege of learning from some of the best journalists in the business. But American newspapers were in a downward spiral even before the internet and everyone in American newsrooms could see it. John Snell, an affable veteran reporter who had worked for the *Oregonian* for more than a decade, hung a small sign on his file cabinet that could summarize the mood in newsrooms all across America. The message, printed in bold black type on a letter-sized sheet of copy paper, read simply:

**THE BEATINGS WILL
CONTINUE UNTIL
MORALE IMPROVES.**

Still, survival skills honed as a Catholic schoolgirl-turned-runaway seemed to pay off for me as a journalist. I could think on my feet, navigate new and tricky environments, and talk to anyone regardless of class or race. At the end of the summer internship, *Oregonian* editors offered me a full time staff writer position. I worked as a general assignment reporter for the Oregonian for three years before tiring of the rain, dreary Oregon winters, and the corporate approach to the news.

Wanting to focus more on investigative journalism, I accepted a job at the *Dallas Observer*, a controversial weekly investigative tabloid in Texas. I worked for the *Observer* for three years before quitting in a chaotic scramble of racial and class tensions.

During my tenure at the *Observer*, I often found myself in a tug-of-war between white editors and black activists. Before I finally quit, the New Black Panther Party had issued a death threat against me for a headline calling them toothless that I didn't write. The famously polarizing black commissioner, John Wiley Price, had refused to speak to me because of a *Dallas Observer* story alleging he raped women that I hadn't written. And a white slumlord had sued me for libel for writing about favorable treatment he received from the city despite owning hundreds of substandard properties in poor minority neighborhoods. The city officials who gave him that special treatment were often black. They didn't like me either. Editors said I was difficult because I often objected to the descriptions of black people they habitually strived to insert under my byline. Glenna Whitley, a freelancer who would soon join the *Dallas Observer* writing staff, wrote a hack piece for *D Magazine* about my departure that began floating around the Internet around the same time I sued Allstate.

The headline read, "Playing the Race Card at the *Dallas Observer*."

That's how I ended up in Mexico. I sold everything, packed up my Jeep Grand Cherokee, and eventually drove south to finish my book, *Making Myth of Emily*.

"I was sick of white people, AND I was sick of black people," I often explained, tongue-in-cheek. "I decided, 'Screw it! I'm moving to Mexico!'"

But it was also a practical move. Mexico was affordable and offered a never-ending supply of cultural pleasures. I wanted to live the writer's life and to live a life of service. In Mexico, I could enjoy a rich, socially fulfilling lifestyle without fretting over how to pay the bills and, at the same time, build a future as a writer and advocate. I knew that I never again wanted to work in the corporate world. It required concessions I just couldn't make.

I rented a house in Guanajuato for three years, taught English at the University of Guanajuato and Academia Falcon, and published a small bilingual magazine. In 2001, I won a two-year fellowship that required me to move temporarily to Montana, where I worked at the Indian Law

Resource Center in Helena. My job there was to help the non-profit law firm share indigenous stories, especially in the areas of human rights, with the news media. The founder Tim Coulter, a member of the Citizen Band Potawatomi tribe, worked with indigenous communities, tribes, and nations across the United States and the Americas. It was an eye-opening experience for me and further convinced me that information was key to a community's defense against abuse and theft. I learned a lot from Tim Coulter.

When the fellowship ended, I returned to Mexico. This time I settled in a tiny desert village in the Altiplano region of San Luis Potosí. Tucked deep into the high plains of the Chihuahuense desert, the Catorce municipality was so remote some residents referred to Mexican visitors from out-of-town as foreigners.

There I founded the Auris Project, a 501c3 non-profit organization dedicated to helping communities access key development and rights information. In the remote Altiplano Potosino, that meant connecting people to people, so I started an international volunteer program. Volunteers came from the U.S., Canada, Europe, and South America to join the program. They lived with Catorce families, helped contribute to small development programs, and improved their Spanish. I ran the program for a couple of years. But the organization, so full of promise, was not growing. We needed better internet service (Catorce was still on dial up) and more reliable postal service. I boarded up my Catorce house, gave the key to my next-door neighbor Doña Queta, and moved back to the U.S. to establish programs on the Eastside of San Antonio, the historically black side of town where I had grown up.

I believed that the Eastside could benefit from improved access to information. The geographic isolation of rural Mexico had its challenges but so did the social isolation of the urban neighborhoods where I had grown up. The plan was to create information programs on the Eastside, apply for funding, and build connections between San Antonio and Catorce. I was doing some of that already, collecting donations in San Antonio – clothes, shoes, toys, and appliances – and transporting them to Catorce for a big flea market. After the big sale in Catorce, volunteers and I would distribute the leftovers to impoverished villagers deep in the desert for free.

I applied to rent a charming little cottage on the Eastside. The young landlady, AJ Garcia, was understandably suspicious. She diligently researched the backgrounds of everyone applying to rent one of her properties, but I came up a big blank. I had no recent credit or employment history in the U.S. I explained, because I had been living in Mexico for the past 10 years. She was obviously skeptical. She discussed this strange new applicant with her husband Cesar.

"She says she's been living in Mexico all these years," she said, "But there is no way I can confirm that."

"What do you think of her as a person?" he asked.

"I like her."

"Well, you have great instincts."

She rented me the place. We've been best of friends ever since.

To replenish my dwindled finances, I got a job in San Antonio as a coordinator for a senior companion program and began buying and selling items from government auctions. Fueled by my love of books, I quickly built an online bookstore as a way to raise funds for the Auris Project. I would buy boxes of books at auctions, scoop up bins of discontinued books from libraries, and browse thrift shops looking for rare out-of-print books. I had a knack for it. I could pay a dime for a rare book near the trash pile only to sell it later online for more than $100. Before long, the Auris Project had an inventory of thousands of rare and out-of-print books.

One day, while crossing the international bridge spanning the Rio Grande River on my way to check on my house in the Altiplano Potosino, I felt a sense of accomplishment and hope. Things seemed to be coming together. I was living the life I had always wanted. I was a published writer. I had won journalism awards. I now enjoyed dual residency in Mexico and Texas. The Auris Project had just received a large donation that would help the organization become sustainable. The future seemed bright.

I didn't know it then, but that would be the last time I would see my Mexican hometown of Catorce.

Allstate would soon make it entirely too dangerous to even visit.

San Antonio de Bejar

I missed Mexico, but I loved being back in San Antonio. It truly is a special place, with a unique history and culture.

Named after a 13th century Portuguese Catholic priest, San Antonio is the oldest city in Texas. Landlocked and resting about 150 miles from the Gulf Coast, the city was officially founded in 1718 by Spanish settlers. It briefly became part of a remote province in Mexico after that country gained its independence from Spain in 1821. It became a principal city in the short-lived Texas Republic after Texas won its independence from Mexico in 1836.[36] Known as San Antonio de Bejar in colonial times; it now serves as the seat of Bexar (pronounced "bear") County.

San Antonians are famous for their Tex-Mex culture and food, festive spirit, and laidback hospitality. The city is vibrant, unique and cultural. Despite being one of the fastest growing cities in the United States, it still manages to feel like a small town. A popular tourist destination, it is home to the world-famous Alamo. Millions flock to the colorful River Walk and tour its three other historic Spanish missions. Few teams in the NBA enjoy a more raucously devoted fan base than the San Antonio Spurs. City growth has outpaced once larger cities like Dallas. It is now the seventh most populous city in the United States. It's geographic location and military installations make it strategically important to national security.

It is also the most economically segregated city in the U.S.[37] It has terrible social index scores in poverty, health, and education. It is the poorest of the nation's biggest cities.

City managers have struggled to keep pace with growth. San Antonians have weathered repeated corruption scandals, easily traced back to historically poor administration of city institutions and budgets.

Corruption in San Antonio is historic and endemic.

Historically, it was common for city council members to extort developers.[38] By the turn of the 21st century, local government agencies had uniformly poor reputations. Many decent contractors and developers refused to work with them.

By the mid-2000s, spurred by a string of embarrassing public corruption scandals, then-mayor Phil Hardberger met with local billionaire and city father Red McCombs to discuss ways to clean up the city's act. McCombs, a well-known automobile dealer and philanthropist, agreed that the city had a problem. What the city needed, the men agreed, was a strong city manager. A nationwide search ensued. The men wanted someone with strong management skills, budget savvy, and a reputation for integrity. They began wooing a young deputy city manager out of Phoenix. Sheryl Sculley had earned a reputation for getting things done. Hardberger and McCombs wanted her bad. She resisted at first, but the men were persistent. Sculley finally accepted, swayed by the challenge of managing the country's seventh largest city and a $3 billion annual budget. A hefty $300,000 annual salary made her the highest paid city manager in the country.[39] On September 1, 2005, the San Antonio city council approved her hiring.

Sculley found a city government teeming with fraud, waste and abuse. She strived to bring a professional management style to a major city run politically like a south Texas cow town. She wrestled the budget into something akin to sensible. She recruited accomplished people from other cities to lead chaotic departments. She fired supervisors caught in graft schemes. She was a skilled, determined tactician.

She made many enemies, the most vocal being the local police union. She became a polarizing figure. Still, the woman had skills; there was no doubt about that. She seemed unflappable, hyper-focused, supremely sure of herself.

"She's playing three-dimensional chess while everybody else is playing checkers," San Antonio political consultant Laura Barberena told the *San Antonio Current*. "She's as hard and corporate as they come. You could be on fire, or she could be on fire, and she'd still maintain eye contact."[40]

But even Sculley, sophisticated, shrewd, and tough-as-nails, knew she had barely scraped the surface of the city's corruption problems.

4 | REGULARS

How to get rid of poor folks

AFTER A FEW MONTHS OF legal research, I crafted my original petition against Allstate using templates I found online. I sued Allstate; Teresa Butolph, who held the Allstate policy for the car I was driving; and James Keller, the motorist who plowed into me. I waxed from anticipation to dread to defiance.

Legal research was tedious at first. Then I discovered Google Scholar. Tucked away in the search engine's "more..." tab, Google Scholar lets researchers search for scholarly literature. But it also archived what for me was a game changer: appeals court and Supreme Court rulings from both federal and state courts. Even better: searches were free.

The first time I used Google Scholar, I searched for terms like breach of contract, fraud, and insurance liability. The results were thrilling.

I felt like Google was giving me a free legal education. I learned about statutes, rules, remedies and civil procedure. I read online case files, poured over judges' detailed opinions, and took notes on grounds and evidence. Finally, I was in the research zone that I enjoyed, where one tidbit led to questions that could only be answered by digging deeper into the archives.

Before long, I had completed my Plaintiff's Original Petition. I styled it *Denise McVea v. James Keller, Teresa Butolph, and Allstate*. It was time to file suit.

I headed to the historic Bexar County Courthouse, and joined the already ample parade of citizens roaming confusedly through the courthouse complex. I encountered a troubling tableau.

On the civil courts' side, unrepresented plaintiff's wept on benches. Smirking lawyers sauntered down the halls, gleefully reliving their victories over some hapless citizen.

"And then she was like, 'but that's not fair!'" one young lawyer chortled to his snickering companion as they strolled.

Scowling clerks directed harried citizens in what appeared to be an orchestrated series of wild goose chases.

When I finally found the filing clerk, she directed me to the staff attorney's office.

"You can't file a lawsuit without getting approval from them," she said.

She handed me a sheet of paper. It was an information sheet about the staff attorney's office. It stated the same thing, gave the location of the office and warned that using the attorney's office would result in a long wait to see a judge. The words on the sheet were sharp, demeaning, addressing the reader in the same way a juvenile prison guard might address a group of delinquents. "The staff attorney's office does not represent you," it concluded tersely.

In the staff attorney's office, law school graduates who had recently passed the state bar milled about with case files in hand. The office seemed slapdash, temporary. The staff attorney's office was a very strange creation. It seemed tasked with managing the flood of pro se litigants seeking justice in the courthouse, but staff attorneys adopted a hostile stance against the people forced to interact with them. The vibe was less "let's help them" and more "let's get rid of them." The staff attorney's office does not represent you, the young attorneys reminded us at every turn. Get a lawyer, they liked to say.

As if it was our fault the judicial system was unwell.

The day I filed my complaint against Allstate, the office was bustling. Finally, one of the young lawyers looked over my paperwork. She was impressed, she said. She found no reason I could not file my lawsuit.

I walked the petition down the hall, rode the elevator down to the basement, trudged the underground tunnel to the more modern Justice Center next door, ascended the elevator to the second floor of the that building and stood in line at the District Court Clerk's Office. When it was my turn, the clerk stamped the petition, cover sheet, and copies.

I had sued Allstate.

I also handed her an affidavit of inability to pay court costs, a form that stated I was too poor to pay court fees. My legal research had revealed that Texas law – at least on paper – followed the concept that poverty should not stop someone from accessing justice. I would soon learn that the Bexar County civil courts did not share the state's view.

If you wanted to access justice in Bexar County, the one thing you could *not* be was poor.

Not long after I filed an affidavit asking the court to waive court fees, I got a letter from the staff attorney's office. The court clerk, Donna Kay McKinney, had contested my affidavit of inability to pay court costs.

"Based upon a review of the information you provided in your affidavit," the letter stated, "we have decided to contest your affidavit.... *Please be advised that a failure to appear at this hearing will result in the Court striking your affidavit of Inability to Pay Costs.*"

It was signed by Staff Attorney Dinah Gaines, and her top assistant staff attorneys Brett Vangheluwe and Tiffany Duong.

"If the Court does strike your Affidavit," the letter continued, "then you will be required to pay court costs in order to maintain your action."

One sentence gave a clue as to the court's true intentions behind the letter. Actually, it wasn't a sentence at all, but a dependent clause. It read:

"(I)n order to prove your inability to pay court costs in court."

That was it.

How strange.

Someone had removed the instructions that would have made the clause a complete sentence and ended the clause with a period. But it was more than just an inadvertent grammatical error. Any information about what applicants needed to bring to court to prove they couldn't pay court fees had been deliberately omitted. It was as if someone had said, "Don't tell them that part," deleted the most informative clause, didn't even bother to fix it grammatically, and then bulk-printed the letter.

That odd, redacted notice introduced me to the civil judges' unethical, unlawful, and highly successful plot to block poor people from seeking justice in Bexar County civil courts.

It should have been a simple procedural hurdle. Theoretically, poor people have a right to access justice in America. The Supreme Court of Texas has long clarified how the state should treat the poor trying to avoid court fees.

In 1977, Vivian Goffney had gone to court in Houston to appeal the termination of her parental rights to her two small children. She was a 19-year-old black woman with a ninth grade education. Relying on public assistance and a string of odd jobs, she had been living with her cousin. She was dead broke.

Hoping to overturn the decision that took her children from her, she filed an appeal. She couldn't afford the appeal court's costs, so Goffney filed an affidavit of inability to pay court costs. The Harris County district court clerk challenged the affidavit.

A hearing was held before Harris County juvenile judge Robert L. Lowry. The county attorney, representing the court clerk, argued pitilessly that Goffney did own "a television or stereo set...she had not attempted to sell, mortgage, or pawn it."

Goffney did not own a television or stereo set, her legal defense fund lawyer corrected. She *had* bought a secondhand record player, and it was her only possession.[41] Still, Judge Robert Lowry agreed with the clerk. If this poor, struggling woman wanted to get her children back, she would have to pay the court.

Goffney's pro bono lawyers appealed that heartless decision all the way to the Texas Supreme Court. The state's high court rejected the lower courts' decision, relying on legal principles already established in a 1942 case, *Pinchback v. Hockless*. The *Pinchback* case established that poor Texans should be able to access courts.

The question for the courts was a simple one: could an applicant "pay the costs, or a part thereof, if he really wanted to and made a good faith effort to do so?"[42] The high court stressed that it had no problem requiring a litigant to take out loans or sell or pawn belongings in order to access the courts if he was prosperous. But Goffney's case confirmed that a poor person did not have to further impoverish herself to pay court costs.

"If a laborer was barely earning the necessities of life for himself and family," the Texas Supreme Court decided, "he should not be required to mortgage his hand tools or household furniture in order to raise funds to pay the court costs."

The rules were necessary "to protect the weak against the strong, and to make sure that no man should be denied a forum in which to adjudicate his rights merely because he is too poor to pay the court costs."

Ms. Goffney was obviously poor and so was I.

I just knew that I was poor enough to sue a villainous multi-billion dollar corporation without having to pay court costs.

The hallway hearings

On August 31, 2010, I went to my scheduled poverty hearing. But instead of waiting in presiding court to see a judge, I was ushered into a corner of the hallway. I joined about 20 other people standing in a halfhearted line. They, too, were there to see a judge to make their cases that they could not afford to pay court costs.

We stood around expectantly, waiting to be led to our hearing. After about 20 minutes, three young staff attorneys approached. I thought they would escort the group to a courtroom where the judge would hear our cases one by one. Like traffic court, I thought. Instead, they split the line into three sections each facing an assistant staff attorney. The young attorneys began asking to see our affidavits. They looked over the document indifferently, asked a few perfunctory questions, and then informed us one-by-one that we did not qualify for a waiver.

"Wait a second," I said. "We're supposed to see a judge."

"The judges don't handle these cases," they said.

"Why not?" I asked. "Since when?"

"Ma'am, we have other people to help."

I scoffed. They continued their illegal rejection of our applications until we no longer had any reason to remain in the courthouse. We never saw the inside of a courtroom.

A few days later, I received a notice from the court. A judge had issued a default judgment against me.

A default judgment?

A judge issues a default judgment when a party in a lawsuit fails to take some required action. Most default judgments come when a defendant ignores a summons or doesn't show up to court. It's like a forfeit victory in sports. If one team doesn't show up to a game or shows up without enough players, a forfeit victory is awarded to the other team.

But we had shown up. The courthouse regulars just wouldn't let us play.

So that was the scheme. It was too clever by half.

The staff attorneys' mission was to get rid of all these citizens who had the audacity to come to court without a lawyer and then refuse to pay.

Of course, a bunch of lawyers fresh out of law school had no legal authority to deny our petitions. Common law, and the contest letter itself, confirmed that a *judge* decided in a *hearing* who was too poor to pay court costs – not some snot-nosed lawyer in a hallway. But most poor people going to court in Bexar County don't know that.

So the staff attorney corrals them in a hallway, begins the sham process of pretending to apply some legal standard, and then falsely informs the litigants they have somehow failed the test.

Meanwhile, the judge sits in the courtroom knowing that the staff attorneys are denying people on his docket access to his courtroom. The litigants, now informed they have to pay if they want to have their cases heard, must either come up with the money, or, they think, give up their cases. After the dozens of plaintiffs have been sent home believing the staff attorneys' fictions, the judge then mass-signs the default judgments in favor of the clerk.

Importantly, there is nothing in the default judgment to suggest the dismissal has anything to do with money. Many of the plaintiffs, unable to afford court costs, will not return.

The hallway farce lent new light to the deletion in the contest letter. The missing information telling applicants what to bring to their hearing had been omitted because the staff attorney, judges, and court clerk knew there would be no hearing.

The presiding court judges are then free to while away the afternoon hours in empty courtrooms bantering with bailiffs instead of sitting through the never-ending gripes of the poor, unrepresented masses.

Meanwhile, the official record in the Bexar County court clerk's office, based on the thousands of civil default judgments on file, is compelling evidence that most unrepresented litigants just don't show up for court.

"Keep your voice down."

I eventually got the improper default judgment against me overturned. To do that, I had to return to the staff attorney's office. I wanted to see a judge, I told them. I rejected the default judgment as improper, illegal, and unconstitutional. Court staff responded defiantly, but also nervously. Unsure of what to do with me, the other assistant attorneys would turn me over to Brett Vangheluwe, a 20-something blond lawyer from Houston.

Dinah Gaines's second in command, Vangheluwe barked and yelled at me every time I showed up. He refused to answer my questions. "We don't represent you," he said repeatedly. He could not have been more disrespectful. He was haughty, disparaging, and supremely disrespectful. I grew to detest him. Every time I was forced to deal with him, we bickered.

He constantly tried to send me on wild goose chases. Once, I asked him what rule or statute gave him the right to act as prosecutor, judge, and jury on litigants' requests to waive court costs. The Federal Register, he told me. I laughed at him. The Federal Register is the official journal of the federal government and contained more than 60,000 pages. It had as much to do with the staff attorney's unlawful judging as the bible.

"I'm pretty sure the Federal Register does not make you a judge," I snorted.

"I have other people to help," he would say scornfully, "I don't have time to sit here wasting my time on you."

"I'm pretty sure you haven't helped a single person in your entire life, Brett Vangheluwe," I would retort.

It was always like that when I had to deal with Brett Vangheluwe. Once I asked to speak to Dinah Gaines the staff attorney. I wanted answers to my questions about the judges' default judgments against poor people. I also wanted to complain about Vangheluwe. As luck would have it, she was in presiding court.

Who gave these recent law school graduates the authority to act as judges, I asked her in hushed tones. I couldn't get a straight answer from her, either. We were both whispering but when she had had enough of my questions, she raised her voice.

"Keep your voice down," Gaines blurted. I hadn't raised my voice, but she wanted the conversation to end. She looked over at the bailiff, who began eying us with interest. I could see where this was headed. I decided that from that moment on, I would just put my questions in writing.

I filed a motion challenging the default judgment. I wasn't allowed to see the judge, I argued, so there was no way he could deny my request to waive fees. After a runaround with the staff attorney's office that included more nasty encounters with Brett Vangheluwe, the motion was scheduled for hearing. About three weeks later, I returned to presiding court. I sat through the docket, but my name was not called. I went to the court administrator.

I was supposed to be on the docket, I said. There was a surge of activity, a bunch of hemming and hawing, and then finally, I was handed an order signed by Judge Gloria Saldaña approving my request to waive costs.

Later, someone who identified himself as an FBI supervisor called me and suggested I file a complaint with the local courts about the thousands of people unlawfully obstructed from accessing justice in Bexar County civil courts through the improper handling of their requests to avoid paying court costs.

"I'm not a member of that class," I reminded him.

"Oh," he said. "That's right."

5 | CIRCLING

Bad neighborhood

AROUND THE TIME THAT I sued Allstate, the city of San Antonio was expressing a firm commitment to revitalizing the inner Eastside of San Antonio.

Sometimes referred to as the "black belt" of the city, the neighborhoods I grew up around had long suffered from neglect. President Barack Obama designated it one of several "Promise Zones" a federal program of economic development targeting historically disenfranchised communities. I didn't know then that sophisticated white collar criminal networks already existed to steal that money.

I had been looking to buy a house on the Eastside for about a year. I had already adverse-possessed an abandoned crack house on Martin Luther King Drive.

The old garage I adverse possessed was the perfect place to develop Auris Project information access programs. Auris's rural Mexico programs had been designed to address geographic isolation. The programs I envisioned for the Eastside would address social isolation in an urban setting. I had some ideas already. I knew I wanted to do Freedom of Information workshops. In my mind, there was no reason that only journalists should know how to ask for government documents or know where to look. I also wanted to create an information center to specifically help residents monitor the millions of dollars in federal aid they had been awarded. I had already seen that the local government did not value the public's right to know. (Once, a City of San Antonio public information officer accidently returned an emailed public information request to me that she had meant to forward. It said, "Just got this in. Looks like it's time for another Gaggy Award!")

I found an old farmhouse just off the corner of Hackberry Street. The house, a cedar wood two-story structure built in 1900, was sturdy but neglected. It had asbestos siding over shiplap wood siding, a second-story balcony, high ceilings, and an attic that was tall enough to convert into a third floor. The previous owner had converted it into two apartments. A Section 8 tenant occupied the downstairs apartment. Tedi and I moved into the upstairs apartment and kept the tenant, a middle-aged woman named Ruby.

The house needed a lot of work but we loved it.

It had its pros and cons. For instance, from the front balcony, we had a view of the Alamodome and the Tower of the Americas. From the back kitchen window, we had a view of the drug dealers and prostitutes conducting business on the empty lot behind our house. Business was brisk.

We were excited and nervous. We were glad the city was focusing on the area. I wondered how long it would be before the police would clear the area of overt street crime.

Then I wondered why they hadn't already.

From crack house to information center

The move to the Eastside meant we were now also closer to the old workshop we had adverse possessed, which meant that we could start building the Eastside information center in earnest.

I had been researching adverse possession since coming across an article in Portland in the early 1990s. Many U.S. states, including Texas, had adverse possession laws. The statute allowed people to take over abandoned property, fix it up, and then eventually take formal title if no legitimate claims to title were made after a certain amount of time. In Texas, adverse possessors who had no prior claim to the title could apply for title ten years after taking possession of the property. They only had to keep it up, pay the taxes, use it, and maintain "continual possession."

I had grown up on the neglected Eastside. I had watched as discriminatory city policies had devastated parts of the area, leaving abandoned homes and empty lots scattered across neighborhoods struggling to survive. Municipal cures, if officials bothered to address the problem at all, were limited: demolition or gentrification. Demolition was the easiest route. The city declared the house a nuisance and then hired contractors to tear it down. One day the house is there, the next day it's gone.

Gentrification was much more mysterious. Suddenly, properties were in the hands of developers and others. Neighbors might just assume these outsiders bought the houses at tax sales. Sometimes they had, but sometimes they hadn't.

Adverse possession, on the other hand, offered an incentive for people to take over abandoned property in distressed areas and make those properties viable and useful again. The problem is that most people in poor neighborhoods don't know about the laws and most developers don't want properties they can't immediately sell.

I wanted to change that. Using adverse possession laws, I could turn at least one abandoned property into a viable resource for the community. My plan was to find an abandoned property, adverse possess it, use it for the information center, eventually take title, and show neighborhood groups how to preserve and protect its own housing stock before developers came in and stole everything.

I looked at several properties on the Eastside. When I found one with potential, I would search government tax, appraisal, and deed records. I had to be careful. Just because a house is abandoned doesn't mean that someone won't later make a claim on it. I had to find a property that was truly forsaken.

I found the perfect property. Located on the corner of Martin Luther King Drive and Meerscheidt Street, the property was one block from St. Philip's Community College and a few blocks from Pittman Sullivan Park. It had two structures on it, an old garage that fronted Martin Luther King Drive and a small wood framed house that faced Meerscheidt.

The back door to the house was wide open. Inside, crack vials and dirty syringes littered the floors. Feces sat in dried piles near corners. Copper piping had been ripped away. The house smelled of piss.

I looked up the property records. The owners, Gustavo and Carolina Treviño had passed away in the 90s from old age. Gustavo was a mechanic. He fixed cars in the workshop in the back. Carolina was a grocer. She ran a small grocery from the front room of the wood framed house. The couple lived in the rest of the house. They were devout Catholics with strong family ties to Mexico. They were hard workers and thrifty. When Gustavo died, Carolina Treviño inherited the property. Then she died. The couple had no children.

In her will, Carolina left everything to both Gustavo's siblings and to her siblings. If any of the couple's siblings died before them, the couple's nieces and nephews would inherit their rightful portion of the estate. Most of that first generation's siblings died before her.

Lawyers involved in the probate case identified the potential heirs to the property. There were quite a few. According to probate and tax records, several lived in San Antonio, and several scattered across the U.S. A few lived in Mexico. According to probate records, a battle ensued among second generation heirs qualified as legitimate beneficiaries and how much of the estate any potential beneficiary was entitled to.

By 2000, probate of Carolina's will had stalled.

After Gustavo's and Carolina's deaths, their estate contained enough money to pay the taxes on the property for years. That is why the property had not been sold in Bexar County's rapacious tax auctions. Free from the gluttonous clutches of the county tax apparatus, the Treviños' property sat on the Eastside, abandoned by heirs and ignored by the city. Soon, homeless people, rats, and addicts moved in.

By 2012, the Treviños' estate funds ran dry. By that time, the Auris Project had been in possession for about four years.

Linebarger Goggan sent tax bills to the potential heirs of 1614 Martin Luther King Drive. Responding through lawyers, the heirs signed affidavits waiving any claim to the property. They had no interest, they swore. That was as good as it got for an adverse possessor: sworn affidavits duly filed renouncing all claim to title. There was nothing standing in the way of us one day taking legal ownership of the property. 1614 Martin Luther King Drive would be the Auris Project, Inc.'s nonprofit community information center.

I did not see the plan as vulnerable. The only people with any potential claim to the property had formally rejected it. City officials certainly wouldn't object, I remember thinking.

I mean, they hadn't given a damn when it was overrun with heroin addicts and crackheads.

6 | GLOVES

McVea Deposition, *McVea v. Keller*

"So the vehicle that you marked as (Exhibit) A was executing the same turn that you were executing at the time of the accident...?" Allstate's lawyer asked.

"Well, it appears to be similar, yes," I replied.

"And what kind of traffic was on Hildebrand?"

"It was midday traffic so there were quite a few vehicles."

"Is there a turn lane there on Hildebrand?"

"Yes, there is."

"And you were in the turn lane to turn left?"

"That's right."

"What was the weather like?"

"It was sunny."

"It was sunny, it was clear?"

"It was clear."

It was October 28, 2010 and I was about an hour into a deposition called by Allstate. The insurer had hired three law firms to fight my lawsuit worth less than $15,000. The law office of Gutierrez Wymer was in a small 1950s-era business building on Broadway Street, posted a few blocks shy of the well-heeled bubble town[43] of Alamo Heights.

I wore a business pantsuit. No receptionist came out to greet me. Deposing me was Matthew Wymer of Gutierrez Wymer. He represented James Keller. His partner Albert Gutierrez, who would become a major character in the Allstate tale, did not attend the deposition.

Allstate also hired Steve Katz of Brock Person Guerra Reyna law firm. A slender man nursing a strained back, Katz represented Teresa, although he had neither met nor spoken to her. He asked the fewest questions. He just wanted to confirm that I would dismiss Teresa from the case if Allstate paid the PIP portion of the policy. I told him that I would.

John McGlothlin, a short man with the handsome face of a Hollywood actor, worked for Goldman Pennebaker & Phipps, the law firm that represented Allstate Fire and Casualty Company. They all sat around the conference table as Wymer interrogated me. I felt confident. I had long lost my admiration for lawyers and I wasn't a stranger to depositions. I had sat for depositions twice before, once when a Dallas slumlord sued me for libel, and again when I witnessed a Mac truck run over a homeless man's legs.

Wymer, who had the look and demeanor of a hard partying frat boy, asked most of the questions. His tone was condescending throughout. He asked a series of tiresome questions designed to bore me into agreeing with loaded follow up questions. He asked leading questions. He used words out of context, asking for my agreement.

For me, it was child's play.

Journalists are difficult interview subjects for lawyers. We train in words. We spend a lot of time thinking about what words mean, suggest, convey. We get criticized when we write something that people don't understand. We are also obsessed with facts. Our entire profession surrounds the hunt for and communication of facts. Here's an example:

The day O.J. Simpson was alleged to have killed his wife Nicole Simpson and her friend Ronald Goldman, I was working as a staff writer for the *Dallas Observer*.

When the news hit of the double murders, all work stopped. *Observer* staff began searching for more details about what would turn out to be the crime of the century. Advertising agents and other staff members flooded into the small newsroom. Some staff members huddled around television sets. Some passed wire stories around. Others picked up the nearest phone to call and share the news with family and friends. During all of this, I noticed a peculiar phenomenon. Without fail, when non-journalists described what was happening, they said:

"O.J. Simpson killed his wife."

When journalists described the homicides, they said, without fail:

"O.J. Simpson is suspected of killing his wife."

So it was easy for me to see and avoid Wymer's tricks. I never agreed to something that was not factual, and I made sure we both agreed to terms before answering a loaded question. But my neck was still hurting from the wreck and the pain increased as the deposition dragged on. I struggled to stay alert to make sure I always knew what I was agreeing to. I could tell that I was frustrating him. Every time I began a response with "Using your words...," he changed the subject.

At one point, they tried to get me to testify about the police report:

Q. Referring to the police report, is there anything about the statement that the police officer has indicated here that you disagree with?
A. Yes, the waiting part.
Q. So you were not waiting?
A. No, I was not waiting.
Q. But everything else is correct?
A. Let me check. (Witness reading document.)
A. I feel like something is missing. Actually, I'm missing page four.
Q. This is the copy we've got.

I kept insisting that a page in the police report was missing. The lawyers tried to convince me that they had handed me a complete report. When I could not be persuaded, the lawyers dropped the ruse.

Katz slid the missing last page to Wymer.

"I've just been handed what appears to be a much, much better copy," said Wymer with a straight face. "Let me go ahead and mark this.... Katz has handed me I think a substantially better version and I am going to go ahead and mark this as Exhibit Five."

Even though we had not gone off the record, the final deposition omitted most of the dialogue about the missing page.

The deposition tricks were just part of the plan. Allstate was also drowning me in paperwork. My home office was covered in mountains of motions, interrogatories, requests for disclosures, and other demands from Allstate's lawyers. I struggled to meet their demands in a timely fashion, gathering documents, making copies and running back and forth to the post office.

Meanwhile, Allstate lawyers were ignoring my request for documents. In fact, months after asking for copies of the insurance policies for both vehicles involved in the accident, I realized I had never gotten them.

I brought that up in the deposition. In Texas, civil courts require parties to release requested documents (called "production") within 30 days. Allstate was in violation of court rules. McGlothlin, who worked for the law firm representing Allstate, said he would check on the status of the policy during the next break. After the break, he said that Allstate had not given the lawyers a copy of the policy.

"I have conferred with our office," he said with a straight face, "and we have requested, but not obtained the policy and when we do, we'll produce it to you."

Allstate had hired three law firms to represent its interests for a policy dispute worth less than $30,000. But the company wouldn't give its own lawyers a copy of the policy they were paying them to defend. I was incredulous.

Brushing aside my disbelief, Wymer began haranguing me about documents they had requested from me.

"I thought I had sent you at least some documents," I told Wymer.

"No ma'am, I have not received anything from you on that."

"Well, that's an oversight," I told him. At some point in the deposition, Wymer entered into evidence a medical document and asked me questions about it.

Wait a minute, I thought. He could only have gotten that record from me. I took a closer look at the papers splayed across the conference table. I had provided those documents. He was lying on the record, confident that they had overwhelmed to the point that I would not notice.

"You have them before you," I said at one point. He continued as though I had not said anything.

When I read the deposition later, I spotted the scheme. Someone had changed just enough words to alter my testimony in key places to allow the court to dismiss my case before trial. For instance, I had said the following:

"If Keller were paying attention when he approached the intersection, he would have seen me there and he would have done what everybody else does, which is to stop, let the flow continue and go forward and – that is not what he did."

But in a brazen edit, the deposition record had been altered to omit the word "not," It now concluded "and that is what he did." There were several similar edits.

I realized that Allstate hadn't bothered to provide the policies to its lawyers because it had planned to use the altered deposition to get the case dismissed in summary judgment." I could see that Allstate lawyers had been playing this game against pro se litigants for a long time. They were good at it.

I complained to the court about the alterations. I asked the judge to fine Allstate's lawyers for changing the record. In a motion to sanction, I pointed out how what I said in the office differed from the deposition record.

The judge, Janet Littlejohn, who had the power to sanction attorney misconduct, wanted no part of that. She directed me instead to the state bar. I knew that the State Bar of Texas had a reputation for routinely dismissing citizen complaints against attorneys. Plus, I was running in circles trying to stay ahead of the Allstate lawyers' shenanigans. I would have to let it slide.

Still, I won that round. When Allstate's lawyers tried to get the case dismissed in summary judgment, they were careful not to use any of the falsified testimony in the deposition.

Accord and Satisfaction

A judge ordered us to mediation. We agreed to use Rene Diaz, a former Bexar County judge, as the mediator. Allstate sent Larry Goldman from Goldman Pennebaker & Phipps. After a brief, useless discussion, Diaz placed Goldman in another room. The mediator was respectful and polite as he moved from room to room, trying to mediate a needless dispute.

At one point, with Goldman in another room, I told the mediator that the adjustors had made promises to pay my medical bills but then didn't do it. I told him about the check, and how the company didn't provide me an agreement to sign. They still owed for the medical bills, I told him, and the absence of a signed agreement is proof of that.

"Accord and satisfaction," he said kindly.

"I'm sorry?"

"Accord and satisfaction. That's what you're talking about."

When he left the room, I wrote it down. The mediation, as expected, went nowhere. Allstate refused to honor the adjustors' promises. When I got home later, I looked up accord and satisfaction.

Simply put, it's what Texans sign to show that they agreed to a final settlement, even if it was less than what the contract dictated. Allstate knew that I would never sign a waiver that didn't confirm its adjustor's promises. The company had obviously convinced people in the past that if they cashed the check, they had no claim.

When Allstate tried to get the case dismissed in before trial, I brought up accord and satisfaction. The summary judgment hearing was held in Judge Richard Price's courtroom. The judge greeted Albert Gutierrez, Allstate's lawyer representing James Keller, warmly. As suspected, Gutierrez argued that Allstate had closed out its obligations to me when it issued me the $2600 check and that I agreed with that settlement when I cashed it.

When it was my turn, I argued that Allstate hadn't met any of the elements required to prove accord and satisfaction. Gutierrez was supposed to come into court and show that there was a specific "meeting of the minds," I argued. Allstate had no proof that the check dissolved all further insurer obligations. Something like a signed agreement.

"They do not have that," I repeated, as I recited several elements the company needed to prove.

Judge Price denied the motion for summary judgment. The case against Allstate would continue.

"I'm sorry," the judge told Gutierrez contritely.

"That's all right," Allstate's lawyer pardoned.

Soon after Allstate's failed summary judgment attempt, I would often look up and find some bland, untidy white man staring at me from a distance.

Weeks later, in a courthouse hallway, McGlothlin told me that he was removing himself from the litigation. He was leaving Goldman Pennebaker & Phipps and returning to his hometown of San Marcos about 45 miles away. Then he said something interesting.

"I have a reputation to uphold,' he muttered under his breath. "Judges respect me."

During my deposition I could tell he was confused as to why Allstate was putting up such a nasty fight for an obviously worthy claim. I could tell he didn't want to be associated with something like that.

"You're a good person," I said.

He smiled gratefully. McGlothlin headed out to make a simpler, presumably more decent living in San Marcos.

I thought about him from time to time, wondering if he had ever learned that there was little reason to worry about his reputation with Bexar County judges.

On February 16, 2011, district judge Barbara Nellermoe separated Keller's case from Allstate. That meant that my Deceptive Trade Practices claim against Allstate could only go forward if I won my case against Keller.

Gutierrez and the other Allstate lawyers continued to harass me about documents I had already turned over while withholding evidence I had requested.

And then, seemingly out of the blue, I got charged for a second time with practicing law without a license.

The Unauthorized Practice of Law Committee

Right around the time I sued Allstate, my friend Teresa returned from work to find a court summons thrown on the ground near her front door.

A third party debt collection law firm was suing her for a charged off account she had abandoned during a contentious divorce more than 10 years earlier. They had been reporting it to the credit bureau, hurting her credit. That was illegal, I told her. And now, they were suing her.

She couldn't afford a lawyer so I agreed to help her defend herself against the illegitimate lawsuit. I showed her how to use Google Scholar and helped her draft a response to the suit. She filed her response in the county justice of the peace court. The collection agency/law firm continued calling her and harassing her. She was frazzled. I wrote a letter telling them to stop. I was handling communications as I was acting as her "legal representative" in the matter, I told them.

That turned out to be a poor choice of words, I later realized. The next thing I knew, the debt collector who was reaping millions of dollars by harassing people into paying invalid debts had hauled *me* before the Texas Unauthorized Practice of Law Committee. The complaint was accepted by a UPLC subcommittee in the county where the third party debt collector law firm was located.

It is illegal, the committee wrote me in a cease and desist letter, to act as a lawyer in Texas without a license.

Most unauthorized practice of law cases in Texas are levied against notary publics who charge a fee for legal advice. I was not doing that. I had every right to help my friend wage a defense against unlawful debt collection activity. It's a first amendment right.

A cease and desist agreement was attached to the letter. The committee wanted me to sign the agreement and send it back to the UPLC. And I was to stop engaging in the unauthorized practice of law. If satisfied, the letter stated, the subcommittee would drop the unauthorized practice of law charge against me. If I didn't sign, I might be forced to attend a hearing where the committee may mete out serious consequences.

"This is bullshit," I told Tedi. I wrote the committee back.

I wasn't acting as a lawyer, I responded. Teresa was my friend and I was trying to help her. Mostly, I conducted research, I explained. Teresa had filed the case herself as a pro se litigant and my efforts were mostly to protect her from the continued, illegal harassment of the law firm that sued her illegally in the first place.

So no, I wrote, I would not be signing any cease and desist agreement, because I was not engaging in the alleged activity.

The subcommittee dismissed the charge. Teresa won her case against the predatory debtor law firm and I considered the issue resolved.

But, months later, as I started to gain ground in the Allstate case, Elliot S. Cappuccio, a private attorney and local member of the local subcommittee of the UPLC, filed new unauthorized practice of law charges against me. Cappuccio's cease and desist letter was even more restrictive than the original one.

I had mentioned the UPLC harassment in an Allstate hearing. Now, I knew why Gutierrez spent so much time during my deposition trying to get me to say I worked in the area of "legal rights." He was trying to garner evidence for Cappuccio's sham unauthorized practice of law charge.

I sent Cappuccio the same letter I sent the subcommittee. No, I was not going to sign the cease and desist letter because I was not engaging in the unauthorized practice of law. After months of getting nowhere, he called me. In an abusive call where he yelled, threatened, and mocked me, he tried to terrorize me into signing the cease and desist agreement. I refused. I would later complain about that call and the harassing UPLC charge to the court and the bar, but of course, I got no response. Still, unable to bully me into submission, Cappuccio slunk out of sight, and the second UPLC case against me quietly disappeared.

Cappuccio never bothered me again. I would not hear about him again until years later, when I broke away from Allstate's cyber prison and learned about his brief, humiliating adventure with Scientologists.

The experience with Cappuccio and the UPLC was a lesson: call their bluffs, read everything, and above all else, don't sign anything they hand you when they are yelling.

I was surprising Allstate and its lawyers. Gutierrez's smug smile had waned slightly. He seemed less confident and his thinning hair had gained momentum, with only a few lackluster wisps remaining on top of his skull. They strained wanly up and outward as though lacking the energy needed to escape a toxic host. His suits were dustier. His wife told him that she was worried about what he was getting himself mixed up in. He told her to take care of his house and his three children. He would take care of the rest.

Still, it wasn't turning out to be the breeze he thought it would.

Unexpectedly, I had not only survived summary judgment, but I had exposed for the record clear-cut examples of attorney misconduct that defined Bexar County's civil courts. The record now included examples of record tampering, obstruction of justice, violations of court rules, and an ethics system in complete breakdown.

These potential exposures could not have come at a worse time. With the FBI sniffing around, the last thing Allstate and its enablers needed were credible allegations of widespread corruption and obstruction of justice. I had become a bigger problem than anticipated.

I was promptly arrested.

7 | ORCHESTRATION

False arrest No. 1

ON FEBRUARY 23, 2011, IN what I would later learn was an orchestrated incident, I was denied passage on a Greyhound bus, assaulted by a security guard, and arrested by San Antonio police. It would be the first of several false arrests that seemed to occur the minute it became obvious that I had gathered important evidence against Allstate.

I continued developing the Auris Project. The book sales, auctions, and flea markets were keeping the lights on. We needed another van for moving items for sale. I kept an eye out for an old van on some of the surplus websites open to non-profit organizations.

In February, the University of Texas Health Science Center in Houston began auctioning an old Chevy van that it had retired. The motor ran reliably and the vehicle was in overall great shape. I won it for less than $500. But how to transport it 200 miles from Houston? I decided I would catch a Greyhound bus, taxi to the auction site from the bus station, and drive the van to San Antonio.

I bought the ticket online, but, as usual, there were problems with my online efforts. The site was glitchy, intermittently unresponsive. I kept trying. After several attempts, I was able to print my Greyhound boarding pass to Houston. It looked weird, not at all professional.

Years later, I would understand that hackers had designed the ticket as the first step in a ruse that would play out exactly as intended. But at the time, I did not know that.

The bus was scheduled to leave at 6 a.m. on February 23, 2011.

The day of the trip, I got up early. I decided not to drink coffee, thinking that I would just doze through the three and half hour trip. I would get coffee near the station in Houston, and maybe breakfast.

Tedi dropped me off at the bus station. I walked over to the ticket counter to confirm my ticket and get a boarding pass. That is a boarding pass, the clerk said. It had printed out weird, he said, but it was valid. I asked if he needed to print me out a new one. He said no. Just be in line before six, he said.

I soon joined the line forming at the bus that would take us to Houston. I desperately wanted a cup of coffee. I had no doubts I would be able to sleep through the trip. The driver stood at the bus entrance and began taking tickets. He was a short, thin middle-aged black man. I later learned his name was Gary Daniels. There were about eight people in front of me. About 15 passengers queued up behind me.

When it was my turn, handed the driver my ticket. He immediately started yelling. "This ain't right," he barked. "This ain't right!"

I looked around in dazed confusion. The other passengers were also perplexed. None of us was expecting this level of energy or hostility.

I told Daniels that the ticket had been approved at the ticket counter and that there was proof of purchase at the ticket counter if he had doubts about the ticket's validity. It is unclear to me if Daniels heard the entire explanation because he continued to yell throughout my explanation. I asked Daniels why he was yelling.

People began murmuring behind me. Several people looked at me with sympathy. There were murmurs of confusion and disapproval. I turned back to Daniels and out of the corner of my eye saw the security guard, later identified as David Galbreath, quickly approaching. I again turned to Daniels and asked him why he was yelling. "Because you are not hearing me," he roared.

Galbreath stepped closer in a menacing fashion. A Statewide Patrol badge was stitched onto his uniform. He was handsome, in his fifties. Sporting a blonde crew cut and muscular physique, he looked like a former exotic dancer who had aged out of the business. The bus driver rudely ordered me out of the line, gesturing with his hand that I should get out of the way.

I was confused and annoyed, but also uncaffeinated, so my response was muted, befuddled. What was going on? I felt that this was not the first time that these two men had harassed and abused a Greyhound customer. Years later, I would understand that the whole thing was contrived and that was why I couldn't make sense of it.

"Well," I said, "I am going back to the ticket clerk, since you do not know what your own tickets look like."

I turned and began walking back inside. Galbreath immediately walked up behind me and said in a threatening voice, "you do not talk to Gary that way."

I continued to walk and responded, "I will talk to him how I please."

Galbreath inched closer to me. Gesturing with one arm, he growled, "You get out."

He pointed at the garage exit to the street. At this point, he had come within reach of me. He was extremely threatening.

"I am going to talk to the ticket clerk," I said, speeding up.

"I'll put you out," Galbreath said and positioned himself even closer to me. This guy is trying to put me in a full nelson, I thought. When I turned my head to the right to see him, he stepped to the left to be at my back. I knew he was about to attack me, and I could tell that this was something he had done before. He was extremely muscular, very tense, and completely sociopathic. He would hurt me badly if he thought he could get away with it, I thought. I looked behind him to see if the other passengers were watching this scene, but a second bus was obscuring us from the passengers' view.

My mind was racing. I needed to keep an eye on him. It was not lost on me that he moved in for the attack after we had passed the bus that blocked the other passengers' view. If he grabbed me, I decided, I would scream, break free, and run back to the crowd at the bus.

I turned to face him and began walking backwards. "You lay a hand on me," I said, still walking backwards, "and you will rue this day."

"No, I won't," he said, but he backed off. I scurried to put distance between us.

We continued bickering as I entered the building. At this point, the argument had escalated into a series of insults flying back and forth. Galbreath told me that I didn't deserve to be there, that I was not going to get on any Greyhound bus. I told him that he would lose his job for his behavior. He told me that he didn't care. He called me crazy. I called him an idiot. He asked me if I was bipolar. He asked me if I was schizophrenic. Later, I would understand that this orchestrated attack and arrest was the beginning of the plot to paint me as mentally, violently unstable.

By this point, I was extremely agitated. I approached the ticket counter and complained to the ticket clerk that I was being harassed by Galbreath and that the bus driver would not let me board the bus. The ticket clerk instructed me to keep my voice down. This was nothing new to him. I told him my voice was raised because I was afraid, provoked, and agitated by how I was treated. He was unsympathetic.

Galbreath told the ticket clerk to give me a refund so that I could leave. That was strange.

Why would he offer me a refund if he didn't think I had paid for my ticket?

The refund order unintentionally revealed the scheme. Up to that point, Daniels and Galbreath had acted under the pretext that I had not paid for the bus ticket and that was why I was not allowed to board the bus. His refund instructions destroyed that pretext.

The ticket clerk handed me a sleeve similar to the one that he had placed my ticket in, but there was nothing in it. Galbreath continued to hurl insults at me, making it very difficult for me to have a civil conversation with the clerk. Galbreath again told me to leave; I ignored him. I told the ticket clerk that I wanted to speak to a manager. He responded that the manager would not be in until 9 a.m. I asked him to call the manager. He refused. I told him that I would wait for the manager. I turned and made my way to a nearby chair. Galbreath followed me and told me that I was not going to sit down. "Get out," he growled. I worried that he would hit me or start dragging me out of the chair. I turned to the other passengers, who were looking on the altercation with interest. I made an announcement.

"We deserve better than this," I said in a calm and modulated voice. "We deserve to be treated with respect at all times." Galbreath didn't like that. Now everyone was watching with avid interest.

There would be no confusion about who was the aggressor. I would soon learn that it didn't matter how many witnesses saw what was happening to me. They couldn't tell what happened if no one asked.

I sat down.

Galbreath stood over me and continued verbally assaulting me, calling me crazy, schizophrenic, and trash. Standing over me, he told the ticket clerk to call the police. I told Galbreath that I wanted to talk to the police because I intended to file charges of assault, intimidation, and terroristic threat against him. He said he didn't care. He walked away.

"I am the police."

I called Tedi. At this point, the energy level in the room had returned to normal, and I felt relatively safe and calm. I told her what had happened. She told me to press charges. I told her that I would when the police arrived. She asked me if I had already called the police. I told her that Galbreath had already called the police.

Daniels and Galbreath walked up to the ticket counter. I overheard the clerk telling my abusers that the ticket was valid and that there was no reason to deny me entry onto the bus.

Daniels and Galbreath looked slightly worried, but neither men approached me to apologize or offer me my seat back on the bus. I was very upset, but I felt it was important to remain calm. I didn't want to alarm Tedi or get off on the wrong foot with the manager when he arrived.

In other words, I showed incredible restraint.

A few seconds later, SAPD officer Robert Muñoz arrived. What followed would be a pattern of SAPD misconduct that I would experience and document many times. Muñoz approach the security guard, who pointed at me as he talked. I was sitting quietly on the line with Tedi, waiting my turn.

Muñoz approached me. The bus station environment was once again quiet. I hung up the phone and greeted the officer.

"What's the problem?" Officer Muñoz asked, politely.

"Can we step outside? I asked.

"Sure," he said. We stepped out the door and stood near a wall in the garage.

I could feel my voice trembling as I recounted the assault. As a talked, Muñoz studied me, first looking at my hair, then my clothes, then my tennis shoes. When I finished recounting the incident, Officer Muñoz said: "Ok. Now I have heard what you have to say, and now you have to leave."

I was dumbstruck for a moment. "I'm sorry?" I asked.

"I listened to what you had to say and now you have to leave."

"But, I want to press charges against those men for attacking and harassing me," I told him. He shook his head.

"They no longer want your business, so you have to leave," he said.

I explained to Officer Muñoz that I had a valid bus ticket, I was refused entry on the bus for no reason, and that Galbreath had physically threatened me and verbally abused me out of the blue.

"That's what happens when you act a fool," the cop said.

I told him that I did not believe that Galbreath's illegal behavior could on the face of it be taken as representative of Greyhound and that the manager was on his way. I told him that the manager, who was not accused of assault and threat, would be the person to determine if I had consent to be on the property.

The officer asked me for my Texas driver's license. I handed it to him. I asked him to go interview the passengers who stood in the line with me. "They can tell you what happened," I insisted. He refused. I told him that there were numerous witnesses to my interaction with Daniels and Galbreath and that they were still on the property.

I begged him to go and interview some of the other passengers who were in line with me. He again refused. I told him that I was going to call the police.

"I am the police," he said.

I shook my head. "No you're not," I said. "If you were the police, you would be doing police work. And that would mean you would be interviewing the witnesses on the bus. They would tell you that he's lying."

Muñoz shook his head again. He could not be persuaded to talk to the witnesses.

Another cop arrived and immediately began telling me to get off the property. I tried to explain to him what was going on but he rudely waved me off. I asked him to interview the other witnesses present before their bus departed for Houston. He also refused.

Officer Muñoz told me that if I did not leave immediately, I would be arrested. I told him that I could not leave until we had either confirmed with the manager that I did not have effective consent and issued a refund, or the police officers present conducted a proper investigation by interviewing the witnesses to the incident that he was called out on. He told me to turn around. I did. And for what would be the first time of several, a SAPD police officer arrested me after I had been a victim of a readily verifiable crime.

He put handcuffs on me and handed my purse to the unidentified officer.

The unidentified officer walked me to the street side of the police car and opened the back door. I asked him again if he would interview the other passengers. He said in a rough voice, "get in the car," and shoved me down. I did not enter the car but turned and looked at him sadly. That got to him a little bit. He said more respectfully, "Get in the car, ma'am."

I awkwardly climbed into the back of the squad car.

From the backseat, I could hear the two officers talking. Officer Muñoz grumbled that I had forced him to do paperwork that he did not want to do. He asked the unidentified officer to take my purse to the property room. The unidentified officer complied. The two men made a thorough search of my purse, and then the unidentified officer took the purse and departed.

I later was unable to identify the officer who inserted himself into the scene even though he took possession of my belongings, because he used Muñoz's name and badge number to check my belongings into the property room.

So much for chain of custody.

This was another example of problematic, routine misconduct that SAPD officers freely engaged in: the mishandling of evidence. I would witness several incidents where police officers signed records attesting to "facts" that they had no independent knowledge of. If they ever had to testify in court, they could just rely on the record and let the judge or jury think they had created the document.

(In 2021, the capital murder trial of the man accused of brutally murdering beloved HEB deli specialist Paula Méndez Boyd came to an abrupt halt when the court learned that police had not provided key evidence to either the defense or prosecutors.)

From the squad car, I could see the cop and the Greyhound security guard chatting amiably. I watched as Officer Muñoz patted Galbreath on the back before turning to walk toward the squad car.

He got in.

"Do you think I am the police now?" he asked.

I repeated that police officers actually do police work, and that since I had not seen him perform any, I did not consider him police.

The cop laughed.

"You probably do this all the time," he said as he put the car in drive. "Running around acting a fool." I told him that was not true, that I had not "acted a fool" in Greyhound, and that he would know that if he had performed even a modicum of police work.

Galbreath approached the driver side window and asked Muñoz for my driver's license. He took it from Officer Muñoz and walked off. He returned a few minutes later, handed the card to Officer Muñoz, and thanked him.

"No problem, buddy," Officer Muñoz said warmly.

"What, is that your boyfriend?" I asked sarcastically. Officer Muñoz did not respond.

I said, "Everyone is subject to the law, officer, and that includes your friends."

"Those guys have to deal with this all the time."

"They are victimizing people who they perceive as being defenseless and they can count on you to allow them to continue breaking the law. That security guard is a brute and a bully and you are an accomplice to his crimes."

The cop laughed again.

Muñoz labored for nearly an hour over the police report. He settled on a fictional paragraph to explain why he arrested me:

> Upon arrival I contacted V1 and W1. V1 stated that he is a bus driver and he explained to AP1 that she had the wrong ticket and needed to get the correct ticket to enter the bus. V1 stated that AP1 started yelling and using profane language and would not calm down. W1 who is a security officer at location heard the disturbance and immediately responded. W1 stated that AP1 was yelling and using profane language towards V1 and appeared to be getting combative. W1 stated that he asked AP1 to leave repeatedly. Ap1 refused to leave and went back into the bus terminal and sat down. W1 no longer wanted AP1 business and felt that it would not be safe to allow AP1 on a bus after she displayed her aggressive anger towards V1. I approached AP1 and asked her about the matter. AP1 responded that "you are not the police I don't have to talk to you". AP1

continued to yell and would not listen to what I had to explain. I continued to ask AP1to leave and she refused (and) continued to yell and cause a disturbance. I placed AP1 in handcuffs and she was transported to 401 S. Frio where she was arrested for criminal trespass.[45]

It was a work of pure fiction. Having refused to interview any of the real witnesses, he was forced to make himself a witness. He crafted a narrative to support his abusive arrest.

As I sat and politely tried to reason with him, SAPD officer Muñoz deliberately falsified a police report to depict me as combative and psychotic.

This was a practice I would witness countless times during Allstate' zero sum game. SAPD police officers routinely falsified report and/or scrubbed them of key information, while SAPD supervisors, city lawyers, and local judges knowingly aided in those deceptions.

It wasn't the first time that the Statewide Patrol security guard David Galbreath had lied to police. On January 5, 2011, just seven weeks prior to his attack on me, Galbreath had called police to the bus station alleging that someone had assaulted him. He must have gotten the worst of the scuffle because he apparently tried to press charges. The responding officer referred the case to SAPD detective Troy Marek.

After interviewing witnesses, the detective determined that there *had* been a fight, but Galbreath was no victim.

"After further investigation," Marek wrote in the final report, "It was discovered the disturbance was mutual and there was no assault."

The detective closed the case.

There would be no such investigation of Galbreath's false claims against me even though dozens of witnesses were available to refute him.

They are letting these people get away with murder, I thought. That thought would take on eerie significance years later when local news outlets reported that a Statewide Patrol security guard had gunned down a man in front of his 11-year-old boy. The guard had confronted the tenant for using his apartment complex swimming pool after hours. Despite conflicting official reports and evidence that the guard escalated the incident, no charges were filed. Neither the police nor the news media ever identified the Statewide Patrol security guard who killed the tenant.

Muñoz booked me into jail. I was released later that day after being arraigned by a magistrate. A few days later, I went to the police department to again try and press charges against Galbreath. I spoke briefly with SAPD Officer Justin Carter. Young and slender, Carter told me that I couldn't press charges against the Statewide Patrol security guard. It was a civil matter, he said. I would have to get a lawyer.

This would not be the last time I had been assaulted in San Antonio and then watch helplessly as the police department coddled and protected my attackers. It was an obscene reality that cops had created: I could be arrested on the slimmest of pretexts, while brazen criminal misdemeanors and felonies were routinely dismissed as "civil matters."

I would speak to Carter a few times over the next year or two. Like dozens of other SAPD officer I encountered, he enjoyed mocking me, pretending not to understand me, and generally relishing my powerlessness.

Talk about being *persona non grata*. I just did not matter, and they wanted me to know it.

I wrote a letter to Myron Watkins, vice president of operations in charge of the "customer experience" at Greyhound. I gave him a brief summary of what had unfolded, but so much happened in the years following the incident that ten years later I can't say if I ever got a refund.

The court assigned me a public defender, Audra Bradshaw. But the day of my arraignment, Bradshaw didn't show up. A young defender came out from the back, and showed my bus ticket to the prosecutor to prove I had consent to be on Greyhound property. The criminal trespass case against me was dropped.

Years later, it dawned on me that I had never set eyes on Audra Bradshaw, the court-appointed defense attorney. I made an open records act request to the Bexar County Public Defender's Office, asking for documents related to Bradshaw's appointment as my defense attorney. On December 12, 2016, the chief public defender, Michael Young, replied.

The public defender's office had no records responsive to my request, Young responded.

Young suggested I contact "another department or division of Bexar County, Texas." For months, I tried to contact Bexar County to get clarity on that question, but got nowhere.

Bradshaw remained a mystery.

I did not have time to solve the mystery of the disappearing attorney. Allstate's minions were sending volley after volley of attacks on my home, my finances and my communications. I had to pick my battles. I had to stop letting them pick me.

Audra Bradshaw would have to wait. It wasn't like she was some anomaly. There were hundreds of people who had destructively impacted my life whom I had never seen. She was just one of many. That might be a book in itself, I thought. I tidied up the folder on Audra Bradshaw and filed it away.

The FBI, part I: fidelity, bravery, integrity.

Between 2010 and 2017, I made about five visits to the local office of the Federal Bureau of Investigations. The bureau's San Antonio headquarters rests in a four-story, 150,000 square foot building behind a gated perimeter off Loop 1604 on the city's far northwest side. A sidewalk cuts through a perfectly manicured lawn between the perimeter guard building and the main headquarters. Despite its commanding structure, The FBI's local headquarters appeared to be strategically placed to escape casual notice. It's possible that some motorists driving daily in the area don't know it's there despite a sign near the road that reads, "U.S. Federal Bureau of Investigation." It's imposing, but somehow discreet.

In order to gain entrance, visitors must go through a series of security protocols at the guard entrance along the perimeter barrier. You are instructed to leave all digital devices, including your cellphone, in your vehicle. You are then asked to provide photo identification, fill out a form detailing what you want to discuss with the duty agent, get your bags searched, and then go through a metal detector. After a short wait, you are allowed to enter the main building. Sometimes you are told to walk yourself through the grounds down a pristine sidewalk to get inside the main structure. Other times, a special agent walks to the guard building and escorts you into the main building.

The first two times I visited, I walked myself in. An aging woman in a 1950s-era beehive hairstyle greeted me stoically from a bulletproof booth.

Interviews were customarily conducted in a small interrogation room between the booth and the front door. A two-way mirror dominates that room.

I would tell the agent my story and share the evidence I had collected. As an investigative journalist, I knew to keep it short and to provide documentary evidence for what I was alleging. It was a struggle because there was so much interlocking information and some of it sounded, even to my ears, fantastical. The agents were noncommittal, circumspect, and professional. Not that they had a high bar to overcome but their professional demeanor was light-years above the crass, abusive and ignorant behavior I often saw from local law enforcement authorities.

Still, I couldn't ignore signs that the agency was struggling to gain a foothold in this strange new world. It was ironic that the FBI collaboration with McKinsey & Company only weakened its capabilities, and telling that the country's premier law enforcement agency felt the need to engage with the business consultant in the first place.

Clearly, the FBI was in need of some answers. The agency's responsibility was breathtaking in scope even before the internet. It must investigate literally any federal violation not expressly assigned to another federal agency.

The federal government relies on the FBI to enforce federal law and to *ensure the proper administration of justice* in the United States.[46] In addition to its domestic duties, the FBI is *also* tasked with gathering information necessary for the U.S. government to manage foreign affairs. In short, the FBI's approximately 36,000 employees must detect, investigate, and prevent domestic crimes, protect national security from foreign threats *and* collects intelligence for domestic and international law enforcement. FBI agents have to decide if someone is planning, committing, or hiding from a federal crime. They have to identify, find, and catch highly intelligent sociopaths engaged in fast-moving crimes, including serial killers, pedophiles, and human traffickers. They have to collect spare, elusive evidence needed for prosecution. And then they have to convince an often apathetic U.S. Attorney's Office to prosecute.

To successfully investigate that long laundry list of crimes, our federal bureau of investigation must rely on organizations that are often unreliable. It must contend with corrupt, incompetent, or otherwise compromised local cops in pursuit of genius criminal masterminds. In addition to all those duties, the FBI is expected to provide investigative help to other federal, state, local, tribal, and foreign agencies. It has to deal with Congress. At one point in its history, it had to deal with Donald Trump.

That's a lot, I thought.

Probably too much.

I quickly learned that while the FBI agents were happy to take information, they did not give out information. This made sense. Naturally, the FBI would be extremely tightlipped if they were conducting a major undercover investigation. They were, after all, secret police. I would get few reassurances, although from time to time the agents would let key information slip: there was undercover work going on; the FBI had key subjects they were focusing on, they were aware of the cyber hacking, I was in no physical danger. I was left to wonder if the lapses were deliberate or just slips of the tongue. The agents were extremely hard to read.

As I reeled from Allstate's zero sum game, the FBI was leading a multi-agency task force investigating countless allegations of corruption in Bexar County. The task force had spent the better part of the fall of 2013 wiretapping hundreds of phones associated with the courthouse. My name was sure to come up on some of those federal wiretaps. I was sure my case with Allstate could provide them with ample evidence.

The FBI duty agents[47] I met made it clear they found the information I shared valuable. I could tell when something piqued their interest. They would ask pointed questions and listen intently to my response. They were obviously highly trained professionals. That gave me some comfort. Every now and then, an agent would compliment my research skills.

One offer I made in 2012 got an unusually enthusiastic response: I invited the Federal Bureau of Investigation into my network and devices.

"I am giving the FBI full permission to enter my network and devices at any time," I told the agent. "You don't have to ask a judge or get a subpoena. I give you full and unfettered access. Indefinitely." It took a second for him to deconstruct what I was offering. In federal law enforcement jargon, I had just agreed to "consensual monitoring."

This was an unexpected offer. It could turn out to be quite valuable.

"We need more citizens like you," the agent said excitedly. He thanked me, jumped up, and quickly headed out the room. He stopped midstride in the doorway. He turned back to me as though just remembering I was there.

"Keep your energy up," he said.

8 | IMPLEMENTATION

The NASA engineer

In mid-May 2011, Gutierrez amended Keller's petition. It stated, "out of nowhere a vehicle driven by Plaintiff Denise McVea appeared in the intersection and the two cars collided. Keller was not able to see Ms. McVea."

It seemed like he had made my case for me. Of course he didn't see me. He was looking at the gas station, not the road.

On February 1, 2012, a year and a half after I sued, Allstate finally produced Keller's insurance policy. Allstate's lawyers continued playing dirty tricks. I kept asking the courts, the state bar, and the judicial commission to do something about the rampant misconduct. I got nowhere.

That summer, I formally asked the court to sanction Allstate's attorneys Goldman Pennebaker & Phipps for a laundry list of misdeeds, including violations of the discovery process and falsely telling the court that Allstate was a third party insurer not governed by the Texas Deceptive Trade Practices Act to get a dismissal. Nothing came of my complaint.

And then I caught a break. My good friends AJ and Cesar Garcia mentioned that they knew an engineer who frequently acted as an expert witness for auto accident lawsuits. "Do you want his information?" AJ asked.

I did, very much.

His name was Jack Leifer and he was an associate professor at Trinity University. Mild-mannered with an open, boyish face, Leifer agreed to analyze the wreck to determine what actually happened.

He wasn't cheap, but the engineer had excellent credentials. A Massachusetts Institute of Technology undergraduate, he earned both his

Masters and Ph.D. in engineering from the University of Texas. He had served as adjunct faculty in the area of computational Structural Mechanics at the NASA Langley Research Center.

He was licensed in Texas and Kentucky, taught mechanical engineering at several universities, and served a three-year summer faculty fellowship at the NASA Langley Research Center in Hampton, VA. He had served as an expert witness many times.

I hired him and gave him photos of the wrecked Nissan and the police report. On March 16, 2012, he issued a report of his findings. Using a database of examples, the engineer calculated how fast each car was moving at the time of impact.

At the time of impact, the engineer determined, I was traveling at no more than 5.7 miles an hour.

> This low forward speed estimate does not support the contention of Mr. Keller (driver of Unit 1/Tercel) that Ms. McVea (driver of Unit 2/Nissan) ran the red light and struck his vehicle.48

On the other hand, the engineer found that the incoming speed of the Toyota Tercel ranged between 17.1 - 22 mph.

> The calculated incoming forward speed of the Toyota Tercel supports Ms. McVea's contention that her vehicle (Nissan/Unit 2) was already in the intersection "committed to turning on Blanco" when Unit 1 (Tercel) ran into the side of her vehicle.

It was a slam dunk. A court-certified NASA-affiliated engineer who graduated from MIT had conducted a study and found that everything I had said about the wreck was true. Allstate now had proof that my claim was legitimate.

The insurer's lawyers immediately began trying to get the report thrown out of court.

On May 11, 2012, Albert Gutierrez filed a motion to strike Leifer as my expert witness but stalled on scheduling a hearing. Legally, the motion to strike was worthless. Leifer had already been accepted as an expert on crash disputes. Only a corrupt judge would grant such a frivolous motion. I researched the subject carefully, looking at all the elements needed to prove the legitimacy of an expert witness. Leifer, the engineer who taught at NASA, met or exceeded them all. A hearing was eventually scheduled. I was ready.

Gutierrez entered the courthouse, waltzed into Judge Michael Mery's chambers, and there the two met unlawfully for more than 20 minutes while I sat in court waiting for the hearing to begin.

When it did, it was weird.

Gutierrez gave a disingenuous, convoluted argument that Leifer should be struck from offering expert witness testimony in the Allstate case because, well, he wasn't present to testify in the strike hearing. I had done enough research to know that if Gutierrez had wanted Leifer to testify in a hearing it was his responsibility to subpoena him. Still, Judge Mery nodded supportively. When it was my turn, I outlined all of the reasons why Allstate's motion to strike was meritless. The engineer was more than qualified. I cited key case law that I had found on Google Scholar. I challenged Gutierrez to cite any case law that called for an expert witness to be dismissed from a case based on the arguments he was making. His written motion didn't say anything like what he was spouting in court.

And then things got really weird.

He'd left the case law at the office, Gutierrez told the judge.

"I could perhaps email it to Your Honor," he said.

I objected. Allstate's lawyer had just tried to argue a motion based on false case law and then lied in an attempt to keep his fraud off the record. That he had forgotten to bring support for his argument to court.

That he would email it later.

I wasn't even a lawyer and I knew that American courts don't allow lawyers to argue the law with a promise of emailing support for it when they got back to the house.

Mery accepted my argument. He did so in an uncharacteristically respectful manner. I was not accustomed to Bexar County judges being kind to me. And here was Mery, when I least expected it, showing not only respect for me but for the law. I wasn't, he told Gutierrez, like other pro se litigants.

"She's spitting back the cases," he said.

I was so surprised by this sudden uncharacteristic show of respect for me and the law, I teared up. But Mery kept shooting glances behind me. I turned to see what he was looking at.

Without me noticing, two young lawyers had at some point entered the courtroom behind me. They sat in the otherwise empty gallery exchanging puzzled, slightly alarmed looks. Ah, I realized, there were witnesses. Mery's kindness was a performance.

The unexpected arrivals were a gift from God. Whatever Gutierrez and Mery had cooked up in the judge's chambers had to be shelved.

That would be the last time the Bexar County presiding judge scheduled a hearing after mine. From that moment on, I was always the last or only litigant scheduled for a particular Bexar County courtroom.

Mery was forced to deny Gutierrez's motion to strike. Leifer's report was admissible and, frankly, unassailable. It showed that Keller's defense and Allstate's rejection of my insurance claim were bogus.

Allstate should have simply taken responsibility for its decision to deny a legitimate claim, pay my medical bills and move on, but it didn't. Instead, it ratcheted up its zero sum game.

Around that time, I started noticing that my phone's locator app was showing my phone in places I was not. While I sat on my couch at home, my phone popped up in a toney North Side home, on an alley a few miles away, in the parking lot of the Alamodome, and in a remote rural home in Cibolo. Someone was spoofing my cellular device.

McVea v. Keller, the trial

The trial in my lawsuit against Keller and Allstate was held January 14, 2013. Against all odds I had survived pretrial. I had withstood summary judgment, improper default judgments, record tampering, undisguised judicial hostility and misconduct, covert surveillance, cyber-hacking, illegal wiretapping, assault, and one false arrest.

The day of the trial, I watched a man talking to Albert Gutierrez's assistant attorney Kelly Canales. The next time I saw him, he was sitting on the bench outside of the courtroom. He was a hairy, dark-haired man in his fifties wearing faded jeans. He looked a lot like a certain class of private investigators I'd notice stalking me in and around my neighborhood: seedy, and slightly unkempt. Although he was not a member of the jury, he sat squeezed in on the same bench as the jurors. I noticed him right away. He just didn't fit. For one thing, the other jurors wore juror tags. He did not. For another thing, Kelly Canales, Albert Gutierrez's fawning junior attorney, approached him. The two engaged in a hushed conversation. I couldn't stop watching. She seemed to be giving him instructions. What in the world is going on here? I thought. The next time I saw him, I was walking outside of the courthouse. He was walking a couple of steps behind two jurors who were in a chatty conversation with each other. He did not approach them, but for the first time I formed a vague suspicion of what he might be doing hanging around.

In all, the trial lasted two days. The judge, Janet Littlejohn, was a statuesque woman with a strong Southern accent. She was a no-nonsense judge but seemed fair. She did not berate me the minute she sat on the bench, which was novel, and she didn't seem to care who was watching her proceedings.

My sisters Jacquie and Rene sat in the gallery to show their support. BJ Carroll, my sister-cousin, elected to sit it out. She had worked for more than 20 years in the Bexar County courthouse as a court administrator. She seemed uncomfortable. But call me if you need anything, she said. When I needed an affidavit during the proceedings, she took care of it.

James Keller sat next to Canales. I hardly recognized him. It seemed that life had not been kind to Keller since our wreck. He looked battered, nervous, and tremulous. He faded into the background as I began the court battle with Allstate's favorite San Antonio lawyer, Albert Gutierrez. The Man Who Would Do Anything, I called him derisively. He had finally accepted that he was a bald man and began shaving the few wisps of hair loitering on the top of his head.

During jury selection, I surprised Gutierrez with several objections that the judge sustained. At one point, he asked a potential juror a series of questions and when he didn't get the answer he expected, he asked again, more insistently.

"Objection," I said. "Asked and answered."

"Sustained," said the judge.

This impressed some of the jurors. I suspected that a good number of them had wanted to file suit for one thing or another but couldn't find an attorney they could afford or trust.

I got to see Gutierrez's courtroom demeanor. He was a confident lawyer and was well versed in courtroom procedure. But I could see that he had a likeability problem. He was just so pompous. I could tell that he was rubbing some of the jurors wrong. I tried to keep track of the people who seemed to dislike Gutierrez but the process quickly overwhelmed me. I began spending my energy on making the jurors like me. That turned out to be a mistake.

Several women seemed impressed that I had taken on Allstate. One juror, a well-dressed woman in her early forties, asked the judge if she could ask me a question. The judge allowed it. She asked me how I had learned to represent myself. A murmur of accord came from the jury pool. Many people wanted to know. I explained that I was a journalist by trade and that the law really was about research. I approached the law the same way I approached stories. I asked a question and then conducted research. A few jurors nodded in appreciation. Later, when the jury was selected, I saw that Gutierrez's team was serious about jury selection. None of the people who nodded admiringly made it onto the jury. Allstate's team had quickly eliminated them.

Three people who had given me friendly smiles did make it onto the jury. One elderly man identified himself as a dentist. Another, a Cajun man in his early fifties, identified himself as a manager. And a young woman in her thirties identified herself as a worker for a local museum. I remember the three of them because when the final jury entered the courtroom, all three of them visibly smirked at me. I was caught off guard. The pleasant, encouraging looks they gave me during jury selection had disappeared. Suddenly, they didn't seem to like me at all.

But there was a lot going on and I had to stay focus. The night before the trial began in earnest, my computer and printer froze. Plus, I couldn't print out my notes, the guides I had made for myself, or the case law I had compiled. I spent the night recovering files from back up and placing them on a microcomputer I kept around for emergencies.

The next day, I couldn't help noticing that Albert Gutierrez kept shooting surprised glances at my new computer. He acted as if I wasn't supposed to have it.

The trial lasted two days. I managed to put on a solid case against Allstate and Keller. Leifer, the expert witness Mery and Gutierrez unsuccessfully tried to strike, was able to testified that I was already in the intersection when Keller hit me, shattering Allstate's claim that I had sped through a traffic light and "had come out of nowhere".

When it was my turn to take the stand, I testified that I watched Keller looking to his left at the gas station as he zoomed toward me. He badgered Leifer, but the facts had been established. I had not sped through the intersection but was slowly clearing it when Keller got distracted as he sped through the intersection. Despite his best efforts, Gutierrez's cross-examination was unconvincing – not because he was a bad lawyer, but because he didn't have a case.

When the jury went out for deliberations, I thought it would take an hour or two for the verdict to come back. Hours passed. We waited and waited. As night fell, my sister Jacquie and I waiting in the now empty hallways. I sat exhausted and anxious on a hallway bench as it got later and later. At one point, a Spanish-speaking cleaning lady sat next to me during her break. We exchanged pleasantries in Spanish. She asked me what my case was about. I explained that it was a car wreck. She wished me luck. I thanked her. *Lo necesito*, I told her ruefully. I need it.

Finally, after more than six hours of deliberations, the jury came back with a verdict. Some murder cases didn't take that long, I thought.

The dentist and the Cajun literally sneered at me as the jury made their way back to the jury box. No one else would make eye contact. Then the verdict was read: Keller as not responsible for the accident.

The judge's mouth dropped. She stared in disbelief at the jury. So did I. Several jurors dropped their heads. But the dentist and the Cajun stared back proudly. Gutierrez gave a low, satisfied chuckle. He gave a quick side glance at the dentist and the Cajun, his mouth turned up on one side in a faint half-grin. The two jurors returned his grin openly. The judge took a few seconds to compose herself. Then she was all business as she went through the procedures to close out the case. She thanked the jurors and commended me. You put on a good case, she said. As the jurors filed out, the dentist and the Cajun nodded smugly at Gutierrez. He nodded back, satisfied. I am in a dystopian nightmare, I thought.

People I assumed were handlers for Allstate gathered in the hallway to congratulate a gloating Gutierrez. They had dropped in periodically during the trial but rarely stayed long. Now they were crowded around Gutierrez, who seemed happy and relieved. He said something about people wanting a free paycheck to no one in particular.

The cleaning lady was sitting on a bench near the milling crowd. She asked me how my case went. I told her that it was a great injustice, but that was how life was. Allstate's handlers abruptly stopped talking and stared at me, surprised to hear me speaking Spanish.

Oddly, Gutierrez broke out in Spanish, addressing the cleaning lady whom he otherwise would not have given the time of day. It was a convoluted sentence that neither I nor the cleaning lady could parse. Not because he couldn't speak Spanish, but because he had nothing to say. We both just looked at him. I turned back to the lady. I thanked her for her interest and told her that I hoped things went well for her. "*Que le vaya bien,*" I said.

"*Igualmente,*" she responded kindly. I appreciated her.

The jury began filing out. I stood my ground, and put my hand out. "Thank you for your service," I said, and shook the hand of each juror who filed past me. Most did not look me in the eye, but two people, a man in his 20s and a woman in her late 30s, looked me long and hard in the eye. It was if they wanted to tell me something. The jury count had been 10-2 in favor of Keller and Allstate.

The Cajun approached me jovially. He put his hand out. I shook it.

"I'm sorry, he said, smiling, "but I just couldn't agree."

He wanted me to know it was because of him that I had lost the case. He wanted me to know that he had stonewalled until the other jurors, wanting it all to end, finally caved and gave him what he wanted. He looked so pleased with himself.

"I understand," I said.

He turned to shake hands with Gutierrez, who rewarded him with another ghost of a smile. The juror responsible for wearing down the other members bounced proudly out of the courthouse. Allstate handlers followed.

Before closing the record, Judge Littlejohn had explained that the jurors would exit the building one way and the parties would exit the building the other way. She would show us out, she'd said, so we waited for her in the hall. Soon she appeared.

"I'll show you how to get out of here," she said, and Jacquie and I walked with her to the elevator. As we waited for the elevator to arrive, Canales and Gutierrez walked up behind us.

The elevator door opened. Jacquie and I followed the judge inside. She turned to Canales and Gutierrez. "You can catch the next one," she said.

Did I detect a whiff of revulsion?

The elevator door closed.

I didn't know what to say.

"Thank you for your service," I said.

She didn't respond. I looked at her. I wondered if I saw shame.

She was a true jurist, I thought, a dying breed. I was not surprised when she did not run for re-election. Judge Price, the judge who apologized to Gutierrez for following the law in the summary judgment hearing, also did not run for re-election. At least I got to experience what it felt like to be in the presence of two judges who actually followed the law, I remember thinking when I heard the news. Now they were gone.

When Jacquie and I walked outside the courthouse, a grey drizzle was falling. Fitting, I thought. Behind us, Gutierrez and Canales walked to their car. Gutierrez was pontificating self-importantly. Canales listened with rapt attention.

Tedi was waiting up for me when I got home. "How did it go?" she asked.

"I lost."

"How?" she asked incredulously.

"They tampered with the jury," I said.

The Appeal

Meanwhile, things were heating up at the information center. I had started actively looking for volunteers to help us speed up the repairs to the property so that we could begin operations. I placed Facebook and Craigslist ads recruiting volunteers.

I was a surprised at the enthusiastic response. Several people answered the ads, including Air force cadets, a gaggle of Brackenridge High School honor students, good Samaritans, and a college students looking to earn community service points. A few neighbors stopped by to offer help. More than one person exclaimed that the information center was much needed in the neighborhood. A real buzz started happening around the center. People began checking in to ask if we had set an opening day.

I was touched by the interest in the center. We were welcomed. St. Philip's College let us hold meetings in some of its empty classrooms. Neighbors and Facebook friends signed up to be volunteers. Various groups made donations. It was clear that the community could see the benefits of the center and wanted to support it. Despite the ongoing scourge of Allstate and the corruption I frequently encountered in city and county government, I was excited about the possibilities. Everywhere I turned, residents of the city and Eastside encouraged us to hurry up. There was so much work to be done. Tedi often worked by my side. Her organizational skills saved the day many, many times. Money was tight. We kept afloat with book sales and auctions, buying low and selling high. Donations continued to trickle in.

Over and over again, I heard concerns about property on the Eastside mysteriously transferring ownership. Property transfers would be a top priority once the information center was up and running, I decided.

At the same time, I headed to appeals court.

The Allstate lawsuit had been a travesty. I had no doubt the jury had been tampered with. Hell, they *wanted* me to know it. There was only one thing I could do about it. When we met in court for a post-trial wrap up, I had asked the judge to overturn the jury verdict on the ground that it was against the overwhelming evidence. Littlejohn could have overturned the verdict, but she wanted none of that. It's more appropriate for you to appeal, she said.

I soon learned that appeals court had its own rules and so I set about learning appellate procedure. Reading motions and petitions online, I thought the appeals court seemed more straightforward than district court. I would appeal the verdict based on a single concept: the verdict was in conflict with all of the evidence presented in the case.

The engineer's crash report clearly showed not only that Keller was at fault, but that Allstate's position was fraudulent, malicious, and abusive of the court system.

Gutierrez had presented no evidence whatsoever. By appealing the insane Allstate verdict, I could put the obvious difference between the verdict and the evidence on the record.

If Allstate handlers thought that a jury-rigged verdict would send me on my way, they were wrong. I filed an appeal in the Fourth Court of Appeals.

SAPD cops arrested me a second time.

9 | MALICE

False Arrest No. 2

ON JANUARY 21, MARTIN LUTHER King Day, 2013, I became the first person in San Antonio history to be arrested and jailed for allegedly having a garage sale without a permit.

It just so happened that the information center was located on the route of San Antonio's famous Martin Luther King Day March. Despite having a relatively small black population, the city held the largest march in the nation.

We decided to run a flea market. It would be a good opportunity to introduce the information center to citizens, fundraise, get rid of excess auction inventory, and stump for volunteers. We set up a table with information and sign-up sheets. People walking to the march browsed the items displayed between and promised to come back after the march. I was excited. It looked like we were going to have a productive day.

But things went south pretty quickly. A half dozen Eastside cops descended on the place when I called to complain that a drunken vendor across the street was blasting his music and grabbing his crotch and thrusting toward my volunteers. (I now understand he was probably paid to do that.) The cops looked keystone, running to and fro as though on a desperate manhunt. I could not make sense of what I was looking at.

One of the cops, Joseph Swan, asked to see our garage sale permit.

I explained that the event was an organizational event and that as such, no garage sale permit was available. "This is a business," I said. "Plus this is not my home. You can only get a garage sale for your homestead."

He ignored me. "Y'all need to put this stuff back," he said.

And just like that, I was in another encounter with San Antonio police determined to haul me off to jail. I tried to reason with the cops, first Joseph

Swan and then his supervisor Sergeant Daniel Scott. I was engaging in a misdemeanor offense, the cops told me, and if I didn't remove the items immediately, they would issue me a citation.

I had never heard of a misdemeanor garage sale violation. This fact contained no irony. It had never been enforced because it didn't exist.

When it became clear that they were determined to disrupt our event, I asked them what probable cause they had to believe a crime was being committed. Scott went to his car and began talking on a cell phone. He was gone quite a few minutes. When he returned, he said he had spoken to code enforcement and that the code enforcement officer had confirmed that I was engaging in a misdemeanor criminal offense.

I didn't believe him. Code enforcement is closed today, I said. I told him to go ahead and give me the citation, that I would fight it in court.

He issued me a citation. And when you sign this, he said, you have to put this stuff back or you will be under arrest.

"That's coercion," I said. I would not sign the citation if it meant that I would have to stop my event. And you don't have probable cause to arrest me for any crime, I insisted. He ordered Swan to handcuff me. It was an overt violation of the Fourth Amendment, which protects Americans from unreasonable searches and seizures. Swan was clearly reluctant, but he did as he was told.

Handcuffed in the backseat of the patrol car, I saw Scott gesturing aggressively at the volunteers. Heads down, they began quickly picking up items and taking them inside. I could tell that they were scared. Swan drove me to the Bexar County Detention Center. He pulled into the jail's parking lot, and slowed to a stop. He sat there for some time unspeaking, the patrol car idling, unsure of what to do. Finally, he marched me inside. The intake guard asked what the charge was.

"Garage sale without a permit," he told her.

She stared at him in disbelief. Her look of shock was so comical an involuntary laugh burst from me. He whispered something to her, pleading. She resigned herself to the jailing. I sat in the holding tank for hours. I spent three months running on wild goose chases through the courthouse before the case was finally dismissed for lack of evidence.

Looking back, I can see that the second arrest had three major objectives. The first objective was to disrupt my gains in court and to overwhelm me so that I would not have the time or energy to examine and document the widespread judicial misconduct my cases were exposing. The second objective was to disrupt the building of the information center. The third objective was to traumatize me so thoroughly that my general demeanor matched the image of the psychotic, delusional woman painted in the police reports.

The lawyers and judges who'd signed on to Allstate's zero sum game had not expected things to go this far. The threat of exposure remained. The people who had taken action on the company's behalf had participated in a series of high crimes and misdemeanors. Folks were worried. I could see it on their faces. Their expressions seemed to be saying, "This better work."

Allstate's operatives were now under even more pressure to protect the officials and other informants who had contributed to the insurer's illegal campaign. More needed to be done to neutralize the odd writer in the old farmhouse off Hackberry. That would mean heaping more abuse on me. Allstate operatives were more than willing to "do whatever it takes."

But even in this corrupted system designed to provide impunity for just about any misdeed, there were some vulgar crimes that even San Antonio's most corrupt officials simply would not do.

For that, they had Kristina Combs.

How to get away with burglary

On September 7, 2013, under cover of darkness, four people entered the site of the information center and broke into the house at 1614 Martin Luther King Drive using bolt cutters. It was just before 8 p.m.

It had been a blistering late summer day so Tedi and I had waited for the sun to go down before heading over to work on the information center. When we arrived, we saw the group stepping out of the house exiting the back of the property at Martin Luther King Drive. A slender middle-aged white man and a short, a stumpy white woman contemplated us silently. The woman, in her 30s, wore a white, oversized man's t-shirt over wide hips and a protruding belly. A Hispanic couple hovered awkwardly in the background. I drove onto the property and jumped out of the car.

"What are you doing on this property?" I asked.

The lock on the back door, I could see, had been snapped. The door stood ajar. The white man placed bolt cutters in the back of a truck.

We bought this property, she said.

No you didn't, I replied.

Yes, we did.

Show me the paperwork, I said.

The white woman refused to give her name. The older man walked up with his arms crossed and began challenging me.

You show us *your* paperwork, he said.

I don't have to show you anything, I told them. We just caught you illegally breaking into this property. We are in legal possession of this property and you are committing breaking and entering.

The white people seemed unfazed, emboldened. The Hispanic couple stood off to the side, quiet. Eventually, I would learn the names of all of the burglars. The tall white man was Roger Combs. He was the father of the pudgy white woman. Her name was Kristina Combs and she was "a practicing attorney." Combs was representing the couple, she said, who were heirs to the property.

"No they aren't," I said.

I had done ample research before adverse possessing the property. I knew that the potential heirs had already signed away their interest in the property.

I demanded that the burglars show proof that any one of the burglars had been awarded the property. They ignored my request. There was no way these two people were heirs to the property. I began loudly challenging them. The stumpy white woman refused to show any paperwork. I told Tedi to call the police.

When the police arrived, they made a beeline for the white couple. The leader of the pair was Detective James Phelan. The uniformed cop, James Tullis, stood back, allowing Phelan to take control. Phelan immediately approached Roger Combs and Kristina Combs and in low, respectful tones consulted with them. Tedi and I waited patiently, but when he turned to us he began to yell. Prove you are the owner, he barked.

I told him to look in San Antonio Police records. They would establish that I was the person legally in possession of the property. Plus, I have the key and they have bolt cutters, I said.

Since I had established that I was legally in possession of the property, why are they not being required to show they have legally taken control of a property that they had to use bolt cutters to open?

He ignored the question. It was an ugly, frightening scene. A San Antonio Police Department detective brazenly was assisting a group of burglars who were breaking into a property under darkness of night.

I stood and watched as Phelan coached Roger Combs on how Combs could take control of the property. You need to file your papers in Bexar County deeds office, he told the group. Then, the detective then turned to me, and in belittling, hostile tone, ordered me to hand my keys over to Combs. I refused. He looked at me a moment, calculating what he could get away with in light of my refusal. He order everyone to stay off the property until the "case was resolved."

Shaken, Tedi and I locked up the property as the larcenous group filed off the scene. Once the property was secure, we headed home. Passing

Pitman Sullivan Park, we saw Phelan and Tullis meeting in the park's parking lot with Kristina Combs and Roger Combs. They huddled under a lamplight, while the Hispanic couple hovered nearby. I pulled into the parking lot.

"What's this?" I asked.

"Back off, ma'am," said Phelan. "I'll deal with you in a minute."

I leaned against a truck as I waited for an explanation for the cops' bizarre meeting with the burglars of my property.

"Get off my car," said the male member of the Hispanic couple.

"Make me," I said calmly.

He turned away. Phelan continued to caucus with the burglars.

"I'm going to call the police," I said.

"We are the police," said Phelan.

"No you're not," I insisted in what had become a mantra. "If you were police, you would be doing police work, which means you would be arresting burglars who are breaking and entering, not meeting with them in a parking lot."

I called SAPD dispatch and explained that my property had been burglarized and that the police were assisting the burglars.

More cops arrived.

I was deeply frazzled by this point. I ended up talking to a female cop on the scene, who seemed mildly sympathetic to my plight. She acted like the whole thing was unusual, but not very. She told me to contact my city council person.

That was probably the first time that I thought, Oh, shit. The cops can't even handle these bad cops. Phelan and his ilk had free rein to indulge in all sorts of crimes without any fear of pushback.

This is very, very bad, I thought. I had already had my experiences with the courts in Bexar County. I could see the writing on the wall.

Eventually, I would get my hands on the police report for the burglary. Even after everything I had seen and experienced before, I found it shocking. The cops had recorded that someone had died and left Roger Combs the property. That had been the third story the burglars had told police, it was provably false, and it was directly contradicted by the false claims that Roger Combs's daughter, "practicing attorney" Kristina Combs, would eventually file in court.

Even though I was the verifiable occupant of the property who had called the police to report the burglary, I became the "other person" in the police report. SAPD designated Roger Combs as the "reporting person," even though I was the one who had called police and was the proven occupant of the property. A reader of the falsified police report would not know that Roger Combs changed his story several times, had no history to the property, had no key, and no proof of his morphing claims. I added the police report to a growing list of SAPD reports that were obviously, provably false.

I thought again about the constant failures we were witnessing from our national intelligence agencies and shuddered. If San Antonio was any indication, any government agency relying on street patrol records for information or intelligence were severely disadvantaged. It was trash data.

The MLK burglary police report, ostensibly prepared and filed by officer James Tullis, stated that "each party presented paperwork showing they have a right to be at the location." That was false. Combs had provided no documentation.

"I advised both parties that the situation was a civil matter and the court date will determine who has a right to be there," Tullis would later write in the false police report.

But there was more.

Detective Phelan, who controlled the burglary call from start to finish, did not appear anywhere on the police report.

There was no one I could turn to in Bexar County to address this obvious criminal conspiracy. The scheme was in play and if every conspirator played his part, the property at 1614 Martin Luther King would be illegally transferred like clockwork.

They did and it was.

Offense case #SAPD13196530 would turn out to be valuable evidence. It essentially showed how a corrupt cop could descend on a crime scene, assist the criminals in the criminal act, and never even be mentioned in the official police record. It wasn't the first time corrupt SAPD cops had performed that act, and it would by no means be the last.

I was never served any notices, but I knew that wouldn't stop the courts from ruling in Combs's favor.

I decided to go in person to the SAPD Eastside substation to file a burglary report. I was referred to Detective Reginald Freeman.

I walked to Freeman's desk, where he greeted me jovially. Two plainclothes cops sat at their desks nearby, unmoving, heads cocked. Freeman and I engaged in a roundabout conversation where Freeman did everything in his power to dissuade me from pressing charges. He had heard about the case, he said, and he understood it was a civil matter. From time to time, he would involuntarily shoot glances at the two white detectives listening to our conversation and so I would, too. They were keen on what was going on at Freeman's desk.

I told the detective what he already knew. I repeated that Combs had no claim to the property, told conflicting stories to police, and could provide no paperwork supporting her claims. I said the burglary was part of a pattern of wild illegality meant to cover up other crimes associated with Allstate's vicious zero sum game in San Antonio. I said that she and her cohorts needed to be arrested for breaking and entering.

Freeman responded that he had spoken to Combs and that she had shown him the deeds to the property. She hadn't shown them to me, I said. From what he understood, he said, she had filed the necessary paperwork in the deeds office. She had also filed an eviction suit in County Court No. 4. I have not been served anything, I told him. He shrugged.

I pointed out that people can't evict someone from a property they don't own. "Everyone in this room knows that," I added, making a dig at the detectives listening nearby.

Freeman stood up, indicating the interview was over. Sounds like a civil matter to me, he said.

Then it hit me. Freeman had been the detective assigned to investigate a burglary of the MLK property a few years earlier. That case was also rife with bizarre police conduct.

The search

It had been 2010 and I had driven over to MLK to do some filing after returning from a trip out of town. As I approached the information center, I noticed a slim, bedraggled man in his 20s pulling at what seemed to be a steel panel that had been pried off the large sliding garage door. I pulled across the street and parked behind the car wash. I watched as the man slid under the panel and disappeared inside the information center. I called police and waited.

Officer Jesse Mendoza, Jr. arrived. He was curt, inexplicably rude. I explained that I watched a burglar make entry into the building and that he was still inside. Another officer arrived and I unlocked the door to let them in. At that point, the place had been little more than a storage unit. Already in disarray, it had been ransacked. Several computers were missing. The thief had been making return trips, treating the warehouse as a piggy bank.

"Lots of places to hide," I had said. I went into my little office while the cops searched the premises. He never left, I told them. I couldn't see how the burglar had gotten out without me seeing.

"There's nobody here, ma'am," Mendoza said impatiently. "We've done a thorough search."

"Okay," I said. Maybe he slipped out when I was dialing my phone. I didn't understand why the cop was being so rude. The cops left and I went back into the inner office, organizing paperwork at my desk. An hour later,

I looked out of the inner office door and saw a foot move under a dresser in the warehouse. The burglar was still in the building.

"Goddammit!" I yelled. I grabbed my bag and purse and fled outside, slamming the heavy metal door behind me. The burglar jumped up and tried to follow, but the door could only be opened with a key. He was trapped. He started pleading with me to let him out. "No!" I yelled.

He frantically began trying to squeeze through the small opening he had made to enter the place, scratching his back bloody on the sheet metal. He would be free soon, I could see. I ran out into the middle of the street, yelling and waving at traffic. "Call police!" I bellowed. People ran out of the laundromat and houses to see what was going on. The thief, now free, took off running. I followed as best I could, but he was fast. I was losing him.

A teenager who had come outside with his father took up the chase. "I'll get him, Daddy!" he said and took off at a fast clip. I later learned he was a running back for the Brackenridge High School football team. He quickly gained on the thief, and in what looked like a scene from a movie, dived, and tackled him in the street. He held him for police.

The first cop who arrived, a redhead, began yelling at *me*. But they arrested the burglar. His name was Danny Santos, he was 24, and he had a long rap sheet of drug and theft charges.

Detective Freeman had been assigned to that case.

When I met with Freeman to press charges against Santos, he was chatty and flippant. Tedi disliked him instantly.

He had typed up an affidavit of facts that I needed to sign in order to press charges against Santos. He had handed me the sheet and began a distracting conversation, making it hard for me to concentrate on the paperwork in front of me.

"Just sign at the bottom," he had said.

"Just let me..." I said, as I carefully read the affidavit while he blabbered distractingly.

At the bottom of the paper, just before the signature block, Detective Freeman had written that I did NOT want to press charges against the thief Danny Santos.

"Oh!" he had said when I pointed it out, "that was a mistake."

I had believed him at the time, but now here he was again three years later, protecting another set of burglars. I finally understood. He had talked so distractedly back in 2010 so that I would sign the report without looking and close out the criminal case against the thief Danny Santos. It was now obvious that SAPD detective Reginald Freeman did not intend to arrest Combs or the other burglars. He was protecting them. He was a key player in the conspiracy to steal our property. I stood up and began walking to the door. I turned back.

"Everyone knows you all are corrupt," I said quietly. He jumped up from his chair and lurched towards me menacingly, fists clenched. I stood my ground.

"Are you going to hit me?" I asked incredulously.

"You are not going to besmirch my reputation," he growled, leaning toward me. I started to say he was doing that himself. I was ahead taller than him, but I was alone in this room with these corrupt cops and the police records were filled with lies saying I was violently delusional. I bit my lip. I needed to get out of there.

One of the other detectives stood up hastily and ran toward the door, swinging it open with one arm and holding it open with his body.

"Ma'am," he said, beckoning me. "Goodbye, ma'am."

I turned to leave. As I passed the white detective in the doorway, I saw the ghost of a satisfied smile.

The third burglary

The next few weeks were a convoluted, relentless series of attacks as Allstate's operatives rallied their "informants" to steal the MLK property from the Auris Project, destroy the information center on the Eastside, quickly close the record on the thefts, and bury the judges' shady conduct in and around the Allstate case.

Except for a crude notice scrawled by Combs telling me to vacate the property, no one was serving me with any summons or notices. I had to figure out my course of action based on the small clues cops dropped by the co-conspirators and documents I found in record searches. Freeman, the chubby detective, had let it slip that Combs was filing paperwork in the courts.

Combs first filed an eviction suit in County Court Precinct No. 4 and then filed a quiet title suit in civil district court. But I had not received any notices of lawsuits. I ran from county clerk to county clerk to find the suits. I knew by now the system of default judgments and rapid dismissals that the local civil courts engaged in. I would have to stay on top of things the best way I could.

The gang stalking intensified. The petty cons sat in view of my house daily. Across the street, someone was always on the porch surveying my house. The moment I stepped outside, the observer would make a call. To aggravate me, stalkers would approach me in grocery stores and stand in my path, conspicuously holding their phones. Sometimes they would take photos of me. The circling of my house intensified. My network was under constant attack. When I called police to make a report, cops and dispatchers ridiculed and mocked me.

After my meeting with Detective Freeman, the MLK property was broken into again.

This time it was the Hispanic woman pretending to be an heir to the property. She was accompanied by a locksmith and a young Hispanic male who was covered in prison tattoos.

The burglars had broken the lock to the property's street-side electrical box and turned off the electricity before picking the lock to the workshop. The alarm sounded anyway.

ADT, our alarm company, called the police and then called Tedi to report the breach. Tedi called me.

We decided I would head to the property while she called the police to describe the car I was driving so that they would know that I was the complainant.

When I arrived, I saw three SUVs parked on the lawn between the house and the garage. The Hispanic woman was standing beside the white vehicle rummaging through a box of documents she had removed from the building. They had attempted to disable the alarm system inside.

The apparent ex-con exited the building holding a document he had just removed from the property. He showed it excitedly to the Hispanic woman. The locksmith was replacing the lock they had just broken.

I parked the Volvo behind the white SUV. Before I got out of the car, I wrote down the license plates of all the vehicles.

I confronted the woman. "What are you doing here?" I asked. The tattooed guy vanished into the workshop. "It's our property," she kept saying over and over again.

"Which is it? I asked derisively. "Does it belong to you or does it belong to Roger Combs?" I grabbed the box of documents and put them back inside. The workshop was already in some disarray before this second breaking and entering incident, but could tell that they had been rummaging through items.

The police arrived. Once again, they asked me for proof that I owned the property. I was ready for them this time. I showed them the ADT contract with the property address on it.

"It was our alarm company who called you," I reminded them.

These new cops were not as belligerent as Phelan and Tullis the week before, but they were following the same script. They asked us for proof of occupancy and when I showed it to them, they ignored it. When the fake heir was unable to show them anything valid, they ignored that, too. And when the police report came out, I went from being the complainant to the trespasser. Someone reading the police report about the burglary reported by my security company at my property would have no idea who tripped the alarm.

"I showed you my proof," I told them. "Where's her proof?"

She didn't have any. First, she told the cops that the title company was on its way with proof of ownership. She then called Combs and handed the phone to one of the cops. I demanded that the locksmith hand me the new keys. He passed them over.

"Yes, I know," the cop was saying sympathetically into the phone. "Yes, I know."

I continued to plead with the officers to get physical, documentary proof that they had a right to the property. I had shown mine, I reminded them.

"Officer Freeman has the deed," the woman was now repeating. "Officer Freeman is handling it." She said the detective was scheduled to come to the property to let them in.

In our meeting, Freeman had said he'd received a copy of the deed, but when I asked to see it, he recanted. It was all smoke and mirrors.

"Each party presented paperwork showing they had a right to be at the property," the cops lied in the police report. That was a lie. I was the only one to show any proof. The report continued: "I was advised that a court date was set to determine ownership. I advised both parties that the situation was a civil matter and the court date will determine who has a right to be there."

The fake heir started complaining that I had parked my car behind her and blocked her in. "Female who is trespassing is arguing with Complainant," the police wrote in the police report.

I replaced the lock on the door and reset the alarm. The fake heir complained that I had blocked her in.

"Now, complainant is blocked in," the report stated. Somehow, in the police report, the fake heir in the white SUV became the complainant and I became the person trespassing, even though it was my alarm company who had called the police.

Tellingly, the cops did not write down either my name or the name of the woman pretending to be an heir to the property. Like the first breaking and entering incident, this second burglary was coded as a miscellaneous disturbance.

The police were covering up a felony theft in broad daylight. It was truly horrifying.

Later that night, a man identifying himself as Sergeant Custer called me while we recuperated from the trauma of the day at home. The people who had broken in had shown proof that they were the true owners of the property, he lied.

No they aren't, I said.

Yes, they are, he said. He was sending a patrol officer to the house to pick up the key I had taken from the locksmith.

You need to give the key to the officer, he said.

I'm not going to do that, I said.

You're a squatter, he yelled. If you have a complaint, go to Internal Affairs.

I had already been to internal affairs twice. The first time to complain about a cop who, after visiting amiably with drug dealers and pimps on Hackberry, ignore my request to speak to the responding officer about illegal soliciting of motorists behind my house and then falsified his incident report. The second time was after the false Greyhound arrest. In the latter visit, the Internal Affairs detective rudely informed me that there would be no investigation because the police department had already met its quota of disciplinary actions for that year.

That's another thing corrupted officials like to do: send you to departments they already know won't help you.

I told Custer I had no intention of going to SAPD Internal Affairs, but that I did intend to go to the feds.

He didn't like that. Still yelling, Custer barked that he was not taking sides. This was a civil matter, he yelled.

If this is a civil matter, I responded, then why are you calling me?

He abruptly hung up.

I remember the moment after Custer hung up on me. I was sitting in the living room with Tedi and Teresa. They could hear the abuse coming through over the phone. They looked shell-shocked, terrified.

Are they going to come and arrest you?" Tedi asked.

"No," I said. "They wouldn't dare."

But, honestly, I wasn't sure. Nothing I had learned about having civil rights protections as an American was turning out to be true.

10 | FAKERY

The notary fraud

I SET ABOUT FINDING THE phantom deeds Combs and the other co-conspirators kept mentioning.

Evading hackers, I managed to establish a secure connection to the county deeds office online website. I looked with interest at the records pulled up by my search. I was keen to see what could possibly have been filed that would have given the burglars authority to break into the property on Martin Luther King in the middle of the night.

What I found shocked me: several quitclaim deeds reportedly signed and notarized by various descendants of Carolina Treviño signing their interest in the property over to someone named James Michael Kissler.

Combs had filed these purported deeds and alleged power of attorney from Kissler in the deeds office on September 9, 2013, two days *after* she, her father Roger, and the two imposters used bolt cutters to break into 1614 Martin Luther King Drive.

Signed by notaries, the deeds purported to have been executed back in June, but that didn't matter.

I knew immediately that the documents were forged.

I studied the documents intently. They told a compelling story, although not the story Allstate's enablers wanted told. It would all have been comical if it hadn't been connected to so much evil.

If the deeds filed by Combs were to be believed, then James Michael Kissler, a resident of Sierra Vista, AZ, met Kristina Combs in her Austin Highway law office on June 27, 2013 to sign a power of attorney affidavit.

The "office" was actually a mailbox in a strip mall UPS Store.

About a month later, just a few weeks before the Combs burglary, a rash of potential heirs purportedly signed various quitclaim deeds handing their interest in the property over to Kissler.

Even before there was definitive proof of forgery, the documents were clearly fraudulent. For one thing, the signatures of some of the quitclaim signers did not match signatures from past probate records. One signer's middle initial inexplicably changed from a C to a G. Even the notaries own signatures differed wildly from one signature block to another. Two signatures of one notary were clearly signed by two different people. The effort looked rushed, amateurish.

Three notaries certified the quitclaim deeds: Monica Arrellano, Meagan Hollis, and Ofelia Lisa Hernandez. I searched the Texas Secretary of State online record search portal for notary records. Hollis worked for Frost Bank. Arellano and Hernandez worked for Loree, Hernandez & Lipscomb, a law firm on Sonterra Boulevard that specialized in insurance matters. I decided to drive out to Loree, Hernandez & Lipscomb and ask to see Arrellano's and Hernandez's notary books to verify the signatures.

When I got to the office building housing the two notaries' law firm, I saw a white SUV identical to the one driven by the female burglar pretending to be an heir to the MLK property. I checked the license plate.

Bingo.

It was the same vehicle.

Once inside the building, I took an elevator to the Loree & Lipscomb office. I asked the receptionist to speak to Monica Arrellano or Ofelia Lisa Hernandez. "I have some questions about their notary books," I explained. Monica Arrellano came out. She was young, pretty. She gave me a friendly smile.

I introduced myself and requested to see the notary entries for James Michael Kissler. Her face fell. A range of emotions flashed across her face. She looked terrified, dejected, hopeless. She pulled herself together. "You'll have to speak to Lisa," she said. She was suddenly angry, but not with me.

"Hold on," she said and walked back to the inner offices.

"Lisa!" I heard her bark.

She didn't return. I waited for Hernandez to appear. The receptionist, now aware that something was up, asked me again what I was looking for. I repeated myself, careful to be warm and friendly. "It's just for a project I'm working on," I said.

"What's your name again?" she asked.

"Denise McVea."

This time she wrote it down.

She went to the back with the slip of paper. I waited. A man came out, greeted me with a quick hello, and hovered. He must be a security guard, I thought, or a private investigator. Hernandez refused to come to the front. When it was clear she would not be showing herself, I left. When I got home, I conducted a Google search. Ofelia Lisa Hernandez had worked for Loree & Lipscomb since 1995. She was a 2010 master's graduate from UTSA in Justice Policy. She and her husband Erik had registered a new auto business with the secretary of state's office. They gave as the company's address a decrepit storefront on Martin Luther King Drive that had been abandoned for as long as I could remember.

There was a photo of her.

I shook my head and gave a low, mirthless chuckle.

Ofelia Lisa Hernandez had help Kristina Combs break into, steal, and illegally transfer the property at 1614 Martin Luther King Drive.

She was the chief notary on the fraudulent quitclaim deeds.

She was also the woman at both information center burglaries pretending to be an heir.

Kissler v. McVea and Ethics Follies

When I found Combs's bogus court filings, I tried to catch up to the false quiet title lawsuit that was speeding jet-like through Bexar County's civil court system. In my answer, I wrote about the criminality underlying the lawsuit. I subpoenaed the notaries Ofelia Lisa Hernandez and Monica Arrellano and the heir Amelia McKnight to produce records and give testimony. But court proceedings were typical Bexar County Courthouse dog and pony shows.

Tommy Hernandez, one of the principals in Loree, Hernandez & Lipscomb where the forgers worked, filed a motion to quash my request to see their notary books, even though notary books are public record. Almost immediately after his motion to quash, Hernandez's name was quietly dropped from the law firm's masthead. I chased him all over town to confer in the sham motion, but he continued to duck and dodge. A hearing on Hernandez's motion to quash was never heard. Instead, as I waited fruitlessly in presiding court for a hearing that never came, Judge Antonia Arteaga was in the back with Combs, signing a handwritten order to fine me $1500 for non-appearance. They were shameless.

The quiet title "trial" for was set for November 13, 2013 in Judge Barbara Nellermoe's court. That same day, courthouse regulars were excitedly preparing to attend Ethics Follies, a vanity burlesque theatre show popular among the Texas legal set. Courthouse regulars fill the theater as lawyers and judges play themselves, performing a variety of stage scenes about hilarious ethics failures. It's a popular annual event, apparently very entertaining. Attendees earn continuing legal education credits

Nellermoe had no jurisdiction to hear the case because it was part of an open probate suit. In my answer, I also pointed out the deeds were signed by people who had no claim to the property and that in addition to all of that, the deeds appeared forged.

A woman who identified herself as heir Amelia McKnight showed up to court in response to my subpoena. She sat stoically in the hallway. I immediately doubted her identity. When I approached her, she brusquely told me she did not want to talk. She seemed too young for the role, but mostly I suspected her because she had no questions. She had been summoned to court about a property that she had allegedly waived her rights to. A normal person would have questions. I intended to ask for her driver's license when I got her on the stand.

But Nellermoe used the same tactics that Mery had used in the Allstate and Greyhound cases. She avoided establishing any kind of procedure, frequently interrupted me, and ignored obvious and provable facts. There was never any opportunity to call the woman to the stand and in less than an hour Nellermoe was wrapping up the lawsuit in favor of Combs.

At one point, the judge gazed down on me in assessment.

I know you, she said. You are a community activist who maybe wants to do some good for your community but don't really have the resources.

She actually said that. Looking back, I realize that she was talking to herself, convincing herself that I did not have the clout to make her regret what she was about to do.

I was certain that she had had that conversation with herself before, mentally calculating the power level of the victim standing in court before her. Satisfied that the person was without recourse, she would do the dirty deed and quickly move on. Nothing had ever come back to bite her in the ass before. For some reason, I smiled warmly at her. She didn't smile back.

And suddenly, it was over. Without taking testimony, weighing any evidence, or even holding a semblance of a trial, Bexar County Judge Barbara Nellermoe abruptly awarded the property to Combs' phantom client.

"James Michael Kissler has been granted deeds from the heirs of the property, and therefore it is ordered that title to the property located at 1614 Martin Luther King Drive, San Antonio, Texas is quieted in James Michael Kissler."

A quiet title lawsuit is complex, time-consuming litigation. They tend to drag on for years as the court wrestles with property and probate laws. But Nellermoe quickly, efficiently dispensed with the law to illegally transfer the title to a person, who, for all she knew, didn't even exist. To do that, she engaged in judicial misconduct, official oppression, and obstruction of justice.

Then off she went, without any irony at all, to doll up for Ethics Follies.

The woman purporting to be the heir Amelia McKnight quickly slipped away.

To add insult to injury, Nellermoe gave me two days to remove all of the Auris Project contents from the MLK property. I complained that the order was arduous because the Auris Project had tons of valuable equipment, libraries and furniture inside the structures on the property. She ignored me.

I spent the next two days writing a request for temporary injunction. On November 15, 2013, the day Nellermoe told Combs she could take official control of the property, I filed a temporary restraining order. At the very least, the court could allow us to take inventory.

I went to the courthouse. Temporary restraining order requests are one of the few times a litigant can meet with a judge when the other party is not present. Tiffany Duong, the assistant staff attorney, walked me up to Nellermoe's office. Duong looked like she was getting sick of all this. She led me into Nellermoe's chambers and departed.

Nellermoe was pleasant, but was completely devoid of empathy. I handed her a copy of the motion for restraining order I had filed and asked for more time to take inventory and remove items from the property.

I reminded her that Combs had alleged in open court that criminal charges were being pursued against me for theft. I needed time to conduct the inventory, I told her. She listened to my arguments with a kind, attentive look. Then, smiling warmly, she refused to sign the restraining order or take any action that might stop the brazen theft.

"You better hurry up," she told me. "You don't have a lot of time to get your stuff." She beamed at me in the loveliest way.

These people are deranged, I thought, a bunch of raging sociopaths.

Nellermoe called out to the bailiff sitting outside her office door.

"Please see Ms. McVea out," she requested mildly. "Be gentle. She's a nice lady."

The forgery report

Months later, during a lull in Allstate's burgeoning oppression campaign, I contacted nationally noted handwriting expert Wendy Carlson. I asked her to examine some of the quitclaim deeds Combs had filed in the county deeds office. A court-certified forensic document examiner and registered investigator, Carlson agreed to examine the quitclaim deed signatures. I couldn't afford to examine all the documents so I asked her to focus on the deeds containing the signatures of notaries Monica Arrellano and Ofelia Lisa Hernandez, heir Amelia McKnight, and James Kissler.

After a "meticulous examination" using peer-reviewed methodology, Carlson issued her findings in a report entitled "Questioned Document Examiner Letter, June 4, 2014." In court records, I referred to it as the "Carlson Report."

According to the report, the signatures in the quitclaim deeds had indeed been forged.

It had been a good, old fashion forgery party:

The person who signed notary Monica Arrellano's signature also signed buyer James Michael Kissler's signature. A second Arrellano signature did not match the first signature. In one instance, the purported signature of notary Ofelia Lisa Hernandez was actually signed by the person established as the signature of Monica Arrellano. And the person who signed Hernandez's signature also signed the signature of the purported heir, Amelia G. McKnight. The report reinforced my suspicions that the woman who showed up for Nellermoe's kangaroo quiet title trial wasn't McKnight at all, but an imposter. No wonder Nellermoe worked so hard to quickly end the trial. She did not want that person to take the stand. If it had been McKnight, the notaries would not have needed to forge her signature.

Later, I made an open records request for Ofelia Lisa Hernandez's notary files from the Texas Secretary of State. More of the puzzle fell into place.

In the quitclaim deeds, the notary signatures were very different. The person signing Ofelia Lisa Hernandez's signature had light, spidery handwriting. The Secretary of State documents showed that Ofelia Lisa Hernandez had bold, heavy, loopy handwriting in the signature.

Ah, I realized, Ofelia Lisa Hernandez signed Monica Arrellano's signature on the quitclaim deeds.

It didn't take a forensic expert to understand that notary Ofelia Lisa Hernandez, the fake heir repeatedly burgling 1614 Martin Luther King Drive, had also forged the signature of the phantom buyer, James Michael Kissler.

The Carlson report was powerful evidence.

It proved what I had been saying for months, that the claim to the property was fraudulent and part of a criminal conspiracy. Even before the report, it was obvious that the quiet title case before Bexar County District Judge Barbara Nellermoe was defined by wild illegality. I had argued in court that the quiet title suit was brought as part of a criminal conspiracy to harass, defraud and inflict emotional distress upon me and that Kissler was a front, either knowingly or not.

But I was making that argument to a co-conspirator.

I attached the report to a motion for new trial based on newly discovered evidence. I wrote:

> This new evidence supports McVea's contention that the eviction and seizure of Auris Project property was affected through fraud. Even if Bexar County Probate Court had properly designated heirs to the property as required by Texas Laws of Descent and Distribution (it had not), and all of those designated heirs signed quitclaim deeds to Kissler (they did not), the new evidence unequivocally impeaches Combs' fraudulent claim that James Michael Kissler legally gained title through the quitclaim deeds filed in this court - because the signatures on these quitclaim deeds were forged. The evidence supports McVea's belief and contention that James Michael Kissler is a "straw buyer" who may or may not be aware that his name is being used in a fraudulent manner.49

In my motion for new trial, I added other evidence: the burglaries, the failure to notice, the burglars' false statements to police, the tax records showing the heirs had renounced the property.

But when I tried to file my motion for new trial based on newly discovered evidence, I was turned away. The District Clerk simply refused to file it. That case has been closed, a deputy clerk told me.

By this time I was dead broke. The property and all of the assets inside had been stolen and resold. I had suffered a devastating loss.

Plus, I was already deeply embroiled in two awful lawsuits, the federal civil rights lawsuit against the cops who arrested me on MLK Day for the bogus garage sale crime and the malicious criminal assault charge used to cover up Kristina Combs' deed fraud and theft of Auris Project assets. All I could do was use the motion as evidence in the two trials I was currently dealing with. My efforts now had little to do with accessing justice and almost everything to do with preserving evidence against corrupt officials in San Antonio.

But the evidence was clear: Combs had appeared with forged quitclaim deeds and a fake client to illegally transfer real estate property on the Eastside into her name after she had already broken into the place. According to public record, she was assisted in that crime by several principal players: notary Lisa Ofelia Hernandez, notary Monica Arrellano, former county commissioner Tommy Adkisson, attorney Tomas Hernandez, attorney Robert "Woody" Wilson, Judge Karen Pozza, Judge Antonia Arteaga, Judge Scott Roberts, and Judge Barbara Nellermoe. She was also assisted by former District Attorney Nico La Hood, current District Attorney Joe Gonzales, many prosecutors, and numerous cops. There were many others, but the ones mentioned here unwisely exposed themselves on the public record.

But the public record could be scrubbed.

I kept making copies, kept filing them away.

Dear Judge

The next few years would be defined by my efforts to recover from the devastating theft of Auris Project assets and to survive Allstate's continued zero sum game against me. The cyberhacking and gangstalking continued.

At some point, I learned that Antonia Arteaga, one of the judges expediting the MLK theft, was running for re-election.

She thinks she's gotten away with it, I thought. On July 21, 2015, I wrote Arteaga a letter urging her not to run. I wanted her to know that I had not forgotten what she and other district judges had done.

In the letter, I explained my professional background, mentioning some of my publications, awards, and my social justice work with the Auris Project and New Voices. I then delved into the some of the misconduct I witnessed in the Bexar County courthouse, including the illegal default judgments against pro se litigants. I also documented Arteaga's part in the criminal conspiracy to steal the property at 1614 Martin Luther King using forged quitclaim deeds. I wanted Arteaga to know that I had found the quitclaim deeds and that I knew that they were fraudulent. And I reminded her of her contribution to the crime, that on October 31, 2013, she illegally met with Kristina Combs in a back room while I sat in presiding court waiting for a hearing that never came.

"With court provided paper, Kristina Combs then was allowed to handwrite an order sanctioning me and fining me $1500, ostensibly for not showing up for the hearing. You signed that illegal order.... For this reason alone, you must not run for re-election."

I notarized the letter and mailed it certified mail, return receipt requested. I also sent certified copies to the chief of police, the county commissioners, city council members, and state legislators. Not a single person responded.

Years later, I encountered Judge Arteaga as she ran presiding court during my divorce proceedings. She would pretend that we had never met.

I knew that what I was witnessing was not happening in a vacuum. I had only to go on Facebook to see the stories of countless people victimized by the Bexar County court system, the SAPD, the county at large, and the city.

"We are fighting for our lives," one activist had said, and I knew exactly what she'd meant. I had also spoken to people representing government entities in other Texas towns. They all wanted to know: What the hell was going on in San Antonio?

The plot to steal the MLK property was cynical, well planned, and confidently executed. Clearly, this was not the first time cops, judges, lawyers, notaries, and title companies collaborated to steal property on the Eastside. But it was probably the first time that a trained journalist had documented the theft. It was all starting to come together, and I began to understand how local corruption fit into Allstate's decadent business model.

The relentless attacks overwhelmed and traumatized me, but I couldn't help thinking: *this is a good story.* If I didn't have a great story to tell, I knew, Allstate wouldn't be spending millions of dollars to silence me. *Keep going,* I repeated to myself.

Keep going.

I had covered enough stories to know that when the public was made aware of things much less horrific than what I was witnessing here, something got done about it. All I had to do was tell the story, show the proof, and the cat would be out of the bag.

I didn't feel sorry for myself.

Instead, I thought that all the other victims now had proof.

I just had to get the story out. That story had to be clear, concise, and levelheaded.

I got arrested a third time.

11 | ERRORS

False arrest No. 3

ON NOVEMBER 16, 2013, "PRACTICING lawyer" Kristina Combs, now armed with the fraudulent order from Nellermoe awarding her phantom buyer the MLK property, began moving furniture, documents, books, and other inventory items out of the information center at 1614 Martin Luther King Drive in earnest.

The entire eviction was illegal. It was affected by a crooked judge making an unauthorized order based on obviously forged documents.

A team that included Combs, her mother, her brother Roger Combs, Jr., and a man I had never seen before ransacked the place.

As a matter of law, items still present in a property at the time of an eviction must be placed outside on the sidewalk. I knew I would have to wait for Combs and her family to start tossing my things on the sidewalk and then, like a scavenger, pick through and claim what I could of my own stuff.

I was exhausted. I had no idea how I would get the strength to reclaim the thousands of items inside MLK, especially heavy furniture like bookshelves and desks. One of the items was a gorgeous wooden file cabinet that covered a whole wall worth thousands of dollars. There were also revolving metal bookcases in mint condition, also worth thousands of dollars. There was no way I could move those items in the timespan that Nellermoe illegally ordered. And then there were the books, the tens of thousands of books. How in the world would I be able to safely gather and transfer the thousands of books that made up the Auris bookstore and law library?

Maybe, I thought dazedly, I could dig through the piles and find some of the out-of-print collectibles or first editions in what I expected to be a horrific pile up on the sidewalk. They were extremely valuable. If I could find those, I could potentially resell them and help replenish Auris's shattered finances as I figured out my next steps. Again, I had underestimated exactly the number of laws Allstate's minions were willing to break to reach Allstate's objectives.

The day of my third arrest, I was lying in bed, fatigued in both body and mind. I was also limping, having dislocated my knee weeks earlier in an ill-conceived effort to ride a miniature horse without a saddle.

Tedi offered to go pick up a pizza. I asked her to swing by MLK to see if Combs and her family had started placing things on the sidewalk. She swung by. When she returned home with the pizza, she reported what she had seen. They were there, she told me, but they weren't putting things on the sidewalk. It looked like they were stacking items in a truck.

That was illegal.

I dragged myself out of bed and headed toward 1614 MLK. I parked at the closed and empty carwash across the street. Sure enough, Combs, her brother Roger, her mother, a preteen boy, and a grinning man I had not seen before were putting my books into the back of a late model pickup truck. I couldn't help but recall that I had unwisely expressed in front of Combs the day before that it was the loss of the books that I lamented most. And here they were, brazenly stealing books to the exclusion at the time of all else. You keep playing into their hands, I berated myself. Not a single item had been placed on the curb.

I turned on my phone's video recorder and got out of the car.

"What are you doing?" I asked. "You are supposed to be putting my property on the curb."

They ignored me. The boy disappeared inside. I never saw him again.

Combs and the unknown, weirdly smiling man kept toting boxes of books out and putting them in the back of the truck.

That's illegal, I told them. That's theft.

They ignored me. I would need proof that they had stolen the bookstore and library.

I made sure my camera was working and stepped toward the pickup to take a picture of the boxes of books. Combs, who had just deposited a book in the bed of the pickup, came charging my way. "Get... off...the...property." She grunted as she charged toward me, arms flailing.

This bitch is trying to hit me, I thought in disbelief as she charged, her arms swinging wildly.

I stepped back. The pain that shot through my injured knee reminded me that I was at a physical disadvantage. I still could not put full weight on the left knee. I risked falling to the ground if I did. I could not really avoid her attack. Forced to stand my ground, I blocked Combs's wild haymaker with an upward block and countered with a jab to get her off me. Her face contorted into a look of surprise. Limping, I immediately began retreating backwards. Combs recovered from the jab and began pursuing me as I sought the safety of my car. Behind her, the odd smiling man followed, yelling, "You hit her! I saw you!"

Combs' mother piled out of the second building. "You hit her, you hit her!" she yelled. "I saw you!"

The small crowd chased me. I had a vague feeling as I limped to my car that I was being hounded by a family that Kristina's whole life had been considered by neighbors as nothing more than trash. Ignorant and bellicose, this was a family of morally bankrupt, often-dismissed, brutish thieves and drunkards. Now, one of them had somehow miraculously passed the Texas State bar exam with no substantial knowledge of law, and the family was mysteriously empowered to claim free property on the Eastside. Looking back, I can see that this shabby family was doing the illegal work that even Bexar County officials, who would do just about anything for money, wouldn't do.

I made it back to the car and quickly jumped inside, slamming the door shut behind me. Combs ran after me, and with a grunt, kicked the driver's side door. She then ran to jump in the truck that held Auris's books and drove it into the street, essentially blocking my car in. I got out of the car.

Kristina's mother came barreling across the street. She was her daughter's doppelganger, pudgy and short with extremely wide-set eyes.

"I saw you hit her," she repeated.

I began calling them thieves and bitches, but the mother was as defiant as her daughter. We began to argue. Only once did uncertainty cross their faces. In the middle of the bickering, I began naming some of the lawyers I knew were behind this latest outrage. I named them one by one: Albert Gutierrez, Matthew Wymer, Todd Lipscomb, Robert Loree, John D. Carlos, Larry Goldman, Martin Phipps. Upon hearing those names, the mother stood there for a second, her mouth agape in surprise. I wasn't supposed to have any idea about what was happening to me. I wasn't supposed to know about these people. Her reaction made that obvious.

I began scolding them about doing the dirty work for the elitist lawyers. They consider themselves high society, I blustered, and they use people like you to do their dirty work. When it all comes out, I harangued, you will be the ones left holding the bag. You're nothing but a bunch of pawns.

Even after everything I had seen from the Combs family, I called them pawns instead of what I really thought they were: white trash. They looked like the sort of people who stood on the sidewalk hurling insults and empty water bottles at neighbors. They were kind of doing that now.

The mother quickly regained her composure.

You're crazy, she said.

Trapped, I stood outside my car, trying to figure out what to do next. A woman who had seen the altercation came to my rescue.

"Ma'am," she said to Combs, alarmed, "What are you doing? You can't park in the middle of the street like that."

Combs ignored her.

The woman looked over at me. She could see that I was surrounded and under attack. "Ma'am," she asked me. "Are you alright?"

I said something about them being part of the cabal who was stealing property on the Eastside.

She wanted to help me. She turned back to Combs, repeating her earlier objection. My first thought was to get her name and number as a witness. My second thought was that I needed to protect her. She was a black woman on the Eastside and the cops were on their way. Nothing good could come from her willingness to help me. I knew that with certainty.

"Ma'am," I said, "these people are very dangerous. Just go. Thank you, but just go."

She left.

Standing in the heat, leaning up against my car, I could feel my injured knee starting to swell and ache. I didn't know what to do. I couldn't move the car because Combs had illegally blocked me in. I started to walk home. I got a few blocks before a police patrol car came up behind me, lights flashing. The officer exited his vehicle and, handcuffs in hand, told me to turn around. I kept walking.

"I haven't done anything wrong," I remember telling him. He grabbed my left wrist and began to handcuff me. I tensed up.

"Relax," he said. I stopped straining. He put me in the back of his patrol car. Through the window, I could see another cop arrive, and then Kristina Combs. The three huddled together while I sat handcuffed in the back of the patrol car. From police reports, I would learn that one cop was named Martinez; the other named Jesse Mendoza.

One of the officers, Martinez or Mendoza, I can't remember which, came to the back of the squad car where I was handcuffed. I asked him why I was under arrest.

Because you assaulted the other female, he said.

That's not true, I said. She attacked me, and I have a video to prove it. It's on my phone. You can see for yourself.

It's okay if I look at your phone? he asked.

Yes, I told him. Struggling with the handcuffs, I awkwardly handed it to him. He took it and walked over to the other cop, Martinez or Mendoza. Immediately, I regretted giving the phone to him. What if he erased the video? I would have no way of showing that I was the victim of assault. The two officers fiddled clumsily with the phone. It looked like they didn't know what they were doing. He brought the phone back to me.

Did you see the video? I asked.

Yes, he said, he had seen the video. It showed that you attacked her, he lied.

My heart sank. I was going to jail again. But I was also relieved. After watching their fumbling and hearing him lie about what had been recorded, I knew that they had not seen the video. And if they couldn't access the video, they couldn't erase it either. I had proof.

In the police report, Jesse Mendoza repeated Combs' lies almost verbatim. According to the police report, Mendoza was dispatched to a disturbance and learned that officer Martinez #595 told him he "had the female causing the disturbance in custody."

According to police report SAPD13252834, Combs, the purported victim, was on the property when I approached "in an aggressive manor (sic) and demanded to collect more items from the listed location." When Combs told me I needed to leave the property, the report stated, I "struck her in the mouth twice with a closed fist," and then walked off.

Mendoza, the author of this false police report, was the same cop who had left me inside the information center with the burglar in 2010. And the video showed that he also wrote false police reports.

For what that was worth.

Off I went to jail for the third time in Bexar County in less than three years.

While I sat in jail, Combs and her family emptied out the information center, stealing everything inside. The bookstore and law library were gone, and so was the information center. Furniture, electronics, antiques, tools, auction inventory, books, artwork, and documents were all gone, stolen by the state of Texas in collusion with brazen criminal actors.

As I sat in the holding cell with the other inmates, I grieved my losses. I was exhausted, overwhelmed, and beaten down. I had lost just about everything I had worked for. I had no choice but to keep fighting. I had little left to lose.

This time, I did see a magistrate. The state of Texas was going to prosecute me for allegedly assaulting and causing physical injury to Combs. I prayed that the cop hadn't erased the video. I stayed in jail for hours as Tedi worked with our friend Janice, a bail bondswoman, to get the paperwork together to bail me out. It was starting to feel routine.

The constant harassment was taking a toll not just on me, but on Tedi as well. I didn't know how she was still with me.

The billboard attorney

I started looking for a lawyer who could help me fight the bogus Combs assault charge. I knew that with all that was going on I needed a lawyer in the criminal case. I was exhausted. I did not know the first thing about criminal law and did not feel I had the energy to learn it.

But my internet searches continued to bring up the same two or three pages of lawyers. I had already tied several to the corrupt networks supporting Allstate. For instance, Cappuccio, the lawyer harassing me through his position on the Unauthorized Practice of Law Committee, was listed as a civil rights attorney.

I knew I couldn't trust any of the lawyers listed on the webpages. I had learned enough to know those pages were being spoon fed to me through Allstate hackers' man-in-the-middle campaigns.

Driving around town, a billboard featuring criminal attorney Joe Gonzales caught my eye. I had never thought much of billboard attorneys, but my circumstances were dire. I needed help, and so I jotted down the phone number of Gonzales' law firm. That would turn out to be a costly mistake for me, and an important opportunity for him.

Days later, sitting in his peach colored waiting room on Main Street, I still had misgivings. His paralegal passed me a handout listing all of the assault cases Joe had won. I was impressed. The paralegal sent me back to his office. He was awkward and a bit stilted, but polite. I showed him the video of Kristina Combs attacking me. I also explained the background.

He seemed sincere about his winning record and he had made no gaffes like other attorneys before him. I signed the contract.

He explained that he would show the video to the prosecutor on the case. The evidence was so strong that he had no doubt the case would be dismissed. He charged $3500 to represent me in pretrial. If for some reason the case goes to trial, he told me, it would cost an additional $3000 to see the case to its conclusion.

"But you don't have to worry about that," he told me. "With your evidence, there is no reason this won't be dismissed pretrial."

I chuckled sarcastically. "You would think," I said.

Gonzales told me his office would get right to work – upon receipt of the $3500. I had to borrow the money from my mother.

On November 20, 2013, billboard defense attorney Joe Gonzales notified the court that he would be representing me in the Combs criminal assault case, officially known as *The State of Texas v. Denise McVea*.

That same day, as I sat with dozens of other defendants in County Court 12, my lawyer asked me to pull up the video showing Combs attacking me on my phone. I watched as Gonzales walked it up to prosecutor Matthew

Ludowig. The two bent over the small screen. Ludowig shook his head. Gonzales walked back to me and handed me back his phone. "I'll let you know," he told me.

Gonzales then stopped answering my questions. He was noticeably vague about the criminal justice process. He suddenly had no time to discuss strategy. He hemmed and hawed.

Once, he brought in another lawyer, David McLane, who he said might want to represent me in a battery case against Combs. McLane asked pointed questions about my case. Unaware at the time that the lawyers were violating attorney-client privilege, I answered freely. I showed him the video, apologized for my repeated use of the word "bitches" as I ran from my attackers, and explained about the crimes and cover-ups I had already documented. Both men were completely engaged and interested, which I at first took as a good sign.

But, certain aspects of the meeting troubled me. When I referred to Kristina Combs as an illiterate criminal thug who did not have the intelligence or grasp of the law to pass the state bar exam, the men shot quick glances at each other. The hairs on the back of my neck stood up when Gonzales asked me kindly not to mention that again.

"It's true," I said.

When I called McLane discuss my case against Combs, he told me he couldn't discuss the case until the criminal charges against me had been dropped. Looking back, I can see that the meeting was for his benefit, not mine, and that he was there on a fact-finding mission.

Years later, I would come to understand that the information I gave those two lawyers that day probably helped define the strategy against me that played out in criminal court for the next two years.

Soon Gonzales passed me off to a chubby lawyer he introduced as a junior associate. This new attorney also offered no strategies or information. "This is an important case, rife with official misconduct," I told the young associate. "You can be a hero."

He shrugged dismissively. He couldn't have been more disinterested. Being a hero for his fellow citizens held no appeal for him all.

Gonzales' law firm filed no motions to dismiss, habeas corpus, or any pretrial motion challenging the false prosecution. When I called him for an update, he talked in circles.

And before I knew it, Joe Gonzales, my criminal defense attorney and soon-to-be Bexar County District Attorney, stopped talking about pre-trial altogether. He started telling me what his plans were once we went to trial. He hadn't filed a single challenge to the obscenely malicious prosecution of his client.

As he talked, he offhandedly slipped in that representation for trial would cost an additional $3000 before quickly changing the subject.

I realized that, by hiring Joe Gonzales, I had made another forced error.[50]

12 | COLLUSION

The informant

MEANWHILE, THE FBI WAS WIRETAPPING District Judge Angus McGinty, defense lawyer Al Acevedo, and hundreds of other people circulating through the local courthouse.

The feds had found a key witness in its investigation into corruption in the Bexar County Courthouse: Michael Oliver Otten. A San Antonio mechanic, Michael Otten was also a career criminal facing deportation when he told federal investigators that his criminal defense attorney was bribing Bexar County judges. It was not the first time that Otten had used his knowledge of the criminal underworld to escape prosecution or deportation. Feds were always ready to strike a deal with people facing prison time if they thought the information could lead to important arrests. Otten was a fast talker, and he knew how to work the system. Twenty years earlier, a Bexar County judge had reset Otten's theft case more than a dozen times before eventually dismissing the charges against him, according to the *San Antonio Express-News*.

This time, Otten offered the feds a state district judge.

He was working on that judge's car right now, he told agents, an aging Mercedes Benz S430. The judge, Angus McGinty, sat on the 144th district court. Otten's lawyer, Alberto Acevedo, had picked the car up from the judge and driven it to Otten's shop for repairs.

It was a classic back-scratching scheme that Acevedo apparently ran often. The lawyer would pay for the repairs to McGinty's Mercedes himself. In return, the judge would repay the lawyer with favorable rulings from the bench. That's how they do it in Bexar County, Otten told the FBI.

The feds halted deportation proceedings against him. The next time Otten met with Acevedo, he wore a wire. Unaware that the feds were listening, a cocky and boastful Acevedo quickly implicated himself and others.

In conversations recorded over the next several months, Acevedo and McGinty incriminated themselves repeatedly in federal wiretaps. Acevedo bragged that he had other judges in his pocket, but not only was McGinty corrupt, he was cheap.

ACEVEDO: He's (McGinty) been doing a lot of shit for me.

OTTEN: Really? So, if I ever get in any problems, God forbid, he'll help me out?

ACEVEDO: Oh, this guy (McGinty) is better than (the other, unnamed judge who is now a prosecutor in Comal County). You think (the former judge) is good? This guy (McGinty) is better, man.

OTTEN: Is he cheaper, though? That's the main thing. ...That fucking (other judge), man, was costin' a grand every couple of days, man.

ACEVEDO: This guy (McGinty), you know, I'll give him cash and he won't say nothing. You know, I don't do anything, you know. You know, it's like the way I keep the immigration judge. I ask her for shit and she just does it.

The FBI soon captured Acevedo getting his money's worth. In August 2013, Acevedo asked McGinty for an order to release one of Acevedo's criminal clients from electronic monitoring. Sure, said, McGinty, no questions asked. He also revoked an arrest warrant for another of Acevedo's clients and released an Acevedo client from alcohol monitoring conditions.

McGinty summed up his motivation for betraying the public trust in six words. That, too, was captured on federal wiretaps.

"Well," the Bexar County judge said, "I'm a whore for money."[51]

The killing of Michael Oliver Otten

Acevedo and McGinty were soon arrested and charged with a host of federal crimes. In the summer of 2014, a federal grand jury indicted the pair on bribery and corruption charges.

In announcing McGinty's indictment, the FBI used its usual superhero language.

"A fair and impartial criminal justice system is one of the cornerstones of our democracy," said San Antonio's Special Agent in Charge Christopher Combs. "Judges in particular are expected to protect the public's trust in the fairness of the judicial system. This case should serve as a strong warning to those who might consider similar alleged behavior. No one is above the law, and everyone is accountable for their misdeeds."

"Yeah, right," I grumbled.

Because corruption and conflict of interest ran so deep in South Texas, the feds prosecuted the men in New Mexico.

Both men eventually pleaded guilty. Acevedo was the first to flip. For a time, McGinty continued to deny wrongdoing, asserting that he followed universally accepted actions in the course of his judicial duties in Bexar County. Federal prosecutors mocked that justification, pointing out that federal law does not offer an "everybody's doing it" defense. When Acevedo turned state's evidence against McGinty, the judge stopped pretending he was innocent. Acevedo received a one-year sentence in federal prison. McGinty received two years. He served 18 months.

The conspirators could have spent more time in prison. But Otten, the government's chief witness, was gunned down before trial, the victim of a targeted shooting in the garage of his home on Linda Drive. Four men were in the garage on January 15, 2015 when the murder took place. According to media reports, an argument between the men erupted. The killer, Frank Campos, reportedly left the garage and returned with a firearm. He shot and killed Otten and another man, Anthony Reem. He left the fourth man alive. Directly after the hit, Campos jumped in Otten's car and fled to the Eastside. When police located Otten's car on St. James Street, it was empty. Ramos later surfaced down in the Rio Grande Valley. He holed up in Beeville for a bit before a friend convinced him to turn himself in. Campos would eventually plea bargain and receive two consecutive life sentences for the murders. After the sentencing, he sang as he left the courtroom.[52]

Police and the local media were careful to suggest that Otten's murder had nothing to do with the federal investigation into corruption in the Bexar County Courthouse or his work as an FBI informant.

Of course, they couldn't really know that.

I followed the case with interest. One day, I opened the newspaper and saw a photo of McGinty leaving the federal courthouse.

"I know that guy!" I exclaimed to Tedi. I'd recognize the bald head and watery blue eyes anywhere. He was the same judge who refused to dismiss the bogus criminal garage sale violation charge against me.

But McGinty was not a municipal judge. He was the judge for the state's 144th district court. Why would a district judge be involved in a municipal court case?

Suddenly, all of the bizarre conduct I witnessed during my plea hearing made sense. There were all sorts of shenanigans that day. I had been assigned a courtroom at the last minute and then had to wait out in the hallway as the judge made a late entrance. Grinning cops and lawyers walked in and out as I sat waiting. When the hearing finally started, I was the only defendant in an otherwise empty courtroom. Despite pressure from the prosecutor, I pleaded not guilty. I asked the judge to dismiss the case because prosecutors had charged me with a misdemeanor crime that did not exist. He denied my request. He scheduled a jury trial.

That judge was Angus McGinty.

When I returned for my jury trial a month later, a prosecutor wordlessly handed me a dismissal order. I wondered how many Bexar County residents had been forced to plea bargain on non-existent criminal charges.

Certainly, the false criminal misdemeanor proceeding against me had been off the books. It was essentially a shadow court performed in the courthouse but untethered to court rules or the law. The courtroom had apparently been staged, and McGinty had evidently been tapped to star in it. I wondered how much he had been paid to do it.

He was, after all, a whore for money.

I didn't have time to get to the bottom of it; I was being battered by one Allstate orchestrated attack after another. I had a dozen fires to put out. I tucked McGinty into the back of my mind.

Two months after the mechanic's murder, prosecutors reduced the federal corruption charges against McGinty from 15 to five. On April 13, 2015, McGinty pleaded guilty to a single honest services wire fraud charge. As part of his plea agreement with federal prosecutors, McGinty admitted depriving the state and Bexar County residents of his honest services by "soliciting and accepting bribes intended to influence his judicial decisions."

At the writing of this book, the public still does not know the identity of the immigration judge or the Comal County prosecutor implicated by Acevedo. Not only have they not been held to account for their alleged crimes, but they conceivably continued to occupy places of public trust.

The McGinty/Acevedo corruption case was anti-climactic. Despite overwhelming evidence of systemic corruption and widespread criminal misconduct by judges, lawyers and other public officials, the FBI had managed to arrest just two men in its Bexar County Courthouse corruption probe.

Neither man was a genius.

McGinty tries to drop a dime

In December 2013, FBI agents confronted the crooked lawyer Al Acevedo. He had been under surveillance, they told him, and his phone had been tapped. They had audio-recorded evidence of him admitting that he bribed judges.

The jig was up. Acevedo, eager to save himself, quickly turned on McGinty and started naming others in the courthouse he alleged were engaged in corruption. He identified Alan Brown and Jay Norton of the Brown & Norton criminal defense firm, "as examples of other attorneys who had gotten favorable rulings from McGinty."[53] (He would later walk back that statement somewhat, saying that it was mostly just a hunch based on what he saw around the courthouse.)

By January 2014, word of the FBI investigation had gotten around the courthouse. The entire legal community in San Antonio was abuzz. Acevedo, the corrupt lawyer, made the rounds, discreetly meeting with several Bexar County judges and lawyers about the investigation. One judge asked Acevedo pointblank if he was "debriefing with the feds on public corruption cases."

Although Acevedo made several stops in his notification campaign, he didn't tell McGinty. McGinty first learned he was the target of an FBI investigation when he got a call from Jay Norton, the same criminal defense attorney Acevedo fingered as a corrupt lawyer getting favor from judges like McGinty. In the call to McGinty, Norton urged McGinty to meet him for an "urgent" meeting in a restaurant parking lot.[54] Norton told McGinty that a Bexar County prosecutor had tipped him and Brown to the federal probe.

While Norton was furtively meeting with McGinty in the restaurant parking lot, Brown was meeting with two other judges. According to McGinty, Brown had talked to other judges and lawyers in the legal community to try to stanch any fallout from the investigation. Brown reportedly warned one of the judges that he too had been implicated in the corruption probe.[55]

All of this activity was going on at the same time that I was fielding a relentless series of attacks from Allstate, often facilitated by local lawyers and judges. I wondered which judges had been implicated in the probe. I was sure one of them was Michael Mery.

Norton warned McGinty: If the FBI contacts you, don't answer questions.

Two weeks later, FBI agents paid McGinty a visit. At first, a nervous McGinty lied about how he got his car fixed. Agents listened to his tales and then calmly showed him some of the evidence they had collected. McGinty examined it with a sense of increasing doom.

"This looks really bad," McGinty said.

When the Justice Department indicted McGinty in June 2014, Norton & Brown, the lawyers fingered by Acevedo for corruption, offered to defend McGinty free of charge.[56] McGinty quickly accepted that unexpectedly generous offer.

His new lawyers let him know they were "very upset" to hear that he had met with the feds. They started pressuring McGinty to keep his mouth shut. If he cooperated with the FBI, they allegedly told him, he would be labeled a snitch. If that happened, his life would surely be in danger. They would have no choice but to drop him as a client.[57]

A conflict of interest issue regarding Brown and Norton representing McGinty soon came up. After all, McGinty's co-defendant had implicated McGinty's new defense lawyers as willing participants in the same bribery schemes that he was now under indictment for. The judge assured the court he wasn't worried about it.

McGinty eventually signed a plea deal with prosecutors but he didn't get the same sweetheart deal as Acevedo, who had quickly turned states' evidence.

McGinty soon started to feel used. He had wanted to plea bargain from the beginning, he would later complain, but Brown and Norton had talked him out of it. Belatedly, he tried to drop a dime on his own defense attorneys.

He asked to speak to the FBI agents. At the meeting, McGinty told the feds that he had received favors from several lawyers while serving as judge, including Brown and Norton. The bribes came in the form of cash and free legal services, he revealed. Brown and Norton were just as corrupt as he was, McGinty insisted.

The federal agents pressed him for specifics. Well, McGinty offered, Brown once gave him an envelope of cash in payment for McGinty setting bond for one of Brown's clients. He once also accepted a bribe from Brown in exchange for sentencing one of Brown's clients to probation rather than prison, he admitted.

It was too little too late. The FBI agents later stated in court that McGinty's tips could not be substantiated.

McGinty then tried to get a new trial. He argued that his lawyers had a conflict of interest. Looking back, he told the court, he could see that their efforts in his defense were primarily to cover up their own crimes. They were just as corrupt as he was, he essentially argued, so he shouldn't be the only one getting in trouble. In fact, he pointed out, he wasn't the only person to suggest that Brown was corrupt. Acevedo had also said so.

Alan Brown was no stranger to the FBI. In the early 2000s, an Austin federal grand jury indicted the lawyer for tax evasion after a five-year federal investigation into income he reported from his law firm. But after 29 days of testimony and more than 140 witnesses, a San Antonio federal jury took less than 90 minutes to find Brown not guilty on all charges.

It had been a contentious, convoluted investigation that surfaced while the feds were investigating one of Brown's clients for drug trafficking and money laundering.

While investigating Brown's client Sammy Naranjo, the FBI began suspecting that Naranjo was laundering money through Brown's law firm accounts with the help of Brown's office manager, Kelly Houston.[58] Naranjo and Houston, it turned out, were lovers.

The FBI began secretly wiretapping the law firm's phones. Even though agents alleged that drug money was being laundered through Brown's law firm accounts, investigators did not suspect Brown of being involved in Houston and Naranjo's money laundering scheme. Brown, feds stated, cooperated fully with the federal investigation against Naranjo. According to court records, Brown gave his secretary an ultimatum: end the affair with his client Naranjo or resign. She chose her lover. When she left, she took some of the law firm's financial records with her. She would later offer the records to federal investigators in exchange for a lighter sentence for Naranjo. They accepted.

Those documents became central to the federal government's tax evasion case against Brown. But Brown put on an aggressive, sophisticated defense. Ultimately, Brown's attorney, the "high-stakes" white-collar litigator Michael McCrum, convinced the jury that the government had miscounted Brown's finances. A Bexar County jury acquitted Brown of all charges.

Brown's luck held. McGinty's allegations against Alan Brown and Jay Norton got no traction with either federal investigators or the courts. He lost his bid for a new trial. The federal appeals court reasoned that if McGinty knew his lawyers were corrupt, he shouldn't have hired them.

"McGinty knowingly, intelligently, and voluntarily waived the purported conflict,' the U.S. Appeals Court found.

In other words, McGinty got exactly what he asked for.

Allstate's kitchen sink

For the next few years, I lurched from one harrowing series of attacks to another as Allstate's handlers intently tried to cover up what had become a widespread, undeniable criminal conspiracy involving some of San Antonio's most prominent officials. I was being battered by people in nearly every conceivable local, state, and federal agency I encountered.

Catherine Stone, chief justice of the Fourth Court of Appeals was expediting the dismissal of my Allstate appeal, while the district clerk, Donna Kay McKinney, delayed providing me the trial record that I had paid for. At one point, I remember checking the public access terminals at the courthouse to find that Stone had quietly dismissed my case without informing me. For a major portion of that appeal, the Bexar County Clerk's Office under Donna Kay McKinney delayed providing me with a trial record. An appeal cannot start without it. McKinney refused to tell me the cost of the record and then filed a notice of late record.

I made a motion for reconsideration, and requested an extension to file my appeal. I explained that I was not getting sufficient notice amid a backdrop of official and unofficial abuse.

Stone canceled the dismissal but in a terse letter told me that any other requests for extension would be "looked on with disfavor."

On February 5, 2014, a mere few months after I appealed the unsustainable verdict in the Allstate insurance case, Catherine Stone, chief justice of the Fourth Court of Appeals of Texas, dismissed my appeal for want of prosecution.

It was a well-timed dismissal. I was still under criminal bond for the false misdemeanor assault prosecution, and all of my organizational assets had just been stolen.

Kristina Combs, the thuggish "practicing attorney" who had worked with registered notaries to forge quitclaim deeds, had quickly transferred the MLK property into her name and sold it. It was her reward for her crucial and necessary part in the criminal scheme. The plot to steal Auris Project assets, disrupt the development of the information center, and impoverish and traumatize me had been a huge success.

As front person for the conspiracy, Combs had an impressive support team. It included state district judges, civil lawyers, title companies, debt collectors, county constables, and Allstate. For probably the first time in her life, Kristina Combs was in high cotton. And she was top dog.

One of the most haunting moments of the entire conspiracy was the image of one Bexar County District Court judge, Karen Pozza, standing silently in her own courtroom, face ashen, as Combs rebuked her for not following orders. I will never forget it.

A long list of buyers stood by, ready to quickly buy and sell the MLK property and bury Combs's illicit transfer in deed records.

James Kissler, the phantom buyer, evaporated into the ether.

I tracked the rapid transfers, sending letters to each new owner, stating that the property was under dispute and a subject of fraud. The new owners quickly sold the property, ignoring the notices. When the taxes came due, Tommy Adkisson, the former county commissioner, paid them through his Alamo Title company franchise. That's how I learned what title company certified the illicit title transfer. Adkisson would be implicated in other questionable title transfers on the Eastside. I started a file on him.

Over time, I would come to think of the 2013 burglary at 1614 Martin Luther King as the first piece of the puzzle into understanding how properties in distressed areas are systematically and illegally transferred to new owners. But that's the subject of another book.

On August 22, 2014, Southwest Recovery Services, a Dallas-based debt collector, sent me a demand for payment on behalf of "practicing attorney" Kristina Combs. The fraudulent sanction issued by Antonia Arteaga had quickly grown to $3247.50. "This is an opportunity for you to resolve a debt," wrote SWRS collection manager Steven Dietz. "If you do not remit balance due, or make satisfactory arrangements, we will advise our client that additional action may be necessary." The letter stated I could pay by phone, certified funds, funds transfer, or credit card.

"Like hell I will," I muttered.

I dashed off a letter disputing the debt. I said that the charge was fraudulent. I described how Judge Arteaga conspired in a back room with Combs to sanction me for non-appearance while I sat waiting in court. Do not contact me again, I wrote SWRS. I made three copies and mailed them to the credit bureaus. The bureaus removed the charge.

Every couple of months, the agency would report the debt to the credit bureaus and I would have to repeat the dispute process all over again.

The tax collector

On March 5, 2014, I received a letter from Linebarger Goggan Blair & Sampson, the county's tax collector, for a late payment on an 1899 house on the Westside the Auris Project had bought as investment property. I had waffled about what to do with the house. Did I want to fix it up and flip it, use it as office space, or rent it out?

My strategies and plans were constantly changing as I ran from one Allstate-inflicted travesty to another. The house, located directly across the street from an elementary school, had sat undisturbed on Ruiz Street for years. Now it was the target of repeated vandalism. On one visit, I found seven windows had been broken. On another visit, the wood panels we'd nailed over the broken windows had been pried open. A few times, I would drive up and see people walking toward the property. These were not teenage vandals but grown men. When they saw me, they abruptly changed course.

We could see that the vandals kept trying to enter the house through a floorless, attached shed in the back of the house.

My sometime handyman Chris Covarrubias proposed rigging the place with booby traps. I wasn't sure that was legal. "Can you booby trap a house?" I wondered.

"Well, they're not supposed to be back here, anyway," he argued.

He had a point. The situation reminded me of Catorce, Mexico, the tiny desert village I lived in for several years. A place like Catorce has no government animal control so when residents got fed up with dogs and cats scattering trash around their homes, they put rat poison in cuts of meat and fed them to the offending creatures.

Living in Bexar County, I could see why people would start to take the law into their own hands. It happens in failed governments all over the world.

Chris scrounged up several large pieces of plywood and hammered dozens of large nails through them. Then he laid the lethal-looking squares strategically throughout the small room and covered the nails with dead leaves.

Before nailing the room shut, I perused his work. I could not see the nails in broad daylight. There was no doubt in my mind a nighttime vandal would step on the nails and be in a world of hurt. The thought made me smile.

As I battled to recover from the latest series of Allstate-inspired attacks, Linebarger Goggan filed suit against the Auris Project for unpaid taxes on the Ruiz property. But I was having typical difficulties getting information from Lilia Ledesma about how to resolve the tax issues for the Ruiz property. And soon, I was being sued for back taxes.

"Your immediate attention to this matter is required to avoid possible foreclosure action," the letter warned. It was signed by attorney Lilia Ledesma. I recognized the name. Ledesma had made an appearance on the record in the fraudulent MLK quiet title suit for Kristina Combs. That was the day I sat in presiding court waiting for a hearing that never came, only to be served a $1,500 sanction by Judge Antonio Arteaga for non-appearance. I remember it was Halloween that day, and Arteaga was wearing a black witch's hat to match her black robe.

I had called Ledesma to ask her why she had made an appearance in the MLK case. What did Linebarger Goggan have to do with the case? I asked her. She chuckled lightly. She wasn't there, she said, and didn't know what I was talking about. She was having a grand time, almost giddy as we spoke. I made copies of the appearance notice that the assistant staff attorney Duong had given me with Ledesma's name on it and tucked them away in a safe place. That notice would be significant one day.

Later, I would look closer at Linebarger Goggan. One of the nation's largest government collection law firms, Linebarger Goggan Blair & Sampson rakes in billions by pursuing debtors for local governments. Founded in 1970, the company collects debts for courts and governments in 22 states.[59] It has a structured but sometimes inaccurate system for collecting property taxes, toll violation fees, water bills, and parking tickets for municipalities.[60] It is relentless.

Linebarger Goggan also has a long history of criminality and corruption. The firm's partners live lavish lifestyles fueled by hefty fees tacked onto sometimes small debts. It is not above adding a whopping 25 percent collection fee to even the tiniest outstanding balance. It has been accused of frequently violating fair credit laws. It has allegedly intimidated debtors by threatening jail. According to multiple news reports, it grew into a national powerhouse in part by financially seducing local and state politicians.

In 2004, Linebarger Goggan partner Juan Peña pleaded guilty to bribing two San Antonio city councilmen to guarantee the firm won a city contract. Peña also pleaded guilty to guaranteeing a bank loan to San Antonio attorney Jack Pytel for $25,000 even though he knew the credit application he submitted was false.[61] Peña's name was removed from the company masthead before he skipped off to prison, but the firm kept up business as usual.

In 2008, the firm settled accusations it used bribes to rig bids in Dallas County, Houston, Corpus Christi, Beaumont, Port Arthur and other Texas municipalities.[62]

According to CNN Money, Linebarger Goggan "doles out more on lobbying state lawmakers than ExxonMobil, American Airlines, and Halliburton." No wonder Ledesma was so confident. It was clear that she worked for a corporation that had no fear of the law.

Linebarger Goggan, Blair & Sampson is not called "The Debt Collector that Runs Texas" for nothing.[63]

I understood the game behind Judge Arteaga's abusive $1500 sanction. "Let's add Ledesma's name to the appearance card to keep her guessing," someone probably suggested. "That way, when Arteaga sanctions her $1500 as she's hunting for the other lawyers, she'll be distracted about why Ledesma is on the appearance sheet."

Ledesma was obviously fine with Arteaga, Hernandez, Combs, and their handlers using her name to assist their criminal ruse. She worked for a company that had gotten away with *way* more than that.

It was all good fun.

Dark tinted windows

Meanwhile, Tedi and I tried to get on with our lives. We wanted to start a family. In an effort to get pregnant, we began seeing a fertility doctor near the Medical Center on the prosperous north side of town. Allstate goons followed us there. For the first time, I started to get glimpses of several of the cockroaches stalking me in their cars.

The same three or four cars had been following me for months, but I could never see past their heavily tinted black windows. On our visits to the Medical Center, however, I could get clear glimpses of the drivers. They were white men, in their late 30s and 40s, of the seedy private eye type. They wore baseball caps and sunglasses. But why are they revealing themselves to me now? I wondered.

It took a minute, but then it dawned on me: *they had to roll their windows down.*

They must be getting traffic tickets on this side of town, I realized. They could confidently haunt the Eastside from behind blackened car windows even though the heavy black tint they installed were illegal. But when they followed us to the pristine, impeccably landscaped avenues of the Medical Center area, they had to roll their windows down if they didn't want to get stopped by north side patrols.

13 | KANGAROO

Detective Val Garcia

MONTHS LATER, A PROPERTY CRIMES detective contacted me and asked if I still wanted to file theft charges against Combs and her co-conspirators. Finally! Yes, I told him eagerly. He introduced himself as Detective Val Garcia and told me to bring all of my documentation of the burglary to the Eastside substation so that he could collect it as evidence. He was pleasant and respectful as I handed him the documents, including reports from our security alarm company, our property paperwork, the fake deeds, and the massive inventory list of our stolen property, including furniture, electronics, donations, thousands of books and the law library. He seemed very happy to have all of that information, almost excited. He eagerly made copies and returned the originals to me. I thought that I had finally met someone in SAPD who wanted to enforce the law.

But a few weeks later, after giving me the run-around, he told me that no charges would be filed. "The DA has rejected the case," Garcia told me. He seemed sheepish. I knew that the evidence I had provided him was overwhelming. How could the DA's office refuse to file charges?

Years later, I would make an open records act request for Garcia's case file related to my charges of theft, burglary, battery, and fraud.

The city responded it had no responsive records.

McVea v. Swan

I EVENTUALLY SUED THE CITY of San Antonio for the phony misdemeanor garage sale permit arrest. It was a clear violation of my constitutional rights to be free from illegal search and seizure. It was obvious that the alleged permit violation was a pretext.

The city assigned two lawyers to the case. City attorney Michael Seimer represented the city; Mark Kosanovich, a private attorney on retainer with the city, defended the officers. Because I invoked civil rights violations under the Fourth Amendment, my case got transferred to federal court. Maybe I'll have a better chance in federal court, I thought, but instantly dashed the thought.

For one thing, the Justice Department had been so concerned about conflict of interest in San Antonio it prosecuted the judge Angus McGinty and the lawyer Al Acevedo for corruption in New Mexico federal courts. If the DOJ couldn't count on local federal judges and U.S. attorneys to do the right thing, what chance did the rest of us have? Still, I held out slim hope. Maybe, for once, I thought, someone would follow the law.

The first time I stood before local federal judge David A. Ezra, he made it very clear he had no intention of doing that.

It was a strange and hostile proceeding.

Seimer, the city's attorney, opened his address to the court by telling Ezra that I had accused Judge Barbara Nellermoe and others of corruption, not just the cops who illegally jailed me. It seemed odd that he had mentioned Nellermoe by name. I wondered briefly if she and Ezra were friends. But things were moving quickly in the courtroom and I needed to keep up.

The judge was already glaring at me from the bench. A transplant from Hawaii federal courts, he wore a dated boxcar mustache that was just hairs away from the toothbrush mustache style popularized and then de-popularized by Adolf Hitler.

Ezra began berating me. The federal judges don't like pro se litigants either, I thought. But somehow this seemed personal. Like other judges before me, Ezra mildly asked questions of the city's lawyers and waited patiently for their answer. If they misspoke on some fact or procedure, which they often did, he would patiently clarify or offer a kindly correction. When it was my turn, his tone turned discourteous, dismissive. He frequently interrupted me. He did not respect me and wanted me to know it.

Kosanovich and Seimer, the city's lawyers, exchanged surprised, delighted looks. This was going better than they had imagined. They struggled to wipe grins off their faces. I assessed the judge glaring down at me. Two years earlier, I would have been trembling with nerves. By this time, I had lost any respect I might have held for the judges lording over me.

Small people in big robes, I called them.

Ezra deliberately antagonized me. At first, I thought he wanted to get a rise out of me to prove that pro se litigants were emotional, unfocused, time-wasting drains on court resources. Later, I would understand it was to keep me rattled so that I wouldn't be able to analyze what was happening to me. They needed me to stay rattled. Otherwise, I might be able to put two and two together.

I knew that if I rose to his bait, he would have the ammunition he needed to sanction me, or dismiss the case altogether. I struck a posture of indifference, calmly resting my hands on the podium in front of me. As he rebuked me, I offered him a steady gaze.

I could tell this took him by surprise. They are all so racist, I thought. They fully expect to have their way with me. I was determined to teach them otherwise, no matter how long it took.

Reading over transcripts of the hearings years later, I was at once proud of myself and mortified. I never rose to his bait. I come across on paper as extremely courteous, almost obsequious, while he repeatedly belittled me.

I had to take it. What choice did I have?

Despite a diverse set of constant attacks in all vectors of my life, I kept building my case. Using audio recorders, video equipment, and traveling notaries, I deposed SAPD officer Swan and Sgt. Scott, who I was suing in their individual capacities. I questioned Swan about the SAPD criminal code he used to justify the arrest. He didn't know. I drilled Scott about his claim that the city code enforcement office confirmed that he had probable cause to arrest. He said he didn't remember the name of the code enforcement officer he spoke to.

The city provided Captain James Flavin to be deposed. A graduate of the FBI National Academy in Quantico, Flavin was a rising star in the police department. I deposed him to establish that the city had never arrested anyone for having an unpermitted garage sale before me and to reaffirm that the SAPD had no code for justifying the arrest.

At one point in Flavin's deposition, I asked for a break so that I could replace a memory card in my camera. The minute the camera turned off, both Kosanovich and Seimer began loudly verbally abusing me. Kosanovich really got into it. He was so abusive that a shaken Seimer shouted his name to reel him in. I turned to Flavin for help. He just looked back, indifferent.

The camera was off, but the abuse was captured in an audio recording. Because I could never be sure if my recording devices were infected with malware, I would make sure to take several recording devices to depositions. On the day of the obnoxious verbal assault, I simultaneously audio recorded the meeting while the camera rolled.

"Let me turn this off," I said when the tirade was over. I pulled a small audio recorder off my lap and put it on the table. They looked shocked.

"I thought it *was* off," Seimer blurted.

I had proof of their misconduct. And, the depositions of SAPD cops accomplished exactly what they were supposed to. None of the cops could show that a crime had been committed, that the city had ever arrested anyone for having a garage sale without a permit, or that the detention was permissible under the law or even the police department's own policy. I, on the other hand, had loads of evidence of widespread misconduct and illegality. After all three cops' deposition, it was clear that the cops had falsely arrested me on a pretext.

When it was my turn to sit for a deposition in the illegal MLK Day arrest, Seimer and Kosanovich spent a good 30 minutes trying to get me to characterize the flea market as a form of hawking. I later learned why: door-to-door hawking is a code enforcement violation that qualifies as a criminal misdemeanor. Garage sale permit violations do not.

That was more evidence that the cops knew they had no authority to detain me, but arrested me anyway.

Many facts established the falsity of the arrest: the absence of a criminal code to book me under; the jail guard's astonished reaction when she heard the charge; the lack of operational procedures for the arrest; the city's own website outlining fines for garage sale permit violations; and my hasty release from jail when it was time to bring prisoners before a magistrate.

The only ambiguity that remained was the question of probable cause. Sgt. Scott insisted that his call to code enforcement gave him probable cause to believe I was committing a criminal offense.

Everyone involved knew that Scott had made no such call, but I needed proof. I formally asked the city to produce Scott's phone records for that day. Not only would the phone records destroy Scott's probable cause argument, it would prove him a liar. His credibility thus wrecked, even a South Texas court would have to acknowledge that the arrest was against the law.

Theoretically.

The city ignored my request for the call log. Kosanovich and Seimer stalled on providing the phone records so long, I filed a motion to compel. I also made a DVD of the abusive outburst at the deposition and asked the court to sanction the lawyers for their misconduct. Magistrate federal judge John Primomo refused to sanction the lawyers. Instead, he rebuked me for not answering questions the way the city wanted me to. And when I attached evidence of the widespread abuses cops and state judges had facilitated against me, Ezra berated me for "frivolous" filings.

Despite seeing clear evidence of a criminal, racketeering conspiracy, (or, rather, because of it) local federal judges sprinted toward summary judgment.

I struggled to keep up. Hackers, aided and abetted by mules carrying IMSIC catchers and signal extenders, continued to make online research a nightmare. Pages froze. Search results were severely limited and often off-topic. Motions I had prepared to file in court would print out as gobbledygook or not at all.

To make matters worse, lawyers could file their motions from the comfort of their desks, while pro se litigants had to drive to the courthouse or mail their motions. Likewise, lawyers got court orders almost immediately after a judge signed them, while pro se litigants had to wait on the mail service. It was another deliberate slight against pro se litigants. In my case, I was at the mercy of a corrupted post office that routinely delayed, opened, or lost my mail.

On December 16, 2014, I stood before Judge Ezra again and asked the court to allow me access to the federal court's electronic filing system. He had lost none of his distaste for me.

He did not like that I had filed evidence of the Allstate conspiracy as support for my argument that the arrest was a pretext to further a larger criminal conspiracy. He began berating me against filing motions that were not relevant.

He was in full protective mode. He didn't want the deed fraud, the bogus title "trial," or any of the past abuses by local cops, lawyers and judges to get onto the federal court record.

"You know you've done it," he said. "You have filed, kind of, documents that don't directly relate to matters before the court in the past, and you know that."

"No sir, your Honor," I responded politely. "I disagree with that. I'm sorry."

"Well, okay, you can disagree but you have. I want you to make sure you file only the things that relate directly to pending motions...."

"Yes, your honor."

Oh, I thought, this is not good. Ezra was revealing that he was going to seriously limit my ability to put the false arrest in the proper context. He didn't want the quitclaim deeds and the judge's default orders on the record. I knew then that he was dedicated to getting rid of this case as fast as possible. But I also knew he would have to break from federal courtroom procedure and law to do it. I comforted myself with the knowledge that the justice system I alleged was diseased kept making my case for me. If I could just get through all of this, I thought.

Years later, I read the transcript of that hearing with morbid fascination.[64] The transcript showed a clear, shared objective. Move the case quickly to dismissal before the plaintiff could put any more damaging evidence into the record.

The alleged call to code enforcement constituted a "fact issue." Under the law, judges can't cases dismiss cases with fact issues in summary judgment.

The city's biggest problem was Sgt. Scott's call log. The city's defense rested almost entirely on Sergeant Scott's insistence that he had relied on code enforcement to determine whether or not I had committed a criminal offense. Everyone knew that Scott could not have talked to code enforcement that day because code enforcement was closed for the MLK holiday. The call log would show that he was lying. More uncomfortably for local officials, it would also show exactly who it was he was talking to when he sat on the phone plotting my illegal arrest. The judges wanted to dismiss the lawsuit before the call log could be put on the record. With no proof that Scott was lying about his conversation with code enforcement, the judges could pretend that no fact issue existed and the case could be quickly dismissed.

During the hearing, Ezra scolded me mercilessly. He would allow me to file electronically, he said, but he didn't want me to make frivolous filings. And, he was going to approve the city's request to move forward with disposing of the case. He had sent my motion to compel production of the phone log to the federal magistrate Primomo, who was sure to deny it. And now, as Ezra rushed to approve the city's request for dismissal, he pretended to know nothing about the city's refusal to produce key evidence. The case, like so many others, would be summarily dismissed while lawyers and judges worked together to keep key evidence off the record.

And that is exactly what happened.

On July 17, 2015, federal judge Robert L. Pittman granted the cops' motion for summary judgment. To support his decision, Pittman essentially cut and pasted from the city's own motion to dismiss. Fudging statute and case law, he ruled that citizens could be "arrested by a city police officer for any violation of the City Code or an ordinance of the city."[65]

"Therefore," Pittman wrote, "The officers had authority to issue Ms. McVea *a misdemeanor citation*, and when she refused to sign the citation, to place her under custodial arrest."

But the judges, lawyers, police, and city attorney's office all knew that a garage sale permit violation was not a misdemeanor crime. I had pointed that out in my responses, but they deliberately ignored that key point.

It was a calculated, deliberate misrepresentation of the law.

In his order, Pittman also legitimized the improper withholding of the phone record, key evidence, before rushing to summary judgment:

> McVea has filed a Motion for Sanctions and a Request for Default Judgment because, among other things, Defendants have not

provided Ms. McVea a call log that shows who Sergeant Scott called. As this Court previously stated, this issue has been "litigated and ruled upon" several times. Ms. McVea has made this unsuccessful argument so many times, in fact, that United States Magistrate Judge Primomo said that "[f]urther requests for the same would result in sanctions." Though Ms. McVea's continued filings regarding this discovery dispute are clearly sanctionable, the Court declines to impose such a penalty at this time. Finding no reason to overturn the numerous previous rulings on this issue, however, the Court denies Ms. McVea's Motion for Sanction and Request for Default Judgment.[66]

Lifted almost verbatim from the city lawyers' motion, the passage is tacit confirmation that the federal judges helped the city hide key evidence in a civil rights case. It also shows that Primomo used the power of the court to intimidate the seeker of key evidence into silence.

The "other things" Pittman refers to was the abusive verbal assault the city lawyers subjected me to, which Primomo, Pittman, Ezra, and chief Judge Fred Biery had all heard, but refused to sanction.

Tellingly, there exists nowhere in the court record, any viable case law that supports the court's ruling to withhold the call log. The judges presented it as a done deal, while cloaking it in ambiguity.

That's what summary judgment by corrupt public officials in South Texas looks like: judges use the deeply flawed and legally unsupported motions of the offending party as a template for their own orders. They help the offender withhold any evidence that might prove their arguments false, and then rush to dismiss the case before it can get to trial and a jury. And the whole time, they are working to keep important evidence off the record. They think nothing of intimidating and abusing citizens.

Ezra performed the same tactics in his order to dismiss for the city. The errors in the orders were obvious. The dismissal was ripe for appeal.

But the judges were also aware of the system of attacks I was being subjected to on a sustained, 24-hour basis. At this point, they were confident that there was little chance of their victim managing something like a federal appeal.

The surveillance camera

District Judge Michael Mery used the same summary judgment tactic to keep video evidence out of my case regarding the false arrest at the Greyhound bus station. Greyhound was still withholding the surveillance video of Statewide Patrol security guard David Galbreath's assault in its garage the date of my first illegal arrest. I filed a motion to compel and asked for a hearing. Of course, the company had the surveillance video, but I understood why its lawyers would not want to produce it.

There was no way that Greyhound could deny what the camera showed. The surveillance video evidence would show the entire interaction between my attackers and me. It would show a drowsy woman standing quietly in line to board the bus to Houston. It would show the bus driver berating the woman, and show the woman looking around in confusion. It would show the people in line behind the women starting to stir, looking around at each other as they tried to make sense of the bus driver's inexplicable hostility to the woman. It would show the bus driver gesturing to the security guard who appeared to be standing at a distance but in view. It would show the security guard approaching and haranguing the poor woman in line before following her as she headed inside to speak to the ticket clerk. It would show the security guard moving to put the woman in a full nelson and the woman trying to get away, moving to thwart that attempt. It would show the woman respectfully talking to the SAPD cop before he placed her in handcuffs and carted her away.

Greyhound's surveillance video would show that everything the SAPD cop wrote in the police report was false.

Now, faced with pressure to release the surveillance video that would show the guard's attack, Greyhound's lawyers were hurrying to get the case dismissed before the evidence had to be turned over.

They relied on the proven method for preventing access to justice: they filed a no-evidence motion for summary judgment.

Presiding Court assigned Michael Mery, the judge who had entertained false case law in the Allstate case, to hear the motion. Any summary judgment while Greyhound sat on evidence would be illegal, but I knew Judge Mery would grant it if he thought he could get away with it. I also knew that given my complaint to the judicial board about the illegal ex parte meetings between Mery and Allstate lawyer Albert Gutierrez, and Judge Mery's overt, on-the-record hostility towards me meant that I could request for him to recuse himself if he tried any funny business.

I sent out a mass email asking for anyone on my Facebook interested in court accountability to attend the hearing. Mery acted more professional when witnesses sat in the gallery. He tended to follow the law in front of observers. In the end, only my friend Teresa Butolph showed up.

Mery seemed visibly discomfited upon seeing the lone woman in the gallery. He did not want to proceed without knowing exactly who she was. He switched to treating me more respectfully. A dark haired man came in, sat in the jury box for a moment and then just as quickly left the courtroom. I knew that he was probably going to call someone to determine the woman's identity. Mery called for a recess. The bailiff rudely gestured for me to leave the courtroom, while gently escorting my opponent to a bench in the hallway. It looked like it was going to be a lot longer than expected. I went to move my car. When I got back, Teresa told me that she watched two men entering and exiting the judge's chambers.

When Mery called us back to the courtroom, he seemed more confident. He proceeded with the plan. Brett Vangheluwe, the assistant staff attorney who helped illegally dismiss thousands of Bexar County civil suits, entered the courtroom.

He sat in the jury box.

"I know that guy," I told Teresa, nodding toward Vangheluwe. "He's one of the attorneys denying access to justice to poor people."

That news alarmed Teresa, who had been watching all of the activity in my absence. He had shed the ridiculous Dutch boy haircut and orange leather tan I had spied him in years earlier. He flashed a salacious glance at Greyhound's pretty, blond attorney before resting a smug gaze on the bench. Mery, his nerves getting the better of him, barked at Vangheluwe about the documents he had handed the judge. Vangheluwe's smirk disappeared briefly. The judge had spent the morning running between his chambers and the courtroom in an apparently frantic bid to determine the identity of the witness. He was in a foul mood. I knew why. What he was about to do was obstruction of justice and his handlers clearly had not fully convinced him that the action could not come back to haunt him. Teresa's presence had rattled him.

Butolph, my only witness, didn't know much about the law but she knew that what she was witnessing wasn't right.

"Throughout the proceeding," Teresa would later explain in a sworn affidavit, "I perceived hostility directed at Denise McVea from the bailiff, Judge Mery, and the presiding judge. In my opinion, these men treated Ms. McVea differently, less professionally, and less cordially than they treated everyone else I saw them come in contact with. When they spoke to Ms. McVea, it was almost always with an aggressive, belittling and hostile tone. In my opinion, Ms. McVea was cordial, professional, and polite. I never saw her raise her voice to any of them."[67]

She felt like Vangheluwe was guiding the judge. What is so complicated about this case, she wondered, that would cause a veteran judge to seek guidance from an outside civil attorney?

"I asked myself why the judge had to continue leaving during the procedures and why was his bailiff so friendly with opposing counsel and so rude to Ms. McVea,' Butolph wrote in a sworn affidavit. "I felt that we were in court but that no one was treating it like a courtroom."

I tried to preempt what I knew they were planning.

Based on the bizarre and biased hearing and his improper behavior in the Allstate case, I filed a motion to have Mery recuse himself.

But in the next hearing, he walked in the courtroom, quickly dismissed the Greyhound case and fled the courtroom, ignoring my objections – and my motion for recusal.

Mery had successfully prevented any chance of the video of Galbreath's assault at the Greyhound bus station getting on the record.

Galbreath, the violent Statewide Patrol security guard who attacked me and assisted in my false arrest, had disappeared. I didn't know where he was.

On September 24, 2014, I complained to the State Commission on Judicial Conduct about Judge Michael Mery. He had rushed to dismiss a case to cover up evidence, I wrote. He was abusive throughout the proceedings, I complained. The commission took no action. Disciplinary proceedings are confidential, the commission letter reminded me.

By this time, every court I had stood before had a copy of the Carlson report showing the forged quitclaim deeds used to steal the MLK information center. Federal, state, and local law enforcement and judicial authorities now possessed a copy of the report and affidavits explaining in detail the context in which the fraud occurred.

I spent my days fighting hackers, recovering from police abuse, trying to keep the Auris Project functioning, and zealously monitoring and correcting the public record in San Antonio.

And the more success I had, the more the harassment on the streets intensified. I was followed everywhere I went by a team of harassers.

I had repeatedly provided rock solid proof of the criminal conspiracy. Every judge who rushed to dismiss my cases did so with the full knowledge that by doing so, they were protecting their friends – and covering up a serious crime.

No wonder San Antonio lawyers were so smug and glib, I thought.

1 | OPPRESSION

The State of Texas v. Denise McVea

MEANWHILE, THE D.A.'S OFFICE CONTINUED the malicious criminal assault case covering up the MLK theft.

I knew that the prosecutors had the video I took of Combs assaulting me and stealing Auris Project assets. It was undeniable, *prima facie*[68] evidence. But they were acting as though that evidence did not exist.

I had been seized by the state of Texas on a fraudulent charge and trapped in a malicious prosecution because I had seen the tools corrupt officials used to abuse Bexar County citizens at the bidding of unsavory criminal elements. Those tools included a well-oiled system of forgery, kangaroo courts, false arrests, and systematic cover-ups.

And ever-present was Allstate, who seemed to be somehow bankrolling any schemes not being financed by taxpayers. But how does a corporation pay for something like this? Allstate, I wagered, paid the private intelligence firms, who then funneled the money to the "informants." I had estimated that by 2021, Allstate had paid millions of dollars in its campaign against me alone.

I would need to get evidence of the cover-up on the record in a longshot bid to force the judge and prosecutor to follow the law.

On July 14th, Judge Scott Roberts heard my request to inspect the prosecutor's evidence in the *State of Texas v. McVea* assault case. As we stood before the judge, Ludowig objected to giving me any medical records showing Comb's injuries, saying that I was not entitled to that evidence. If the prosecutor is criminally charging me with assaulting Combs and causing physical injuries, I argued, he had to show evidence that supported the charge. The law required the district attorney's office to show evidence that the criminal case against me was not fraudulent, I asserted.

The judge had not asked the DA to provide legal support for denying me evidence. But he now asked me for legal support, a common ruse against pro se litigants.

"Do you have a provision of the Code of Criminal Procedure or a case which would show me that you're entitled to discovery of this information?" he asked.

Luckily, I had. "If you'll just give me a second," I said as I rustled through my papers.

I read the provision from my motion. "I am entitled to 'items that are in possession or custody and control of...Texas,' which is Ludowig," I read. "Ludowig understands that he has filed a charge of physical assault against me and he has to prove that."

"That's right, he does," the judge Scott Roberts agreed.

I was getting somewhere! The truth, I knew, was that the prosecutors had no evidentiary basis for the criminal charge against me and the judge knew it, too. But, he also knew that he held all of the power.

"*At trial*, he has to prove that," the judge continued. Oh, these motherfuckers, I thought.

For the record, I reminded the judge that the prosecutor also had seen the videotape of Combs attacking me. And I placed the Wendy Carlson forgery report on the record to buttress evidence that not only was the assault charge against me fraudulent, but it was brought to cover up documented criminal activity.

It was if I hadn't spoken a word.

Finally, Roberts granted me most of the evidence I had requested from the prosecutors. Of the six pieces of evidence I requested, the judge granted four.

The assistant DA did not object to providing me with other evidence I requested.

"Judge," Ludowig said, "we'll make the police report available to the defendant as well as any witness statements that are in the file we'll make available to her before we put on our case in chief."

"Okay," agreed the judge.

I could see where this was going.

I reminded the court that it had been more than a month since I had asked for the evidence. I asked Judge Roberts to order the DA's office to give me the evidence today.

"Okay," said Judge Roberts. "What I'm going to do is, I'm going to order him to give it to you *30 days before trial.*"

That would mean they could keep the fraudulent charges against me for more than two years.

I objected.

"Okay," said the judge.

The State announces ready

On February 15, 2015, the State of Texas announced it was ready to go to trial in the alleged assault of Kristina Combs. It had not turned over a single piece of evidence.

It had been a year and three months since the Bexar County District Attorney's Office had accused me of attacking the "practicing lawyer" Kristina Combs. Since then, half a dozen prosecutors had seen the video recording of not only Combs physically attacking me, but also stealing the Auris Project bookstore, library, equipment, furniture, inventory and more. At all times, Bexar County prosecutors had access to the forensic document showing Combs's claim to Auris Project's property at Martin Luther King to be based on fraudulent documents. Judge Roberts could see from the record that Judge Nellermoe's order handing over the property to Combs was an illegal abuse of power.

And now, Bexar County prosecutors were rushing to trial while withholding evidence the law requires them to provide every defendant.

Still, I had to show up for the dog and pony show. I knew what would happen if I didn't.

"Good morning, Ms. McVea," Judge Roberts said, for the record.

"Good morning," I replied.

"I'm going to take announcement now on the trial setting, so I'd like to hear from the state...."

MS. PEÑA:	Judge, the State is announcing ready.
THE COURT:	You're announcing ready. Is the defendant –
DEFENDANT:	Your Honor, the defense is announcing not ready. Without waiving my right to a speedy trial, I request a continuance because the prosecution has failed to produce discovery that was requested and which the Court granted on July 14th, 2014, particularly as it relates to material witnesses, or barring that continuance, dismiss this cause for insufficient evidence and the unavailability of material witnesses.

They weren't expecting that. A week before, I had met with Dave Thomas, a local lawyer and longtime friend of my cousin BJ Carroll. We had chatted informally about criminal procedure. In 20 minutes, I learned just how much Joe Gonzales had been keeping from me.

Prosecutors and the judge knew that they were violating all sorts of evidentiary, civil rights, and due process rules. They had been counting on me not knowing.

The judge blinked. He turned to the prosecutor. He asked if they had turned over the ordered evidence.

The state had turned over the state's file, she said, but was withholding the addresses of the witnesses. She insinuated that the thuggish witnesses who had forged documents, stolen thousands of dollars of assets, physically attacked me, and created multiple false police reports, were somehow in fear for their safety.

I thought about all of those SAPD police records painting me out to be violent and psychotic. Peña was knowingly tapping into that myth to expand the defamation to court records. They were committed to protecting Combs' criminal behavior while railroading me, Combs's victim.

I was certain they had done this before.

Not today, though. Judge Roberts quickly granted a continuance. But he did not dismiss the case.

Around midnight on April 7, 2015, I watched on my surveillance camera as a male figure walked from next door to stand on the sidewalk in front of my house. The figure shined a penlight on my bedroom window, resting the light briefly on my camera before walking away. A few days later, as I worked at my desk in the middle of the day, I watched the surveillance screen as a car pulled up and parked in front of my house. It was an old wreck of a vehicle. Two obese women, one black and the other white, sat in the passenger and driver seat. They looked like they had just been plucked off the porch of a housing project.

The camera began to move of its own accord. I tried to redirect the lens to focus on the women in the car, but it ignored my commands. Despite my increasingly frantic efforts, the camera pulled up and away from the fat ladies before resting on the clouds in the sky. The hackers had completely taken over my network.

"Like monkeys on a fence."

It was clear that neither the judge nor the DA's office was going to dismiss the malicious prosecution, despite the evidence of corruption and falsity. Rather than dismiss the criminal charge, the DA just kept reassigning prosecutors. At least seven prosecutors had been assigned and reassigned in the two years the Bexar County held me under bond on a false charge:

Matthew Ludowig, Aaron Eckman, Stephanie Lewis, Richard Guerra, Nicholas Kemmy, Ana Liz Deleon-Vargas, and Erica Peña.

Judge Roberts stayed busy trampling my constitutional rights. For one thing, he was careful not to rule on my objections. I had read cases in Google Scholar that had been dismissed on appeal because the judge had not ruled on an objection. In other words, when I made an objection, the judge must overrule (deny) or sustain (approve) the objection. If he doesn't do that, there is nothing on record to appeal. The case gets tossed on a technicality.

I noticed that when I made an objection in the fraudulent criminal assault case, Roberts answered "okay." When I pressed him to sustain or overrule my objections, he would say, "noted." This would give the appeals court a quick and easy way to toss any appeal, according to my research. All I could do was object to the court's deliberate failure to make a ruling on my objections.

I decided to file a habeas corpus motion.

Under the writ of habeas corpus, a person can be released from detention unless the state shows lawful grounds for the detention. I wasn't in jail, but I was on bond, which was a form of detention. I could use the habeas corpus hearing to make sure the record showed the DA's office had access to the video from day one, and force prosecutors to show cause for their continued malicious prosecution.

I researched and wrote the motion, then spent a day on wild goose chases in the courthouse. Finally, I got a habeas corpus hearing scheduled for November 16, 2013. I fully expected to see all sorts of violations of rule and law.

What I needed were observers. Someone who could be a witness to the outrageous behavior of the lawyers, clerks, reporters and judges in the courtroom. I knew that Jim Harrington was retiring from the Texas Civil Rights Project, but thought the egregious nature of the violations in Bexar County might peak his interest. He had, after all authored a report on the impunity of abusive cops in San Antonio. On September 23, 2015, I wrote Harrington a pleading letter about "gross abuse by local lawyers and judges, particularly as they related to handling cases filed by pro se litigants." I also wrote the ACLU, the Texas Civil Rights Project, the Esperanza Peace and Justice Center and the Southwest Worker's Union. No one showed up. No one responded. It's fairly certain those emails were intercepted by Allstate's hackers.

On the other hand, the district attorney's office sent about nine young prosecutors to watch the hearing. It apparently was rare for the criminal courts to have a pro se defendant get as far as I had in a criminal assault case.

A gaggle of young prosecutors descended on the courtroom like a gang of teenagers catching a $1 matinee.

"They were all against you," Tedi told me later. "They were laughing, joking, and making rude comments the whole time. They were like monkeys on a fence."

At least three young prosecutors sat behind the prosecutor's table, staring down at a laptop and feeding information to the lead prosecutors as if we were in the midst of the trial of the century and their careers depended on my conviction for some heinous crime against humanity. Several young assistant DAs ran to and from the courtroom, handing papers over the gallery short wall in response to I don't know what.

These are the people who have Bexar County residents' lives in their hands, it dawned on me. I shuddered.

The bailiff, with whom I had had several confrontations, noticed Tedi sitting in the back of the gallery. He was a young man with a good job, she was a gorgeous woman, and he obviously liked what he saw. He approached her and struck up a conversation. He had no idea she was my girlfriend. He asked her what she was doing in his courtroom. "Just observing," she said vaguely. He shook his head derisively and gestured towards me.

"She sounds like she knows what she's talking about," he told her with a dismissive laugh, "but she doesn't."

Later, when she told me what had happened, I was furious. Not only were Bexar County assistant district attorneys either mocking my efforts at self-advocacy or substantially aiding the malicious prosecution but the bailiff felt nothing about approaching a stranger in the courtroom and ridiculing me. I think it was at this point that Tedi started to see my battle as a lost cause.

I wasn't about to let such a breach of protocol go.

I later asked Roberts's snide clerk, Keysha, to tell me the bailiff's name. She didn't want to tell me. She mumbled something in a voice so deliberately low I couldn't hear. I asked her to repeat herself. She mumbled again.

"Kee?" I asked. "Are you saying 'Kee'?"

"Yes," she lied. His last name was actually Keefe, I later learned.

I wrote Sheriff Susan Pamerleau to complain about Keefe, the bailiff in County Court 12, entering the gallery to mock me to an observer. I pointed out that the assault case against me was a spurious criminal charge being used as an instrument of official oppression.

"It is defined by rampant judicial and attorney misconduct," I wrote. "Deputy Kee has no business approaching persons in the gallery and attempting to indoctrinate them against any litigant."

For the umpteenth time, I asked for an investigation, even though I did not expect anything to come of it. Months later, when I heard nothing back from the sheriff's department, I wrote again, asking why. A woman who identified herself as a captain in the sheriff's department called and said that the matter was addressed. Whatever that means, I thought. But she was polite and professional. That was novel. Years later, I questioned if I had actually spoken to a real sheriff's department official. I mean, I had nothing in writing from the sheriff's department to confirm it. In Allstate's supreme gaslighting world, you just never knew. Still, that phone call, a minor courtesy from the sheriff's department, did make a difference. Looking back years later, I would see that call as the first chip in Allstate's carefully constructed gaslighting campaign. It reminded me that in some government agencies, some people cared about the job they were doing. It was also the first inkling that the disrespectful, dismissive people I was encountering did not always represent the organizations under which they were employed. Allies were sure to exist somewhere, I began to think.

Despite the hostility and abuse in the courtroom on the day of my habeas corpus, I *was* able to show the video. And the video left no question as to the identities of the victim and perpetrator. After getting the video entered into evidence, I pushed the play button. The video started.

It was a clear day and the quality of the video was excellent. It showed Combs and her associates illegally packing my books and inventory onto the back of a truck. It showed me politely asking why they were not putting the items on the curb as required by law. It showed me taking a few steps to capture evidence of the theft by showing that items were being loaded onto the back of a truck, and Combs lurching forward to strike me, swinging wildly. It showed her chasing me to my car and kicking my car door once I was able to get inside. It showed Marty Serratorubio grinning stupidly. It showed me calling them "bitches" repeatedly as I ran for protection.

The video completely destroyed the police report, which had stated:

> "Victim (Kristina Combs) stated while she was removing items she observed Arrested Person (Denise McVea) drive up to the listed location....(McVea) approached her in an aggressive manor (sic) and demanded to collect more items from the location. (Combs) stated she informed (McVea) she need to leave in which (McVea) struck (Combs) in the mouth twice with a closed fist...(McVea) then walked off from the listed location, leaving her car."[69]

In the video, Combs looked pasty, pudgy, morbid, and brutish. When the video ended, I looked around the suddenly still courtroom.

Judge Roberts looked green, nauseated, disgusted. Prosecutor Peña, pale and vapid, fumbled with papers, head down. Some of LaHood's monkey prosecutors in the gallery were sitting forward on the edge of their seats. They seemed less jovial, like the movie they had come to see had taken an unexpected turn and wasn't a comedy after all.

I didn't show the full video, so the judge didn't hear me name the people I knew were behind the attacks and theft. They also didn't see the second time Combs swung wildly at me as I tried to leave or the part where I blocked the second attack and answered with a strike. It didn't show the part of her violent, alcoholic brother coming at me with fists balled, preparing to swing, growling, "Don't you hit my sister," or the bizarrely smiling man checking him from a distance, warning, "Don't hit her."

None of that was actually relevant. The prosecutor's office had expected me to plead self-defense. Not once did that term come out of my mouth. The video showed that I was the victim of theft and assault, and that the District Attorney's office under Nico LaHood had no reason to prosecute me and every reason to prosecute "practicing attorney" Kristina Combs. It showed that the assault happened as Combs was stealing Auris Project's library, bookstore, and thousands of dollars of other assets. It didn't show the forged quitclaim deeds, but they were on the record and everyone who mattered in the malicious prosecution had seen evidence of them.

"This case should be immediately dismissed and Combs arrested for theft and assault," I concluded.

I looked into the suddenly still gallery. A brown-haired prosecutor grinned at me and nodded, much in the way that someone beams at you when they are pretending to be your friend directly after doing something behind your back.

"Noted," said the judge.

How to get away with railroading

Even though the video recording clearly showed Kristina Combs attacking me and stealing Auris Project assets, and the court record teemed with evidence of her and the notaries' document fraud, the prosecutors from the district attorney's office and Roberts maintained the false prosecution for more than two years.

The DA's continued prosecution put more pressure on me to plea bargain. I refused, and continued to hound the prosecutors for evidence in the Combs case. The only evidence in the folder Ludowig provided was the video showing Combs attacking me. Either release the evidence that allows this prosecution or drop this charge, I insisted.

The prosecution continued. I struggled to keep up with the seemingly endless cycle of newly assigned prosecutors.

When prosecutors finally provided the evidence file for inspection, it was empty. DVDs of the exonerating video I had provided to prosecutors earlier were also missing. Ah, I thought, that's why they keep switching prosecutors. They want to bury the video and be able to say they had no idea who might have removed it.

On February 3, 2015, I wrote prosecutors again, asking for the name and contact information of a supervisor. "It is very important that no one be able to say they were not aware of the goings on in Criminal Court 12."

Prosecutor Erica Peña responded. In what was clearly an email drafted by many, Peña ignored my request for a supervisor. Instead, she informed me that photos of Combs with a bloody lip had been added to the file.

And in a calculated cover up, she directed me to a file of the video I had uploaded to YouTube in an effort to preserve the evidence. Combs had given her the link, she lied. "I believe that this recording was taken by you," she wrote. "However I wanted to make you are aware that we have viewed this video and can provide the link to you if you needed."

I saw right through this sham.

The DA's prosecutors were carefully crafting *plausible deniability* on the record. Here is how it would work:

Say, God forbid, that I had been killed by SAPD officers, who justified the killing as the tragic result of a fast moving encounter with a psychotic and violently delusional woman. Say my family and friends, distressed by that defamatory fiction and seeking justice, encouraged the news media to investigate their allegations that I had been the victim of protracted official oppression.

Say that all of the records I had filed in court - the forged quitclaim deeds, the mock court proceedings, the abusive default judgments, the expert witnesses and the video of Combs's assault and theft - had mysteriously disappeared from court records. The video would still exist online, on an obscure YouTube channel that the conspirators could not erase. Say the news media found that video which showed "practicing attorney" Kristina Combs acting like a thug, her assault and theft against me captured and preserved online for all eternity.

The DA's office could conduct an "investigation" and, locating Peña's email, could pretend it was not aware of the video showing I was a victim of assault until 2015. Combs *did indeed* attack McVea not the other way around, the district attorney's office could officially determine, but according to the government's records, the DA's office didn't know that until two years after McVea's arrest.

Judge Scott Roberts was crafting his own path to plausible deniability. Instead of filing his abusive orders with the court clerk, Roberts would scribble his orders on the jacket of the case folder. Those, notations, of course, could easily be scrubbed just by changing the folder on the file. No one need ever know what really happened in County Court 12 in the case of *Texas v. Denise McVea*.

I kept up the pressure.

On March 1, 2015, the Bexar County District Attorney's Office finally sent me a witness list in the criminal assault charges against me.

Six names made up the list: SAPD officers Martinez, badge #595 and J. Mendoza, #597; Kristina Combs; her mother Miranda Combs; Kristina's brother Roger Combs II; and Marty Serratorubio.

That was the first time I learned the name of the weirdly smiling man directing the assault and theft against me at 1614 Martin Luther King the day of my false assault arrest in 2013.

Martin Serratorubio, apparently a resident of California, looked a lot like the dozens of seedy private investigators who had been stalking and harassing me for years: poorly groomed, not prosperous, wearing worn clothes and a ferret-like expression. But he also had a passing resemblance to Kristina Combs and her tatty mother. All I knew was that he had a supervisory role in the theft of my belongings and multiple attacks against my person, and it took two years to learn his identity. Although he was an active presence during the assault, theft, and unlawful arrest, he appears nowhere in SAPD incident reports recorded that day.

And the arresting officer Jesse Mendoza, I would realize years later, was the same abusive cop who had left me alone in the MLK building with the thief Danny Santos in 2010.

A sudden trip to Mexico

After the conspirators stole Auris assets, I got a call from a neighbor in Catorce. A group of people claiming to be lawyers had descended on my little high desert village and claimed ownership of my small cottage. I knew immediately that it was an Allstate scheme. All I had to do was take my paperwork down to Mexico, show it to the director of the town's small credit union, and evict the imposters.

Around the same time, a person claiming to be the brother of a Catorce acquaintance started sending me messages on Facebook Messenger. "How are you?" he asked in Spanish. When are you coming back to Mexico?"

We barely knew each other, but I didn't initially think the inquiry was strange. Mexicans often asked people who frequently cross the US-Mexico border to bring them products from the U.S. that were unavailable or too expensive in Mexico. The most popular items were tennis shoes, small appliances, and electronics. "*Te encargo*," they would say. Loosely translated, it means, "I am putting you in charge (of this task)."

I had been making plans to visit the Altiplano Potosino but with all the fires Allstate was igniting, I could never find the time. Now, because of the false arrest and malicious prosecution, I was under criminal bond and could not leave the county without the court's permission.

I kept receiving Facebook Messenger messages from the brother asking when I would return to Mexico, but he never asked me to bring him anything. That made me suspicious. But he kept asking, and so I kept saying it would be soon. And then he asked a question that made the hairs on the back of my neck stand up:

What time, he wanted to know, would I cross the international bridge at the US-Mexico border?

Suddenly, I remembered that Don Inez, the director of the credit union assisting the takeover of my Catorce house, had hung up on me when I told him my lawyer from the city of San Luis Potosí wanted to come and fix everything. "No lawyers," he had barked in a panic, "Just you!" Suddenly, I could not communicate with my Mexican lawyer.

Now highly suspicious of the Facebook Messenger contact, I hemmed and hawed. I didn't know exactly, I said, but I would let him know as soon as I knew.

I shared the experience with my contact at the FBI.

"I wouldn't be going to Mexico right now if I were you," said the FBI agent.

He knew what he was talking about. Drug cartels, engaged in violent internecine drug wars and clashes with the Mexican Army, were wreaking havoc on the country. The violence had reached such epidemic proportions that some Mexicans driving to work began seeing bodies hanging from overpasses.

In the seven years I had lived in the Altiplano Potosino, I had seen little evidence of cartel activity. But locals had warned me that I lived on a discreet but well-used cartel trafficking route. And there were places out in the desert that I needed to avoid at all costs, locals would warn. As a black woman, I was an extremely rare sight in those parts. "You stick out like a sore thumb," said one friend.

By the time my Catorce house was illegally seized, the cartel's presence in the Altiplano Potosino had become obvious. On February 15, 2011, Los Zetas cartel members ambushed and killed U.S. Homeland Security special agent Jaime Zapata not far from my home, on the same highway I traveled between San Antonio and Catorce.[70]

And on my last visit to Catorce, neighbors told me I had just missed a vicious battle between the Mexican Army and Los Zetas members who had taken over a friend's hotel. The army had won that fight, picking off cartel members with assault weapons from helicopters as the narco-traffickers fled through the mountains near Real de Catorce. I also knew that s*icarios,* Mexican assassins, could be persuaded to put a bullet in the head of a stranger for as little as $200.

I had no intention of going to Mexico.

After a few weeks, I received another Facebook message from the person identifying himself as a resident of the Altiplano Potosino. I decided to conduct a small experiment.

When are you coming down? he asked in Spanish.

I was already down there, I lied. I went by the cyber café, but it was closed. I never saw you or your brother.

He was out of town when you came, he replied.

Ah, I responded, well, I hope to get down there again soon.

The next time I stood in County Court 12 on the malicious criminal assault prosecution, Bexar County prosecutors informed the court that I had violated my bond by leaving the county without permission.

The DA's office would present evidence of my bond violation to the court shortly, prosecutor Peña told the judge.

I stood there, not saying a word.

Of course, nothing ever came of it, but now there was no doubt the DA's office was collaborating with Allstate cockroaches.

The person pretending to be a *catorceño* never contacted me again.

The unavailable "victim"

ON DECEMBER 8, 2015, TWO YEARS after "practicing lawyer" Kristina Combs attacked me and stole more than $100,000 of Auris Project property and assets, the State of Texas dropped its assault case against me.

Judge Roberts and the Bexar County prosecutors conducted the dismissal hearing almost entirely in whispers.

The dozens of defendants packing the gallery strained to hear, knowing that something extraordinary was occurring. Normally, prosecutors enjoyed listening to their voices echoing off the chamber walls, and judges constantly admonished defendants to speak up. Just moments before, judicial officers were talking in voices meant to project across the courtroom.

Now they were murmuring, heads bent over documents, their backs shielding their mouths from the audience. Many in the gallery, noticing this sudden shift, visibly leaned forward in their seats as they tried to catch what was going on.

The state's witness was unavailable for trial, Erica Peña mumbled to Judge Roberts. I flashed a withering glance her way. She stuttered something about Combs working in another jurisdiction.

Oh, you motherfuckers, I thought.

Later, when I tried again to file assault charges against Combs, an SAPD police lieutenant informed me that the statute of limitations for assault had expired. My charge of theft against Combs was still viable, the assigned investigator told me, but the DA Nico LaHood refused to prosecute it.

That was one of the objectives of the malicious prosecution all along: expire the charges against Combs, who was only following orders, just like the rest of the judges and lawyers. Another objective, I knew, was to force me to plea bargain. In order to plea bargain in Bexar County, Texas, defendants must sign away any civil rights claims. It says so right on the plea bargain form they handed me.

What a dirty business.

Still, Bexar County criminal court records teemed with evidence of their misdeeds – at least for now. The record showed that Judge Roberts and the District Attorney's Office violated not just my civil rights, but a host of criminal statutes, ethics standards, and judicial canons. Barring illegal tampering, the court record now showed that the prosecutors maintained a prosecution against a victim of a crime despite having evidence exonerating her of the charge and implicating her attacker. It showed that the judge engaged in tactics designed to rob the true victim, the defendant, of fair hearings. It showed that the judge and the prosecutors had ample evidence to prosecute and convict Kristina Combs but instead conspired to hide her criminal conduct by maliciously prosecuting her accuser. It showed that these judicial officers freely and wantonly made a mockery of judicial procedure. It showed that when some inmates in jail say they are innocent but had been railroaded by Bexar County prosecutors and judges, they are likely telling the truth.

No wonder they were whispering.

Now, the judge and prosecutor just wanted Denise McVea to go away.

Roberts signed the dismissal order. He flashed me a congratulatory smile from the bench. I looked back, expressionless.

He looked away. I noted with some satisfaction that he had aged.

I faced the prosecutor. "Ms. Peña," I said as I turned to leave.

I nodded my goodbye, but she would not look at me.

15 | SHADOWS

Operation Snow White

ALLSTATE'S VICIOUS ATTACK CAMPAIGN CONTINUED unabated. I ran from one Allstate designed catastrophe to another. I was followed everywhere I went. My house was under constant surveillance. I wagered that I had experienced less than 100 hours in the past five or six years where Allstate's gang stalkers did not know where I was, what I was doing, and who I was with.

I continued to battle computer and network intrusions, cyber hacking, and device destruction. I had given up hope that any official action would be taken. I duly reported the attacks just to make sure that there would be a record. To do that, I had to sit through constant mockery from dispatchers on the phone and police officers who showed up at my house. In nearly every case, they would misrepresent what I told them and omit key information. They would often add a simple word to an incident report involving my complaints: PSYCHE.

Stalkers rented homes in the neighborhood. Existing neighbors were bribed to help in the surveillance and the capturing of my network and cellular signal. The house across the street had a camera installed on its second floor permanently trained on my house. If I left town, Allstate operatives tracked me. When I went to retreats, goons followed. If I rented a hotel room, I significantly increased the establishment's occupancy rate. A seemingly endless supply of zeroes, some known to me and some complete strangers, made a living out of making my life a living hell.

Local cops, judges, lawyers, bureaucrats, and politicians were not only failing to intervene, they were in many cases actively supporting the criminality.

But I was in a terrible position. I knew that the tale was fantastical and that the cops and judges were determined to keep any proof of the crimes off the record. I was forced to be silent, not wanting to lend credence to the false police reports. It sounded like a crazy story even to my ears, and I was living it.

If I was to be believed, an American corporation had access to an army of covert operatives who used bribery and quid pro quo agreements to blanket a city with informants, thugs, and criminals, some in high places. Using this vast criminal network, it could target someone, anyone, in orchestrated, covert, criminal campaigns. It could corrupt just about anyone and infiltrate any organization. It could infiltrate an entire government.

That would be very hard for anyone to believe, I knew, especially if it had never happened before.

But I was in luck.

It *had* happened before.

Both Scientology and Allstate have a history of covert criminal conduct. Scientology had pulled off an audacious campaign in the 1970s and Allstate had reportedly engaged in similar acts in the 1990s. When I finally escaped Allstate's hackers, I learned that what I had been experiencing in San Antonio was actually nothing new.

Dubbed the "Cult of Greed" by *Time* magazine, Scientology had long been singled out by the media and anti-cult groups as a dangerous religious movement. Its founder L. Ron Hubbard has been described variously as the man who "solved the riddle of the human mind" by the Church of Scientology; "a mental case" by the FBI; and "hopelessly insane" by his ex-wife.

Since the early 1970s, Scientology has battled numerous branches of the US government regarding its status as a religious organization and its involvement in an array of criminal activities.

By the time Scientologists were teaching business ethics seminars to Allstate managers in the 1990s, the Church of Scientology had already perfected a highly sophisticated system of covert warfare. And it had successfully pulled off a daring secret criminal operation against the federal government.

They dubbed it Operation Snow White.

Launched in 1973, Scientology's Operation Snow White became the largest infiltration of the federal government in the history of the United States. While the main target of the operation was the Internal Revenue Service, Scientology operatives also successfully infiltrated or burglarized more than 130 other organizations, including the Drug Enforcement Agency, the U.S. Coast Guard Intelligence Office, the Food and Drug

Administration, the American Medical Association (Scientologists are famously hostile to psychiatry), and even the Department of Justice. By the time authorities arrested a handful of co-conspirators, tens of thousands of government documents had been copied or stolen.[71]

It all started when the IRS revoked Scientology's coveted tax-exempt status in the late 1960s. Soon, the church owed the federal government millions in back taxes, a staggering amount the organization had no intention of paying. The church demanded that its tax-free status be restored. The IRS refused, saying the church, with its escalating fees for enlightenment programs, was actually a for-profit business.

Scientologists were prepared to do whatever it took to win. They started a freedom of information act letter writing campaign. It soon mutated into a vast criminal conspiracy.[72]

In 1973, Scientologists and their operatives began secretly penetrating federal government departments and other organizations they deemed enemies. The group's main objective was to "clean" these agencies of documents and files critical of Scientology.

The top co-conspirators were all employees of Scientology's secretive Guardian's Office. One of the lead co-conspirators was Mary Sue Hubbard, the third wife of Scientology founder L. Ron Hubbard.

During Operation Snow White, Scientology operatives perfected a host of clandestine techniques, including forged credentials, door key duplication, wiretapping, burglary, blackmail, character assassination, fake identities, and the recruitment and training of covert field agents.[73] They formed front companies, engaged in eavesdropping and criminal conspiracies, obstructed audits, investigated IRS officials, falsified records, and filed more than 2,500 lawsuits.

Scientologists and their agents would apply for jobs as secretaries, clerks, and security guards, and then use their access as employees to break into offices and file cabinets. When moles learned that the IRS planned to hold a meeting about Scientology, a Scientologist working for the agency planted a bug in the meeting room. During the meeting, the bug transmitted the conversations to a van parked across the street at the Smithsonian national museum. When the meeting concluded, the agent simply removed the audio device from the room.

The plot was uncovered when legitimate security guards accidently stumbled across Scientology operatives lurking about government buildings and entering locked offices at night.

The criminal scheme involved thousands of participants, but federal agents made just a handful of arrests. Ultimately, Mary Sue Hubbard and ten other high-ranking Scientologists pleaded guilty to obstruction of justice, burglary of government offices, and theft of documents and government property.

Founder L. Ron Hubbard, the unindicted co-conspirator in the Snow White operation, went into hiding. He evaded authorities for the rest of his life. He died of natural causes in 1986 at the age of 74. In announcing his death to adherents, his controversial successor David Miscavige reported that Hubbard had shed his human form. And while Scientologists eagerly await Hubbard's eventual return to earth (several mansions are prepared for his arrival) Scientology's covert operation against the U.S. federal government was by any rational measurement a huge success. Given the scope of the criminal operation and the catastrophic loss of sensitive government data, the conspirators received relatively light sentences. Their prison sentences ranged from one to six years.

Despite the scope and damage of the operation, and the detrimental impact on national security, governmental operations, and rule of law, the U.S. government never prosecuted the church. By contrast, the organization has been vigorously prosecuted for similar conduct in Canada and other countries.

In fact, the United States is virtually alone in its kid gloves treatment of the Church of Scientology. France considers it a dangerous cult, and the German government views it as an abusive sect masquerading as a religion. Around the world, the reception to Scientology has been "almost universally chilly at best – and at times openly hostile," according to journalist Lucy Morgan.[74]

Back in the United States, however, none of the few Scientologists arrested in the massive Snow White criminal operation even served their full sentences. The organization itself and the thousands of people who contributed to Snow White were inexplicably left alone.

The Guardian's Office, the center of the covert operations, changed its name to the Office of Special Affairs. It continued to run highly sophisticated, successful operations against perceived enemies, including U.S. Attorneys, IRS officials, journalists, the Better Business Bureau, U.S. senators, and local government officials. They had names like Operation Bunny Bust, Operation Big Mouth, Operation Cat, and Operation Devil's Wop. The office was instrumental in the cult's successful takeover of Clearwater, FL.[75]

In October 1993, The IRS awarded the Church of Scientology International and 150 affiliated churches and organizations its long-coveted tax-exempt status. The decision shocked tax experts.

Around the time Allstate managers and executives were attending Scientology-inspired "profit over ethics" seminars in the 1990s, Scientology was also in a decades-long war against the news media, which had been periodically airing or printing exposés about the organization. The church frequently sued news outlets for what it deemed negative news coverage. Before his death, Hubbard taught Scientologists to file lawsuits to "harass and discourage, rather than to win." The cult also continued to use the tactics that had been so effective against the federal government.

The organization sued journalist Richard Behar, who wrote the article "Cult of Greed" for *Time* magazine in 1991. But, he says, the organization also made him a target of harassment and persecution even before the article was printed.

> "[A]t least 10 attorneys and six private detectives were unleashed by Scientology and its followers in an effort to threaten, harass and discredit me . . . A copy of my personal credit report – with detailed information about my bank accounts, home mortgage, credit card payments, home address and Social Security number – had been illegally retrieved from a national credit bureau . . . [P]rivate investigators have been contacting acquaintances of mine . . . to inquire about subjects such as my health . . . and whether I've ever had trouble with the IRS."

The church's tactics have been extraordinarily effective, helping it become powerful and wealthy – and in many ways, untouchable.

"Scientology is quite likely the most ruthless, the most classically terroristic, the most litigious and the most lucrative cult the country has ever seen," said Cynthia Kisser, former executive director of the Cult Awareness Network.

She would know. When the Cult Awareness Network designated the Church of Scientology as the most rapacious of all "deviant cults" in the United States, the Church unleashed a fury of legal attacks against the watchdog group. Having to answer more than 50 lawsuits filed in both federal and state courts eventually drove CAN into bankruptcy. In a final, victorious salvo, a scientologist reportedly purchased the few assets left: CAN's trade name, service mark, and helpline telephone number.

Allstate executives watched all this play out in real time. They saw that the Church of Scientology had used wildly illegal tactics to achieve its lucrative tax-free status and in so doing handily beat the federal government, suffering few consequences.

Allstate as pupil

Allstate did publicly cut ties with Scientology in the 1990s, but things had changed. After the Scientology seminars, Allstate began making major changes that increased its profit margins. According to many agents, those changes included making employees pay more of the operating expenses, pressuring agents to break laws that protected consumers, and targeting highly compensated employees for firing.[76]

When the agents fought back, Allstate responded with tactics that bore eerie similarities to tools used in Scientology's fruitful Snow White covert operation. It was actually quite easy.

Because lawyers and investigators are integral parts of the insurance industry, Allstate had a nationwide army of operatives available to support this new, Scientology-inspired approach to business. Allstate's readymade army was also, as a matter of rule, protected by confidentiality agreements, attorney-client privilege, and lax government oversight.

Many agents complained of covert surveillance, intimidation, defamation, and harassment. Allstate executives reportedly drove some agents to nervous breakdowns. They gaslighted them. They illegally pulled credit reports and motor vehicle records. They even reportedly assigned private investigators to follow agents' lawyers. Pre-internet, they apparently could still tap phones.

After one agent sued Allstate, he began noticing a strange-looking car, "low to the ground, tinted windows, two antennas," passing outside his home. When he left his house to run errands, the car followed him. He began seeing the car everywhere.[77]

Allstate's war against its own agents involved "private eyes, high-speed chases, nasty lawsuits, and threats of violence," journalist Richard Behar wrote for *Fortune Magazine*.

When agents filed civil lawsuits against the company, Allstate worked its litigation magic, "delaying cases, withholding documents, filing voluminous motions, running up everybody's legal bills." An Arizona judge admonished the insurer for its dirty tricks in court.

"In the long run," the judge stated prophetically, "(Allstate's tactics) can only serve to cause disrespect and other harm to the civil justice system."[78]

The company continued to deny it engaged in covert activity, but a former Allstate security officer once testified that the company used surveillance as "standard operating procedure."[79]

After Allstate agent Richard Larkin called senior executives "crooks and cowards," he became a target. He recounted his nightmare to Behar, who wrote:

He says he arrived at his home in Virginia one day last March to find his .22-caliber handgun, which he hadn't used for more than a decade, laying on his dresser. The gun's chamber had four spent cartridges. In Larkin's closet, a row of pants had bullet holes through their backsides.[80]

One story especially resonated with me: that of agent Myles Barchas.

A successful Allstate agent in North Texas, Barchas challenged new Allstate policies he considered illegal and abusive to customers. He blew the whistle, reporting the crimes to the Texas Department of Insurance. Allstate private investigators stalked him for six months. Journalist Behar eventually acquired an Allstate surveillance report. It read in part:

> November 1993 - Barchas made a trip to Dallas yesterday and is on the move again this morning. The surveillance lost him for a while in traffic and had to set up on his apartment and office in hopes of relocating him. The intelligence that has been picked up is that Barchas may be headed to the State Insurance Dept. in Austin. Instructions were given to stay on him.[81]

After Barchas filed a "confidential" complaint against Texas regional managers in 1993 through the company's ironically named "We Care" program, the company sent a supervisor to his house. The supervisor, Barchas was warned, would "break down the door" if necessary. The agent refused to open the door. If anyone broke down his door, Barchas warned, he would be shot. He soon started receiving anonymous death threats. People started following him. His computers suddenly went blank. His customers began receiving letters stating he had retired.

He installed a security system. The installer, a former cop, was so worried about Barchas he invited him to stay in his home 80 miles away. Barchas accepted the offer. Private investigators hired by Allstate followed him. They surrounded the cop's house. Barchas hunkered down inside.

It cost the company today's equivalent of a $250,000 dollars to stalk and harass that one agent for six months. "Everybody who has insurance paid for that [surveillance]," the ex-cop told the investigative journalist.

Allstate began defaming the now former agent. The company fired and stalked him, executives explained, because he had abandoned his customers, was displaying "peculiar behavior," was leaving "rambling" voicemail messages on executives' answering machines and threatened to shoot anyone who came to his house.

The company characterized Barchas's letters soliciting help from then-CEO Wayne Hedien as "garbled, incoherent."

Allstate hired a psychiatrist to analyze Barchas's letter for threats. The psychiatrist determined that the agent only wanted to talk to Hedien.

When Barchas sent audiotapes to the CEO's house that proved Allstate's agents were breaking the law, the company treated the package as a bomb threat.

It all took a toll on Barchas.

"Myles was scared to death," Tim Rose, the Barchas's ex-cop friend told Behar. "There's no way Myles was going to hurt anybody. I was going to teach him how to shoot, and he was so uptight about it he wouldn't even hold the pistol."[82]

Barchas once walked to a parking lot to find all four of his car doors wide open. Later someone loosened the lug nuts on his car. People called his phone and then abruptly hung up. His father reported the same activity at his home. After talking to the journalist one day on the phone, the former Allstate agent got "20 straight hang-ups." Someone then egged his front door. Allstate executives said they weren't responsible for all that. Barchas, understandably, didn't believe them.

The journalist Behar described other incidents from Allstate's surveillance program for the magazine:

> When Barchas flew to Austin to visit state insurance regulators, two Allstate private investigators were on the same American Airlines flight. On another occasion, he drove nearly three hours to see the regulators, tailed by three investigators at speeds reaching 100 mph, according to Allstate's own surveillance reports. Still, the surveillance continued, night and day. When Barchas used his cellular phone, his calls were apparently monitored by a scanning device.

People who helped Barchas were also followed. When the surveillance eased, Barchas began working with a TV journalist to expose Allstate agents' frauds against potential customers. The state eventually fined Allstate $850,000, the equivalent of about six hours' of Allstate's earnings. Allstate easily paid the fine. It admitted no guilt.

In his exacting article for *Fortune Magazine*, Richard Behar talked to several agents who described Texas as a permissive state government in bed with an arrogant, abusive insurer:

> The agents claim they attended a meeting during which a high-level Allstate official bragged about a quid pro quo involving the governor (Ann Richards) that was allegedly orchestrated by Texas Representative Al Edwards, the head of the state's black caucus. According to the sworn statements, Edwards agreed that the governor would not mention Allstate's name on television. Soon

after, the company expanded its minority vendor program through Edwards, according to an internal company memo. Edwards and Allstate deny any such deal. Richards couldn't be reached.[83]

Behar reported that a grand jury severely criticized Texas state government for a "significant reluctance" to investigate insurance company fraud, "undue influence from the industry," and "political pressure on the regulators."[84]

By 2021, the Scientology seminars and Operation Snow White had faded into distant history. But some of the tactics used against Barchas in Dallas surfaced again 28 years later in San Antonio. The target was not considered formidable: a poor black woman with intractable PTSD who had spent the last ten years in Mexico. An independent journalist and activist, the woman was struggling to build a non-profit information center on San Antonio's historically marginalized Eastside. She had little money, no powerful news organization to support her, and virtually no connection to the entrenched African-American powerbrokers who controlled the neighborhoods where she had grown up. Despite all of this, she would unwisely sue Allstate, activating the company's ruthless zero sum game. Allstate knew it had little to worry about from San Antonio's courts, police, city government, lawyer class, black leadership, or state regulators.

This zero sum campaign – largely conducted within a five-mile radius of the famous Alamo mission – was sure to be a cakewalk.

The "Church" at 315 S. Olive.

My house was constantly being circled. Thugs would walk into my backyard uninvited. Several young men would approach me while riffling through their jacket pockets while I worked in my yard. People would step into my path at stores and take photos of me with their phones. My devices were being corrupted on a daily basis. My internet searches continued to throw up the same 10 pages. If I caught a glimpse on Google of something important, my computer froze. If I actually accessed a page that had significance to my fight, my computer might break down completely. If I tried to print a page, my printer would malfunction. There was little I could do. I just stored my suddenly useless devices in the attic. The graveyard, I called it.

Much of the stalking and harassing activity was coming from 315 S. Olive, the small apartment complex at the opposite, cattycorner end of the alley. A rectangular brick, building, we called it the "eightplex" because that's how many mailboxes lined the front-facing wall. In actuality, the apartment had six units.

By the publication of this book, the property at 315 S. Olive had been renovated and transferred to a series of owners.

But back then, the complex had for years been a bustling narcotics operation left unbothered by Eastside police. As addicts and dealers trudge in and out, public records characterized the complex as a church and import business. But the reality was starkly different. Drug dealers, addicts, prostitutes, pimps and johns used the complex as a business hub. Some of the prostitutes looked like minors. When I called the police, patrol officers would slowly drive up to my side of the alley and idle the squad card on Hackberry in full view of the people keeping watch at 315 S. Olive. Catching a glimpse of the squad car idling at the other side of the alley, the criminals would scatter. Only then would the squad car enter the premises. Police reports would state that no activity was observed.

That was one way drug dealing continued to plague the Eastside. I watched it all from my upstairs kitchen window.

Soon, the complex became a center for mules and hackers capturing my cellular and network signal. Vehicles would leave the Olive Street complex, circle past my house and return to the Olive Street complex. When my network and devices began to malfunction, I would turn off and reboot my router, phones, and computers. The vehicles would leave the complex again, circle my home again and return to the drug house/import company/church on Olive Street. This would occur all day, every day, for years. I started writing down license plates.

For weeks, a Black Chevy Tahoe divided its time between my house and the complex on South Olive Street. I wrote down its license plate.

The van

On May 15, 2015, I was working upstairs at my desk when my web pages stopped loading. I looked out my bedroom window. A late model white van sat parked in front of the house. I went downstairs to investigate. It had Florida plates. Most likely a rental, I thought. I took a picture of the license plate.

The next morning, it appeared again. My network began to malfunction. There was no credible reason for the van to choose this exact spot to park two days in a row except to interfere with my network. I went downstairs again, this time determined to get a closer look. No one was inside. I peered into the windshield. A parking permit from Comfort Inn rested on the dashboard. The small hotel was located just a few short city blocks from my house. The ticket gave the van permission to park at the hotel's lot for that day.

I returned upstairs, turned off my modem, and found something else to do. Without me noticing, someone later jumped in and drove the van away. I jumped in my truck and headed toward the Comfort Inn.

And there it was, sitting in the hotel parking lot. I took a photo. But there was something more, something unexpected. The black Chevy Tahoe that had been circling my home and visiting the drug complex at 315 S. Olive also sat parked in the hotel's lot. I took a picture of that, too.

I began examining the plates of other cars in the lot, and taking photos of those that looked familiar. Soon, a burly man in his thirties came out and began eyeing me. I took a picture of him, too. He did not approach me but he seemed to be putting himself between me and the vehicles I was showing an interest in. He looked like a bouncer.

Another man came out and stood behind the Chevy Tahoe, obscuring the SUV's license plate. We watched each other. He showed no signs of moving. I was glad I had already snapped a photo of the plates. The man was in his forties, a slender, fair-skinned black man who looked similar to a man who menaced me in the back of my house weeks before, but I couldn't be sure. I snapped a picture of him.

He didn't budge. He was not going to let me see those plates.

I got you, I thought.

I called the police. I explained to dispatch that I had been complaining of network interference and that I had tracked a suspicious vehicle from my house to this hotel. I said I wanted to make an incident report and get the identity of the person or persons in control of the vehicle.

A group of Hispanic people poured out of the hotel, led by a military-looking black man. The man began ushering them toward the van with the Florida plates, as they looked around uncertainly. I asked a woman in the group what their purpose was in San Antonio. She said in Spanish that she didn't speak English. I repeated the question in Spanish. She wasn't expecting this. She looked around in panic. Their usher intervened, gesturing for her and the others to get in the van. I told him that the police were on their way with questions about the van and that he should not leave. He ignored me. He jumped into the van's driver's seat, took the wheel, and drove out of the parking lot. A man in a business suit came out with a hotel clerk. The clerk approached and asked me what I was doing. I explained that the police were on their way and that I was waiting for them. But the van was now gone, the clerk was hostile, and I understood that it would not go my way if I waited for the police. I decided to go home.

I pulled onto the street and headed back to Wyoming Street. A block away from the hotel, a police squad car sat idling on an empty lot on the side of the road. A patrol officer sat behind the wheel, talking intently on his personal phone. He should have already arrived on the call, but instead it looked like he was getting instructions from someone who was not employed by the police department. I was glad I had decided to leave.

As I got closer to my house, I passed the van, parked on the side of the road. When I passed, it took up a position behind me and followed. My first instinct was to get behind it, but thought better of it. Something told me I was being baited into a confrontation where no one was going to be on my side - especially not the police. I had been down this road before. Nothing good could come from a San Antonio cop on his private phone on the side of the road. Besides, I had some key evidence that needed preserving: the license plate of the Tahoe that had been collaborating with the drug house on Olive. It wouldn't do for me to get arrested *again*.

Once safely at home, I called police to make a report about the van and the hacking. The abusive dispatcher Randy Freeman took the call. He and another dispatcher named Tucker routinely mocked and ridiculed me when I called to report abuse, but of the two of them, Randy Freeman was the worst. Why do I always get these two goon dispatchers who always misrepresent what I say? I wondered. He followed his usual routine, asking questions, interrupting me when I tried to answer, and acting like I wasn't making sense. Do you know who is doing all this, he asked. I have a solid lead, I told him.

We'll get somebody out, ma'am, he said.

Finally, a rookie officer showed up to my front door. Minutes later, another cop arrived and took over the interaction. He looked exactly like the cop sitting on the side of the road talking on his private phone near the hotel. The rookie cop sat silent while the interloper asked the questions.

This was a familiar playbook.

Senior cops like Detective Phelan often showed up, took control of the rookie's call, and then determine what would be included in the police report and what would be left out. Despite the controlling officer being the true author of the incident report, there would be no evidence in the scrubbed police report he was even present at the scene.

Months later, I began researching the Chevy Tahoe connecting the hotel meeting with the drug operation at 315 S. Olive. I had now established that the owner of the SUV circling my house had ties to the drug house posing as a church at 315 S. Olive but also to the suspicious group using the white van to hack into my network. After a little digging, I was able to identify the Chevy Tahoe's owner. An online photo confirmed that he was also the man hiding the license plate at the hotel. His name was Tony Gradney and he was what is often referred to as "a leader in the black community." He had a popular soul food restaurant and served on some local boards. But what did he have to do with the drug house at 315 S. Olive? And why was he here with this group blocking my view of his license plate?

While working on the final draft of the book in November 2021, I sent Gradney an email asking him about that day. I attached a jpeg file of the photo I had taken of him standing in front of the license plate.

"In the interest of clarity," I wrote, "I would like to give you the opportunity to explain your presence at the Comfort Inn that day. So far, it is presented in the book as an open question."

As of publication, he had not responded.

Years later, as I viewed dozens of police reports wrested from the SAPD, I came across the police incident report for that day. It had been prepared by Randy Freeman, the sneering dispatcher.

Freeman had written:

> (Complainant) is saying Mexican Nationals are hacking into (Complainant's) computer from a van outside (Complainant's) home and they are all from Florida and they are there just (to) do that and want to kill complainant/they go to a hotel in the area to sleep at night/have been doing that for two days now....denise stated strange activity taking place. i advised denise i would look into it.

The police report included a now-familiar notation:

`*********psych*********.`

16 | IMPUNITY

"We get a lot of those people in here."

COCKROACHES CONTINUED TO RECRUIT NEIGHBORS and others to harass me. A steady stream of traffic flowed between the Olive Street complex and the house next door. Mules trucked along the alleyway, switching out devices as I bobbed and weaved along the cyber highway. I could tell when I lost my cyber trackers because the next door neighbor would begin to blast rap music from his car parked in the next-door driveway, the pounding bass rattling my windows and walls.

I was at my wits end.

I knew that I could not count on Eastside police officers. On May 16th, I drove again to police headquarters downtown to speak face-to-face with a detective. That's when I met Manuel Perez.

A young Hispanic male in his early 30s, Perez seemed too young to be a detective. He gestured for me to pass through the door he had just exited. I expected to be led to some sort of interrogation room or office. But he stopped at a bench in the inner hall, about two feet from the door he had just closed. Standing there, he turned to me. "What do you need?" he asked rudely. He wore that familiar smirk.

A few days later, while it was still fresh in my mind I would write a letter of complaint to Chief McManus describing the interaction:

> He immediately began to harangue me, asking me incongruous questions and interrupting me before I could adequately answer. Although Perez appeared to have no understanding of cyber security, he told me that the types of cyber intrusions I was describing "just didn't happen." He then asked if I was mentally ill. When I told him no, he asked if I was delusional. When I told him no, he asked me if

anyone had ever told me that I was delusional. He asked these questions in a contemptuous and disdainful manner. When I asked him why he was asking me those insulting questions, he answered, "we get a lot of those people in here." When I told him that I was a journalist, he scoffed, asking in disbelief what newspapers I had ever worked for. He abruptly changed the subject before I could list the dozens of major news outlets I have worked with or the number of national journalism awards I had won.

In the letter, I complained that Perez was no outlier. In fact, I informed the police chief for the umpteenth time, the majority of cops I encountered on the Eastside acted the same way, dismissive, insulting, and ignorant of the law. Many, as if reading from a script, accused me of being unstable.

The three-page letter went on to detail that after I asked to speak to Perez's supervisor, the young detective mocked me from the front desk and loudly told me that the things I was complaining about were not crimes. So I included in the text of the letter the penal codes for the violations I had been complaining about to SAPD officers for years. Perez's supervisor, Sgt. Patterson, never came out to talk to me. The name Patterson sounded familiar. (He was ever-present during police harassment campaigns against me and was probably one of the white detectives listening in on my fruitless conversations with the corrupt property crimes detective Reginald Freeman.)

In the letter, I reminded McManus that Eastside Substation SAPD police officers had arrested me three times on false and non-existent charges while refusing to acknowledge the staggering number of documented official criminal acts against me. I wrote:

> I suppose the hope is that one day I will leave this city and the folk who have had their way with the Eastside can continue their lucrative criminal activities without interference. But this is my home and I have an obligation not to give into these criminal threats – just as you and your officers have an obligation to fight crime, not citizens.

"If drug dealers got arrested as much as Denise McVea," I concluded, "the Eastside would be a much nicer place to live."

I sent the letter to the chief and copied it to both Perez and Patterson. A few days later, Perez called. He struck a very different tone, trying to politely explain why the crimes against me weren't really crimes. Behind his new, friendlier tone, I could hear panic. He asked me to send the letter to his supervisor, Sgt. Patterson. I told him that I already had. He asked me if I had sent the letter to the chief. I told him that I had. He thanked me politely for my time, and hung up. Later, as I reviewed the thousands of documents

I had gathered over the years, I realized that Patterson showed up often in my evidence files, and had played a significant role in stalling and dismissing my complaints against corrupt Eastside cops and the criminal actors they protected.

By the end of the summer, my case against the SAPD in federal court had devolved into an absurd theater whereby the attorneys and judges met behind closed doors to determine how they as a team would perform in court.

Of course, I was not supposed to know about these meetings, but magistrate judge John Primomo inadvertently exposed them himself, when he mentioned something that had not been included in any of the filed motions. He could have only gotten that information from Seimer or Kosanovich – outside of court.

The Texas Civil Rights Project

IT HAD BEEN YEARS SINCE I had contacted the Texas Civil Rights Project. I decided to try that again. After making a few calls that were not returned, I decided to drive to Austin and visit the organization in person.

I woke up early to make my way to the Texas Civil Rights Project,

It was dark when I left the house. The streets were empty. Before I got to the freeway, two cars appeared behind me. The driver side headlight of one of the vehicles was out. When I slowed down, they slowed down, keeping a distance. I made a right, then another right, then another right to end up where I was before on Hackberry. Briefly, I was alone on the road. By the time I entered the highway, the one headlight was behind me again.

I arrived in Austin. I found the Texas Civil Rights Project tucked away in a low brick building in a tumbledown working class neighborhood.

I rang the intercom doorbell system hung to the right of a heavy metal door. "Yes?" came a female voice through the intercom.

"Denise McVea for Mimi Marziani," I said.

A young white woman opened the door and peered at me. "Is she expecting you?" she asked.

"She should be," I answered vaguely. "I'm bringing information from Bexar County."

She let me in. Inside, the building transformed from a dingy warehouse to a hip, minimalist loft of glass, dark woods and recessed lighting. Soon, Marziani was walking toward me, a slender, attractive woman in a form fitting sleeveless black dress and a blonde bob. She looked elegant and wholesome as she greeting me with a welcoming smile. I was surprised. I had expected, at the very least, a muted response to my sudden presence since I hadn't gotten any responses to my letters. I hadn't even been sure she would see me. But here she was, greeting me warmly and wondering aloud behind which shiny glass partition we should chat. Maybe she had responded, I thought, and the cyber attackers had kept her response from me. Despite the harrowing gangstalking, it appeared that heading to Austin was a good call.

We sat in a small conference room, she at the head of the table and me sitting to her left at the corner. I thanked her for seeing me. She nodded graciously and I began my tale. "I don't know if you have received my letters, but I have been trying to get information to you about the court system in Bexar County."

Recognition flashed across her face. Her demeanor changed. "I don't have a lot of time," she said with newfound briskness.

The warmth quickly ebbed from her and the smile disappeared. Then it dawned on me. She had thought I was someone else. That's why she welcomed me so warmly. But she was stuck now, I knew. She had to listen to what I had to say. I got to the point. I told her about the Bexar County civil judges illegally closing non-represented litigants' court cases and I told her how they were doing it. I told her how the staff attorneys were corralling plaintiffs without lawyers and illegally dismissing their applications to proceed with their cases without paying court costs without allowing them to see a judge. When I told her that the judges were closing plaintiffs' cases after staff attorneys prevented them from attending hearings, Marziani gasped. That was a good sign, I thought. Thousands of Bexar County residents had had their cases dismissed illegally, I told her.

But there was no warmth at all from her now. She began to talk about a man who had approached the TCRP about starting a legal library in Austin, and how I should get in touch with him. I asked her how that would help what was going on in Bexar County. She said it looks like it could be a good project.

Marziani stood up to indicate the meeting was over. I managed to give her a DVD of some of the records I had gathered that detailed the court's "no pay-no lawyer-no justice" policy. She hesitated and then reluctantly accepted the disk. As she walked, she gave some vague assurances that she would discuss the matter with the appropriate people. I followed her as she headed for the front door, and before I knew it, I was outside of the Texas Civil Rights Project.

I stood there for a minute, discombobulated. There had been no real closure, no solution, and no advice. Outside of her involuntary gasp, there was no indication that Marziani had been particularly moved by the seriousness of what I had just divulged. I rang the doorbell again. This time, a male voice answered.

"I forgot to get a card for follow up," I told the intercom.

A few seconds later, a man in his late thirties opened the door. He looked like a private investigator. He handed me a business card with the name of an attorney scratched out and another scribbled above it. The last thing I saw before the door closed was the small smirk on his face.

By October, I had not heard from Mimi Marziani or the Texas Civil Rights Project. I visited the TCRP website. My anger grew when I saw in a promo the organization boasting about teaming up with a law firm to fight in the field of "access to justice." It appeared that the whole time Marziani was directing me to the man with the law library idea, she had information that could have helped me as I documented systemic obstruction of justice in San Antonio courts.

On October 1, 2016, I wrote her a follow up letter. I reminded her that for years, Bexar County civil courts had been engaged in a policy to block poor citizens from accessing justice.

"As you know," I wrote, "Texas law leans heavily in favor of allowing persons access to our courts regardless of their ability to pay."[85]

Marziani never responded.

I grew to resent the name of the organization. In my view, Marziani, a graduate of Vanderbilt University, had done good immigration and election rights work. But this well-to-do, privileged white woman had co-opted the civil rights banner created with the blood and sweat of black people in the 1960s while ignoring their plight in the new millennium. It made me sick. I added her name to the list of folks I suspected had somehow been rewarded for turning a blind eye to what was going on in Bexar County.

The same day I wrote to Marziani, I also wrote a follow-up letter to Mike Leary, the editor of the *San Antonio Express-News*. The civil courts were still ignoring my public information act requests in a bid to cover up their policy of blocking poor folks from access to the courts, I wrote him. I again asked for the paper to advocate for the disclosure of public record.

"As San Antonio's only daily newspaper and a major news source," I wrote, "The *San Antonio Express-News* has a vital interest in upholding government transparency laws."

I made it a point to mention the cyberattacks and harassment and reiterate that the best way to communicate with me was through certified mail or in person. As the editor of the daily newspaper, he could have simply assigned a reporter to knock on my door.

I received no response.

I was racking up an astonishing number of letters and emails alleging serious official misconduct that as a rule went ignored. People in charge of crucial protective institutions refused to respond to my concerns. In another world, I would have felt helpless, powerless.

But people who were powerless, I knew, weren't followed everywhere they went.

EVENTUALLY, I LEARNED THAT ONE OF THE NOTARIES who participated in the forged MLK property quitclaim deeds, Meagan Hollis, was a trust administrator assistant for Frost Bank, one of the oldest local banks in San Antonio. I wrote the bank, asking about her notary books.

A few weeks later, U.S. Secret Service agents arrested Hollis, but not for the fraudulent quitclaim deeds that allowed Allstate lawyers to steal Auris Project's assets. The Feds charged Hollis with embezzling more than $76,000 from Frost customers' accounts. According to a criminal complaint affidavit, Frost Bank first became aware of the suspicious activity on March 17, 2015, when the daughter of a deceased customer questioned transfers from her father's account, executives told reporters.

When bank officials learned Hollis had made the transfers, they tried to contact her, the feds alleged in court records. She reportedly called in sick for three days and then resigned via email.

Bank officials then learned that Hollis had also ordered and picked up an automated teller machine card for another deceased Frost customer's account.

Between April 3, 2014, and March 18, 2015, that account saw 124 unauthorized ATM withdrawals totaling $76,664. Most of that money in that account had been transferred from other Frost accounts, the affidavit said.

Hollis, then 42, had faced up to 30 years in federal prison for the embezzlement crime. In the end, however, she got off easy. She was released on bond pending a probable cause hearing set for April 15 before U.S. Magistrate Judge Pamela Mathy. Despite the FBI and police having evidence of her involvement in the fraudulent notarized quitclaim deeds, she has not faced charges for that crime.

Meanwhile, hackers continued to wreak havoc with my financial transactions, my internet searches, and the development of the Auris Project.

On December 6, 2015, I wrote the U.S. Post Office Criminal Investigations Service Center, complaining again about the postal carriers. I characterized the delivery delays, the opened packages, and "lost" mail, particularly of court-related materials, as "purposeful and strategic."

The Sunset Commission

Periodically, Texas takes look at state agencies to see if they are doing the job they are supposed to be doing, even going so far as determining if the agency needs to be shut down.

October 6, 2016, I added my voice to the long line of Texans begging the state of Texas to do something about the state bar.

"I agree with the other citizens," I wrote the commission. "The State Bar grievance process is little more than a sham. It provides virtually no protection to the states most vulnerable citizens – those not important enough to garner media attention – and is a principal factor in the decline of public trust in the Texas legal profession."[86]

I informed the commission of my experiences the past few years dealing with Texas lawyers. I recounted how Albert Gutierrez, Allstate's lawyer, "waltzed in and out of the judge's chambers" in an illicit attempt to strike the expert witness of a pro se litigant and how he falsely quoted case law in court. I explained how "practicing lawyer" Kristina Combs helped forge quitclaim deeds, committed burglary, stole more than $100,000 of private property, and physically attacked the victim of her fraud on video. I shared how billboard lawyer Joe Gonzales collected more than $3000 from a victim seeking legal representation, and then refused to provide legal services in an attempt to extort several thousand more dollars from his victim. I explained that the bar took no action against the actors despite being provided with ample evidence of their crimes. Like many of the citizens pleading with the Sunset Commission, I complained that the confidential nature of the bar's grievance process shielded lawyers from accountability for their misconduct.

I received no response. The Sunset commission approved the continuation of the state bar. Not that it mattered, but it was likely the commission never even got my letter.

The FBI, part II: a struggling agency

Reeling from attacks from judges and lawyers who seemed to have endless impunity and an army of enablers from the street, I began to view the FBI's McGinty/Acevedo investigation as sophomoric and inelegant. I began to worry that the FBI, using outdated Italian Mafia-era tactics, were incapable of fighting the new millennium's well-funded and highly sophisticated criminal networks taking over the judicial system and other public institutions.

The judicial landscape in Texas was littered with corrupt judges and the local FBI managed to snag only the dumbest among them. I was disheartened, to say the least.

For years, Bexar County residents have complained to local federal authorities about actionable, provable instances of oppression, civil rights violations and other crimes against San Antonio residents. Rarely, if ever, has anything ever come of those complaints.

I began to worry that maybe I was giving the FBI task force too much credit. It had been years since the bureau had announced the courthouse wiretaps and an ongoing anti-corruption criminal investigation of the local courthouse. And all the task force had to show for it was the criminal conviction of two not-very-bright men clumsily engaged in a sloppy, low value bribery scheme. Other officials implicated in that investigation, including the judge's own defense team, were not pursued, according to court records. Was the FBI still investigating the widespread corruption plaguing San Antonio? Did they still want to root out the criminality and impunity infesting San Antonio's government? Even after judge McGinty and the lawyer Al Acevedo were trotted off to prison, it was business as usual for corrupt public employees in San Antonio.

Like many Americans, I had begun to lose faith in the Federal Bureau of Investigation.

Even before the Minneapolis cop Derek Chauvin wantonly murdered George Floyd in broad daylight, the public's faith in law enforcement had been at an all-time low. The FBI was itself awash in public disapproval. The American public had come to distrust its premier law enforcement agency almost entirely. I knew this because when I told people about the cyber-surveillance, cyberhacking, gangstalking, and other oppressive actions targeting me, most people didn't immediately think the FBI was ignoring the crimes. They assumed the FBI was committing the crimes. That belief crossed socioeconomic boundaries. Doubters were white, black, Hispanic, poor, middle class, wealthy. I found myself in the peculiar position of defending an organization that had permitted protracted and destructive criminal attacks against me and my family.

Still, if the FBI was involved in an undercover investigation, I rationalized, I couldn't expect them to come to my rescue and possibly blow their cover. They were, after all, secret police. I comforted myself with that excuse for years.

Despite everything I was enduring, I could not bring myself to view the FBI as an enemy of the people. The agents I met had impressed me as intelligent, dedicated, and professional. I wanted to believe that they were smart enough to recognize what was at stake in San Antonio, not for me, but for the country.

But as the years ticked on under Allstate's zero sum game, I could see that the impunity enjoyed by the white collar criminal infesting San Antonio was a direct result of FBI inaction dating decades. In addition, the FBI was deeply distracted by its own troubles. Maybe they are just not up to the task, I fretted.

There was plenty to fret about.

As covert criminal operatives systematically attacked or infiltrated every institution in San Antonio, the FBI was lurching from one humiliating public catastrophe to another. Its reputation had never been in so much jeopardy.

The list of FBI intelligence failures was long and disturbing. They included Osama Bin Laden's successful September 11, 2001 attack on American soil, the ghastly 2016 Pulse Nightclub massacre, and the January 6, 2021 Trumpian mob attack on the U.S. Capitol. In every situation, the agency had warning that the actors posed a danger to the public but took no action.

At the same time, Russian hackers were systematically cyber attacking America's infrastructure,[87] where they found little resistance.[88]

To add insult to injury, an embarrassing video of an FBI agent went viral. It showed the agent performing a back flip in a nightclub, dropping his gun mid flip, and accidently shooting a bystander in the leg when he went to retrieve his weapon. His embarrassed shrug became an internet meme.

The FBI might prefer that I remained silenced rather than add my story to their growing list of failures, I began to think. Maybe that was why these criminals were able to break the law so brazenly. Maybe the FBI had no intention of investigating these organized crimes.

Later, I would learn that my doubt was reasonable. The FBI was terrible at protecting citizens who tried to help them and it often did ignore obvious, provable federal crimes.

Plus, the agency *had* been advised by McKinsey & Company.

By 2015, America's FBI problem was inescapable. Few cases cast the FBI in a more negative light than that of former U.S. Gymnastics Team doctor, serial sexual predator, and pedophile Larry Nassar. The doctor had gotten away with molesting young female gymnasts for years.

On September 2, 2015, after much anguish, top American gymnast McKayla Maroney mustered up the courage to report Nassar's abuse against her to the FBI in Indianapolis.

FBI agents listened aloofly to Maroney's account of horrific sexual abuse by Nassar. When she finished, an agent said coolly, "Is that all?"

The supervising agent, Michael Langeman, buried Maroney's allegations. He didn't even write a summary of her interview. He told no one.

Nassar continued to molest girls.

Under increasing pressure to do something about Nassar, USA Gymnastics officials then contacted the Los Angeles FBI. Agents in LA did open an investigation. They interviewed victims, made phone calls, and wrote reports. Then, they decided they *might* not have jurisdiction. They dropped the inquiry entirely. They also told no one.

For months after the FBI first heard Maroney's painful allegations, Nassar continued to have access to gymnasts at Michigan State University, a high school, and a gymnastics club. He molested dozens of additional young victims.

Even before interviewing Maroney, the FBI knew others had made allegations against Nassar. They had already met with USA Gymnastics officials to discuss mounting allegations against the doctor. They made no official report of that meeting, either. And when USA Gymnastics President Stephen D. Penny, Jr. provided agents with a thumb drive containing crucial evidence, the agents tucked it away, unrecorded.[89]

Later, the DOJ's Office of Inspector General began an investigation into what went wrong. The OIG discovered that the head of the FBI's Indianapolis Field Office, W. Jay Abbott, was applying for a $400,000 top security job with USA Gymnastics when his office buried evidence against a known pedophile.

Once the DOJ started investigating, the agent who hadn't bothered to record Maroney's interview quickly cobbled together a report. Created 17 months after the interview with the victim, it was mostly fiction.

"We concluded that the interview summary...contained materially false statements and omitted material information," the OIG found. "We further concluded that (Abbott) made materially false statements when twice questioned by the OIG about the victim interview."

The inspector general also found that Abbot violated ethics rules and displayed "extremely poor judgment" by applying for a job with USA Gymnastics while covering up serial sexual abuse against young female athletes under the organization's care.

Lawmakers were unanimously disgusted.

"It is shameful that the FBI, who was charged with investigating these horrific crimes and abuse, grossly failed to fulfill (its) duty," said Senator Marsha Blackburn (R-TN). "They sat idly by, they turned a blind eye."

Maroney testified before the Senate Judiciary Committee in 2021 about the cover up. The FBI agents' conduct, Maroney said, was "incredibly disturbing and illegal."

"Not only did the FBI not report my abuse, but when they eventually documented my report 17 months later, they made entirely false claims about what I said," the gymnast told senators. "I was shocked and deeply disappointed. They chose to lie about what I said and protect a serial child molester rather than protect not only me but countless others."[90]

Simone Biles, considered by many to be the greatest gymnast of all time, testified that she was also molested by Nassar. "It truly feels like the FBI turned a blind eye to us and went out of its way to help (Nassar and his enablers)," she said.

Then the four-time Olympic gold medalist asked a heartbreaking rhetorical question:

"How much is a little girl worth?"[91]

Indeed. Not only that, but these little girls were national treasures, some representing the United States at the highest level of international competition. And the FBI was indifferent to their victimization at the hands of a depraved and remorseless pedophile.

Alone and isolated in San Antonio, I knew that I certainly was not worth much. One need only look at dozens of SAPD police reports to see that.

I struggled to not lose hope. I began looking for evidence online that I *could* count on the FBI. I needed evidence that I was not alone and that, despite all of the abuse and systematic cover-ups, my life was not in danger.

I found the tragic case of Kim Groves.

The Desire Terrorist

Kim Groves was a pretty young mother living in New Orleans's Desire housing project in 1994 when she witnessed New Orleans police officer Len Davis brutally beating her nephew. Davis was a notoriously violent and corrupt cop, known in the city's 9th Ward as "Robocop" and "the Desire Terrorist." After the beating, Groves filed a police brutality complaint against Davis and another officer.

When he learned of Groves's police brutality complaint, Davis called drug dealer Paul Hardy and ordered him to kill Groves. On Oct. 13, 1994, Hardy gunned Groves down in the street. It was a day before her daughter Jasmine's 13th birthday.

It turned out that Davis was already under federal investigation for drug dealing. The cop didn't know the FBI was tapping his phone.

The federal wiretap captured his order to assassinate Groves. When Davis learned that the hit had been successful and that Groves was dead, he let out a primal scream of triumph. That, too, was captured on federal wiretap. The corrupt cop was eventually arrested, convicted, and sentenced to death for the murder of Kim Groves.[92] The former New Orleans cop remains on death row.

Groves's murder haunted me for a long time. I couldn't help but think: If the FBI recorded Len Davis ordering the murder of Kim Groves on a federal wiretap, why is Kim Groves not alive today?

I continued to make periodic visits to the San Antonio office of the FBI. I would give them evidence I was collecting, complain about the lack of intervention in Allstate's brutal oppression campaign, and try to glean some sense of what, if anything, federal investigators were doing about organized crime in San Antonio.

Even as they showed great interest in my documents and research, FBI agents listened to my complaints of oppression without expression.

I tried to absolve them for their inaction. Major investigations take time, I repeatedly told myself. Sure, the FBI is not in the business of reassuring informants. But after reading about the Kim Groves case, I began to feel even more insecure. My situation hadn't improved in years. In fact, the conspirators, emboldened by years of official inaction, doubled down on the attacks and the abuse.

I started feeling resentful. The FBI agents were enjoying a prestigious job with good pay and ample benefits while I remained stuck in a never-ending dystopian nightmare, systematically blocked from making a living and provoked at every turn. It didn't seem right. I brought it up on one of my visits to the FBI headquarters.

I pointed out to one duty officer that I had read the U.S. Attorney General's guidelines for FBI domestic investigations. According to the guidelines, domestic investigations, no matter how important, could not violate anyone's constitutional rights. I asked the agent how I could petition for an internal DOJ investigation into whether the FBI's refusal to intervene in my case violated my civil and/or constitutional rights as an American citizen.

That was the only time I saw a similarity between the FBI and local city and county authorities. The agent began to hem and haw, refusing to tell me how I could access the protective mechanisms of the agency. He began to stonewall. I asked how to get more eyes on what was happening in San Antonio so that I could feel safe.

He furtively palmed the nametag dangling from a lanyard around his neck and slipped the tag into his shirt pocket.

"I already know your name, Wagoner," I said.

His jaw dropped in surprise. His expression was so comical I laughed.

He eventually left the room and returned a few moments later with an agent who looked like he had just graduated from college. That agent wasn't wearing a name badge.

"This is my supervisor," Wagoner said. I disbelieved him. I began to cry. They stood there, looking at me silently. They did seem to have some mild sympathy for my plight. At least they weren't smirking, I noticed, which was novel. But they would take no action to protect my privacy, property, civil rights, or life.

That was the job of the local authorities who were committing the crimes.

I could see why people would start to hate the government.

"You people are radicalizing me," I said.

"Be careful," warned the agent.

I knew what he meant by that. The U.S. government does not like radicals, especially brown and black ones.

That's something you are good at, I thought bitterly.

Suppressing people who have had enough.

17 | DYSTOPIA

The gaslighting of America

MORE TIME PASSED. IT HAD been more than eight years since I sued Allstate and I was still under surveillance by Allstate operatives. By this time, the private investigators following me had been expanded and upgraded. The unshaven men in worn clothes and aging sedans were still there, but now so where foreign nationals and white-collar types driving late model luxury vehicles. I noticed it, but I had no context.

Most of the abuses I endured or witnessed were part of Allstate's zero sum game. Sometimes it was just the reality of the corruption plaguing America. It is clear, though, that the zero sum game could not have existed without the other. America had a corruption problem, and it was weakening the country, badly.

In 2020, the U.S. was rated number 25 in the Corruption Perception Index, tied with Chile and just above the Seychelles, who came in at 27. (Denmark, New Zealand, and Finland ranked as least corrupt while Syria, Somalia and South Sudan ranked most corrupt.) But the events I was witnessing in San Antonio suggested that the U.S.'s rightful place was much lower down the list. Not Somalia or Georgia, but probably closer to, say, Portugal, or maybe Botswana.

In fact, according to global indices, the United States is declining in terms of social progress,[93] largely fueled by unchecked corruption and poor education.

And to make matters worse, transnational private intelligence firms were treating the United States like a third world country, operating with the same checkbook impunity enjoyed by paramilitary groups in Colombia, minus the murder. As far as we know.

In 2018, Americans learned for the first time that private intelligence firms were operating freely in the United States.

First, there was Harvey Weinstein, a beneficiary of the phenomenon. Then there was Amazon billionaire Jeff Bezos, a victim of the phenomenon.

Women had for years accused Weinstein of rape, assault, and coercion, but the Hollywood producer managed to keep a lid on decades of criminal activity in part by the use of intelligence operatives. He paid millions to private intelligence firms like Israeli-based Black Cube and Kroll, who sent private spies using false identities to disrupt investigations into his serial sex crimes.[94]

In 2019, Bezos and his lover, former TV host Lauren Sanchez, were married to other people when someone captured passionate texts and racy photos between the pair from his cellphone. Bezos then announced that *National Inquirer* publisher David Pecker tried to blackmail him to get Bezos to stop looking into how the publisher ended up with his private communications.

When the texts and photos showed up in a *National Enquirer* article, Bezos quickly acknowledged the affair and divorced his wife. But how did the tabloid, run by Trump loyalist David Pecker, get the photos and texts from the billionaire's phone in the first place?

Long before covert operatives working for the *National Inquirer* lifted hot photos and texts from one of the world's richest men, I was complaining to local, state, and federal law enforcement authorities that criminals were freely using fake cell towers, known as IMSI catchers or Stingrays, to capture private communications in San Antonio. It was an illegal but effective way to stalk, frame, blackmail, and otherwise terrorize targets.

By the end of 2021, it seemed like SAPD was finally aware of them, too.

A few cops started actually taking down license plates and recording the names of the people I accused of hacking or stalking me. But it was still a crap shoot. I would request a police report only to find that it completely misrepresented what I reported or omitted key information. It was if I was dealing with two police departments: one serving San Antonio citizens and the other serving a clandestine criminal network.

What was left of the good SAPD was hobbled. Struggling to get a grip on this homegrown phenomenon of freewheeling spies running amok in the city, the police department was constantly undermined by its own cops. Legitimate police were at a severe disadvantage against a shadowy, sophisticated foe. Thousands of SAPD police reports, I knew, were works of fiction. How horrible it must be, I thought, to join a police force hoping to be a hero - only to find it so corrupted that you were considered a villain instead.

A record number of SAPD police officers began committing suicide.[95]

Cockroaches, goons, & zeros

By this time, San Antonio was crawling with Allstate operatives and their contract players. Most of the action was managed from a distance by operators for private intelligence firms. Those operatives hired private investigators to stalk me around the clock. They managed criminal hackers who intercepted my phone calls and emails. They orchestrated constant attacks on my finances, privacy, and security.

Intelligence firms are insanely expensive, but their clients get their money's worth. Operators will continue the work as long as they are getting paid. Invisible to most of their clients' targets, they are expert at creating havoc while insulating themselves and their clients from the repercussions of their criminal deeds. Intelligence firms call them "handlers."

Cockroaches, I called them.

Able to operate virtually unregulated in the United States, cockroaches hire local private investigators to add a layer between them and their client's target. Private investigators, also virtually unregulated in the Texas, do much of the legwork of harassing and snooping on their targets.

Goons, I called them.

Cockroaches and goons normally didn't hack my devices, rob, extort, kidnap, or assault me. They bribed a seemingly endless supply of enthusiastic locals to perform those crimes, always managing their workers from an acquitting distance.

Mounting evidence shows that the goons and cockroaches spend their time bribing and managing hundreds of people to do their dirty work. At this level, the number of co-conspirators explodes. Easily bribed, they quickly join the operation in exchange for quick cash or promises of opportunities down the road. It is the one thing that a junkie on the street has in common with the corrupt judge on the bench. They will do just about anything for money.

Zeroes, I call them.

The zeroes have a singular purpose: to do what they are told. The will circle a target's house with **IMSI** catchers or issue a bogus ruling from the bench. Despite major differences in salaries, education, and social status, they have one thing in common:

They are despicable people.

The street zeroes with average social skills will often try to engage the target. The idea is to get the target talking; it's a good way to gather intelligence. I called these zeroes "zombies." Their conversation is severely limited, distracted, manipulative, and inauthentic.

Evidence of the widespread use of covert private intelligence agents operating – often illegally – in the United States began popping up all over the country. One need just google the term "targeted individual" to see a burgeoning number of Americans reporting that they had been a victim of gangstalking. But as late as 2012, the FBI did not keep records of the phenomenon.[96]

I intrinsically knew that a company like Allstate didn't spend millions just to destroy one irksome claimant. I also knew that the level of corruption I was experiencing would show up in other ways and involve other people. I just had to bide my time.

Soon, I watched as zeroes implicated in documented criminal conduct began showing up in places of prominence in the city, often sponsored by the same officials who ignored my constant pleas for help.

Crime fighting, San Antonio Style

In 2016, Donald J. Trump became president of the United States, and for the first time, the country began seeing just how weak and ineffectual our government institutions had become. It seemed that folks in Washington were thwarting, ignoring, and violating U.S. laws at will. But while many bemoaned the national view, I saw the chaos and lawlessness in Washington as a predictable outgrowth of what was happening unexplored at the local level.

In 2016, I sent a settlement demand letter to Joe Gonzales, outlining in painful detail how he had contributed to the malicious assault prosecution and covered up Combs' documented fraud. He ignored the letter.

I filed a complaint with the state bar against Gonzales. By this time, I knew that nothing would come of the effort. My overtures to protective institutions had become little more than exercises in creating records. As expected, the bar dismissed the complaint and reminded me that the grievance process was confidential.

By this time, most of the officials I contacted must have been aware of the harassment and stalking, and I wondered if it served their purposes not to step in. After all, it didn't necessarily breed confidence in the government if organized criminal networks could subvert the law at will, order judges around, and count on an army of arrogant attorneys – which they were clearly doing in Bexar County. If stalkers, hackers, and corrupt officials could make it impossible for someone to expose their crimes, they would also cover up the many failures of government officials. For many local bureaucrats, there seemed to be no upside to intervening on behalf of the powerless Denise McVea.

Hackers continued to intercept communications. Cars continued to circle my home.

Desperate for help, I tried repeatedly to contact my city councilmember, county commissioner, the chief of police, the city manager, mayor, and state representative for help. I could never get through. Emails, phone calls and letters were never returned.

One day, I was canvassing the blocks around my house looking for parked goons when I saw an interesting sight. Michael Helle, the San Antonio Police union president, had just parked his car on a residential side street in the middle of the day. I watched as Helle locked his car, looked around briefly, and then walked down the street to Commerce Street. I followed at a distance. What is he up to? I wondered. He crossed the busy commercial intersection and slipped into a hotel. The hotel had been one of several used by Allstate cockroaches, I knew, but he could have just as easily been skulking in for some illicit sexual interlude. I decided that while his behavior was definitely suspicious, I had no proof it involved the corrupt and criminal activity of the cops harassing me on the Eastside.

But I did not like Michael Helle. From my point of view, he used his position as president of the police union to protect bad cops. He also seemed to be reading from a script. He didn't seem very smart, and yet he always knew what to say. Like Michael Steel, president of the fire union, Helle did not have the brainpower to create and manage the destructive strategies aimed at San Antonio's local government. In other words, I saw Helle as a front man, a puppet, an "informant".

And while Helle and Brockhouse ran interference between bad cops and the city, San Antonio's crime rates soared.

Per capita, the laidback city of San Antonio had more serious crimes than 15 of the country's largest cities, according to a *San Antonio Express-News* analysis.[97] It now had higher rates of serious and violent crime than cities like Los Angeles and Chicago and twice as many serious crimes as New York City.[98]

Perhaps as a tacit acknowledgement that the city was under a crime deluge that threatened national security, federal government surveillance planes, normally used to police the US-Mexico border, began circling San Antonio's East and West sides.[99]

I knew that the soaring crime rates were inevitable considering the obscene level of corruption plaguing the city. We were cursed with a corrupted judiciary, police force, county and city government, and lawyer class. Our suffering was compounded by an unresponsive state government that refused to intervene and a federal investigation that seemed to have stalled in place.

On March 28, 2017, FBI supervisor Robert Krupa asked the public to help fight corruption in South Texas. "If nobody reports it, then we don't know where to investigate," he said.[100]

But I knew the FBI had plenty of evidence.

I wrote letters to city council members and county commissioners. I had written to Judge Arteaga, court administrators, the Civil Rights Project, the district attorney's office, the chief of police and the FBI. Taken together, the letters told a clear story of systematized corruption, organized crime, and abuse of power. The government in Texas just seemed to be a bunch of people who, at best, were taking home steady paychecks without having to do the work. It was no wonder Americans were so disgusted. The country was failing at just about every level. Who could we count on to raise a defense against the evil forces tearing at our social fabric?

I looked in city hall. I looked in county, state, and federal government. I looked in civil society. I looked in civil rights groups and human rights groups. I looked in the police department and I looked in the FBI. I looked in the media, both print and broadcast. ("That's scary," one broadcast journalist told me.) I looked here and I looked there; I looked everywhere. I looked in every nook and cranny. Even when they believed me, there was little anyone could do. I found no heroes.

I guess I'm going to have to be the hero, I mumbled resentfully.

The mayor's police forum

The citizens of San Antonio were getting sick of police misconduct. It was out of control. In an effort to address citizens' concerns about police misconduct, then-mayor Ivy Taylor convened a task force. Citizens focused on accountability. Officials focused on public relations. Taylor invited police brass, city council members, community activists, university scholars, and religious leaders.

In December 2016, I learned that the task force was going to have a public meeting. I decided to attend. I wanted to talk about some of the abuses I had witnessed and encountered and about the fictitious police reports.

A man in sunglasses, baseball cap and full beard slowly shadowed me in a dark sports car as I walked from my car to city hall.

I entered an airy lobby. A security guard behind a security station greeted me politely. He pointed out the conference room where the meeting was to take place. It felt strange: I couldn't remember the last time a person in uniform treated me with respect.

In the room, community representatives shared round tables with councilmembers, academics, and police officers. A local pastor opened the session with a prayer. I was one of about six observers. We sat off to the side in a bank of chairs with a view of the discussion. On the other side of the room, a small contingent of television and print journalist sat, taking notes and filming. The *Express-News* reporter Emilie Eaton and other journalists took up space across the room. Behind them to the left stood two high-level SAPD officers, their uniforms dripping with brass. The chief was absent.

The handsome but diminutive district attorney Nico LaHood sat at one round table like an impish schoolboy forced into detention. Almost immediately after the meeting started, he received a phone call. "I'm on my way," he said dramatically, and with an apologetic shrug toward the mayor, escaped the room.

LaHood is a terrible actor, I thought, but then conceded that he *had* convinced San Antonians that he had changed from the days of his youth when he was a major dealer of Ecstasy.

During my speech at the mayor's police forum, I pointed out that the police officers on the Eastside were providing cover for a lot of the criminal activity that plagued the area. It was a serious threat to public safety and national security, I said. SAPD officers were routinely omitting important information from police reports, I told the group. If the American intelligence agencies hoped to stand a chance in this new world of existential threats, they would have to have access to reliable data. I pointed out that the police patrol report was the first line of data gathering and that it needed to be complete and accurate.

Keely Petty, who had minutes before introduced herself as a pastor from the Eastside, piped up and said I had talked long enough.

I ignored her. When I finished Mayor Taylor responded that I wasn't the first person to point out the problem with police reports. It was something that had been discussed, she said. McManus, the chief of police had arrived and, pushed by an audience member to respond to the issues I raised, said that the police department had asked the FBI for help. He said he would be glad to talk to me about it, but when I called his office to schedule a meeting, I got the runaround.

Tommy Adkisson, the former county commissioner who helped approve questionable title transfers through his Eastside law office also attended the meeting. He shot me a few appraising glances. I made it a point to always return his gaze. I could see that he wasn't expecting that. His eyes dropped every time. Soon he stopped looking in my direction.

At some point, Adkisson popped up and made a quick, self-conscious speech about mental health.

I pursed my lips. To me, his ad hoc contribution to the discussion was scripted, a way to announce his participation in this important public meeting. I predicted that the *Express-News* reporter Emilie Eaton would quote him over a dozen others who had something relevant to say.

I was right. Eaton devoted an entire paragraph to Adkisson's mental health comment even though it had little to do with the topic being discussed.

She left unexplored my comments about misleading police reports.

The day after the forum, although wholly uninterested in what I had to say about fraudulent police reports and their threat to national security, the newspaper ran a large photo of me addressing the mayor's group.

I looked like death warmed over.

Burying the nut at the *Express-News*

In Journalism 101, students quickly learn that the most important paragraph in a newspaper article is the *nut graf.* Sometimes spelled "nut graph," the nut graf tells the reader what the story is about. It is the "meat" of the article, the reason the reader is reading. For a lot of reasons, the nut graf has to be high up in the story.

Editors constantly ask cub reporters, "where's your nut?" meaning that they have been reading for a while and still don't know why. If the nut graf is not high up in the story, the reader may lose interest, or worse, miss the point entirely.

Journalists call that "burying the nut." It is a fundamental failure of journalism.

When it came to covering corruption and abuse of power in San Antonio, the city's lone daily newspaper had a habit of burying the nut.

Some stories that were appearing in the local daily newspaper were almost willfully missing the point of the activity it was reporting on. It seemed the paper framed abuse by local officials in the most benign light possible and rarely used the word corruption.

In general, local print editors and TV producers often treated crimes against Eastside residents as a reality not worthy of further exploration. And they dutifully defaulted to police versions of disputed events, despite communicating to a public that did not consider the police credible. Follow up Metro articles about crime rarely went beyond the ritual laments of Eastside pastors. And despite a growing number of reports of problematic jury verdicts in Bexar County courts, the paper didn't bother to get to the bottom of it.

After years of trying to get reporters to cover the police and judicial misconduct, I began to see the faulty framing as deliberate.

For instance, after George Floyd's murder by Minneapolis cops, Emilie Eaton, the *Express-News* criminal justice reporter, consistently failed to mention that the victim was handcuffed, prone, and cooperating when cop Derek Chauvin suffocated him to death. I finally complained to the paper's new editor when Eaton referred to innocent teen Trayvon Martin as a man when forced to remind readers that Trayvon was stalked and gunned down in cold blood by vigilante George Zimmerman. The next time she mentioned Floyd, she again failed to mention the handcuffs.

And Brian Chasnoff, one of the paper's most prolific writers, was a master at minimizing the citizens' growing alarm at widespread corruption and abuse, in my opinion.

None of the newspaper reporters I had contacted about "really good stories" had ever responded to my tips. Neither had the enterprise editor, David Sheppard. I tried a number of ways to get the paper interested in the civil courts' wholesale default judgments against pro se litigants. I wrote certified letters and sent emails. The paper would not cover this important access to justice story. Conversely, the *Express-News* printed an unhinged article by columnist Gloria Padilla whereby she harshly criticized restorative justice judge Grace Uzomba for being hard working and providing public records to, well, the public. The column was jarring in its outrage given the paper's silence on the illegal rejection of thousands of poor people's civil lawsuits.[101]

I wondered what would happen if I wrote the top editor of the paper. After all, I told myself, maybe he wasn't aware that important stories about abuse of power and corruption were going untold. So I wrote editor Mike Leary and sent the letter certified mail, return receipt requested. I told him about the title fraud, the unconstitutional default judgments, and the police protection of the drug operation at 315 S. Olive, among other things. He didn't respond. No reporter from the *Express-News* called me.

Leary would soon retire from the newspaper and head off to explore Antarctica. Frustrated with my inability to get *Express-News* editors or reporters to cover the well-documented corruption stories imperiling my community, I bade him a snarky goodbye in the comments section of the paper's retirement article. He would always be remembered, I wrote, for his dismissal of the concerns of the people on the Eastside.

"Enjoy, Antarctica!" I wrote snidely.

I had accepted that most of my communications were probably intercepted by Allstate's illegal wiretap program. But I was certain that some of my communications had gotten through.

Just to be sure, I decided to walk some paperwork into the newsroom. The first time, I got no further than the guard stand. The guard took the documents and assured me he would deliver them to the city desk. "I won't read them," he promised, oddly.

The second time, the guard abruptly left the stand when I entered the building. His abrupt departure left me alone in the lobby so I took the elevator up to the city desk. I didn't know what floor the city desk was on so I hit all of the buttons.

Hands down, it was the weirdest elevator trip I had ever taken. The place was like a phantom ship, whole floors empty and abandoned. When I found the city desk, a dozen or so reporters inhabited a bank of cubicles in a corner. I was shocked.

"Is this it?" I asked the receptionist, astonished.

"This is it," she said resignedly. The newspaper was in the process of moving to more modern digs on Broadway, but it was also drastically downsizing. Thirty years ago, I looked over a sea of heads in the newsroom in a city half the size of San Antonio. Now, the *Express-News*, like papers across the nation, had radically reduced staff in a desperate bid for survival. Between 2005 and 2021, more than 2,500 newspapers in the U.S. closed down.[102] The tiny hub of local print reporters typing away was to me a striking visual. I felt like I was looking at a final stage in the painful demise of the American newspaper. It was sad.

I asked to speak to the city desk editor. Audrey Lee came out. She was casually dressed with long brown hair and a kind expression. I told her I had some good stories about corruption and handed her a pack of documents. I gave a quick rundown. "That sounds like something for our criminal justice reporter, Emilie Eaton," Lee said. "I think she's here."

We both looked over to that small gaggle of reporters in the corner. Eaton was there.

The reporter looked up and saw me. A look of pure terror crossed her face. She grabbed the phone, put it to her ear and put her head down. When Audrey Lee tried to get her attention, she ignored her.

"I'll get Emilie to help," Lee told me.

Good luck, I thought.

She walked over to Eaton's desk. Eaton looked up briefly and gave a helpless look. She was on a very important phone call. With the reporter unavailable, Lee decided to hear me out. She took me to small table near a large window. I gave her the packet of information that I held and, trying to be succinct, I told her about the default judgments, the false arrests, the malicious prosecutions, the forgeries, the staggering thefts and abuse, and about how Joe Gonzales took my money and then served me up to county judge Scott Roberts. "It's a lot to unpack," I acknowledged, "but there are some good stories in there."

An hour later, Eaton was still on the phone. Lee walked me out.

Emilie will get in touch with you, Lee told me, but she didn't.

At the mayor's forum I had personally handed Eaton a press release from the Auris Project that outlined how Precinct 4 justice of the peace Rogelio Lopez was helping third-party debt collector Portfolio Recovery Associates violate a federal consent decree by accepting debt cases against thousands of poor Eastsiders without federally required proof.

Months later, when the newspaper finally ran an article about third-party debt collectors operating in Texas, the paper presented Portfolio's illegal activities in the justice of the peace courts as a successful business story.

Once again, the *San Antonio Express-News* had buried the nut.

The activist lawyer

It dawned on me one day that I had not received a single return email or phone call from dozens of sources and advocates I had reached out to.

Over time, as I gained cyber security skills, I realized that there were plenty of hardworking advocates who were doing good work on behalf of the community and who could be powerful allies. They needed my help and I need theirs. But the cockroaches' ability to control my communications meant that they could control who I contacted and who contacted me.

Internet searches brought up pages that my hackers had built. When I made a search for civil rights attorneys, for instance, only webpages for lawyers I had already identified as Allstate enablers popped up. Results for "civil rights" attorneys in San Antonio included divorce attorney Deanna L. Whitley, who berated me for questioning the judges' default judgments against unwitting Bexar County plaintiffs; Cappuccio, who brought false unauthorized practice of law charges against me, and John D. Carlos, the attorney who hovered inexplicably around the *McVea v. Keller* Allstate case.

If someone tried to call me, I would never know it because the criminal operators could easily intercept those calls.

But as I ducked and dodged Allstate hackers online, I began slowly connecting to good people doing good work. One such person was a lawyer out of Austin, Ware Wendell, executive director of Texas Watch.

I visited Ware Wendell in his Austin office. As usual, Allstate goons stalked me to Texas Watch's door.

The organization sat in a small, nicely appointed suite. I didn't have an appointment, but the staff member greeted me politely and said that Wendell was on his way back to the office. When he arrived, he invited me back.

A steady man with a Vandyke moustache, Wendell listened to my tale with respectful attention. I told him about the judges, the arrests, the hacking. I told him about the cybercrimes. "Allstate has become a criminal organization," I told him. "They are engaging in widespread, unchecked criminality in Bexar County."

He didn't seem at all surprised.

He had been fighting to hold insurance companies accountable at the Texas Capitol for years. He took me seriously, but, he warned, Texas Watch was a small organization without many resources and the organization already had its hands full. He asked me what he could do to help.

I realized that I didn't know.

"We could schedule a talk," he suggested helpfully.

The last thing I wanted was to be standing in front of a bunch of lawyers who wanted to help but couldn't make sense of the confusing story I was trying to tell. So many players, so many crimes. It sounded fantastical even to me and I had lived it. The conspiracy was so widespread and complicated that I knew it would be difficult without a full accounting of Allstate's networks, partners, and crimes. I would have to finish the book.

"I - I ... I still have a lot of work to do," I stammered.

But I left with a renewed sense of purpose. Wendell, who had been watching insurance companies and corrupt politicians for years, found little extraordinary about the insane tale I had just shared with him. People who had been paying attention are ready to believe me, I realized. I just had to do the work of making it easy for them.

Hackers continued to intercept my emails in man-in-the-middle attacks, and mules continued to circle my house with **IMSI** catchers.

18 | SPECTACLE

Debates, resolutions, and fraud

By 2018, Joe Gonzales, the billboard attorney who served me up to County Court 12 judge Scott Roberts, was running for district attorney as a Democrat. The newspaper reported that George Soros had awarded his purported civil reform campaign almost a million dollars. All Gonzales had to do was mimic progressive talking points and feign commitment to judicial reform. He had a realistic chance of winning the election, and La Hood had been a major disappointment, so Gonzales got the money.

Meanwhile, I struggled to develop the Auris Project into a publishing company. But I often despaired. I spent half of my days spoofing my own MAC address and jumping from VPN servers all over the world trying to evade my relentless online attackers. Sometimes it worked, but often it didn't. I also spent countless hours, sometimes 12 hours a day, recovering my devices from malware inserted during the attacks.

By the time I staggered into the Democratic Party headquarters during the 2018 primaries, I saw immediately that it was under attack. I visited the local party headquarters in early 2018 but instead of encountering a bustling operation, the place was essentially empty and the lights were out. A woman came in from outside and sat at the front desk. I told her I wanted to talk to Manuel Medina, the local Democratic Party chairman. He's not here, she told me. She was acting very strangely. Rodney Kidd and Adrian Flores, two of Medina's advisors, also walked in from outside.

It was a strange conversation. I asked for information about the county convention where local delegates were selected to attend the state convention to be held later that year in Fort Worth.

The date hadn't been picked, Kidd told me. He would have to get back to me on that. Kidd rambled on about communications programs he was building with Medina. I couldn't make sense of much of what he said. It all seemed so random and untethered. When I asked specific questions, he hemmed and hawed. At some point, he invited me to a back room. That room was also unlit. It was empty except for a single folding chair. A young man sat in the chair, typing on a computer that rested on his lap because there was no table. It was odd. It felt like he had just slipped in through a back door.

I left the office with no sense that the Bexar County Democratic Party was doing much in terms of empowering the Democratic voter. I called and texted Kidd a number of times to get the date of the county convention, but he refused to give me an answer. I ended up finding it another way. When I drove to a far Southside school to attend the event, goons followed. Only a handful of people attended the county convention, that, it turned out, Medina had quietly scheduled on the same day as the popular Cesar Chavez march.

That's how I became a delegate to the state democratic convention; I had no competition. When it came time to suggest resolutions to be adopted by Texas Democrats, I quickly decided to author an anti-corruption resolution. It was unanimously adopted. It read:

DRAFT RESOLUTION
ADOPTED at the Bexar County Democratic Party Convention on March 24, 2018.

Strengthening Anti-Corruption Laws and Oversight
WHEREAS Texas suffers from endemic public corruption, lack of oversight, and reliable penalties for public officials engaging in corrupt acts,

AND WHEREAS corrupt acts by public officials include abuse of authority, graft, nepotism, white-collar crime, and other fiduciary malfeasance and mismanagement,

AND WHEREAS public corruption impedes economic progress for all communities, weakens public safety, and tears at the social fabric,

THEREFORE, BE IT RESOLVED that the Democratic Party calls on Democratic leadership to make anti-corruption measures a top priority of the Democratic Party Platform,

AND BE IT FURTHER RESOLVED that anti-corruption measures be drafted for consideration and ultimate enactment.

Author: Denise McVea, Delegate

Hoping to shepherd the resolution to adoption, I signed on to represent Senate District 19 on the state convention's resolution committee. But by the time the convention rolled around, the draft had been mysteriously moved to the platform committee, where it quietly died.[103]

That was my introduction to Manuel Medina, a sly political operative who had quickly propelled to the top of San Antonio's incestuous political village.

First elected as Bexar County Democratic Party chair in 2011, he had an unconventional backstory. Born in Mexico, he grew up in California, earned a master's degree in engineering from UT Austin, and, according to the *San Antonio Report*, became a successful political consultant in the U.S. and Latin America while at the same time opening a 500-unit call center and a public relations and political consulting firm.[104]

Outwardly charming, Medina would eventually lose his luster.

When he ran for mayor in 2017, he used the Bexar County Democratic Party headquarters as his campaign office. During his unsuccessful mayoral bid, motorists driving down Interstate 10 West could see a large Medina for Mayor billboard resting atop the party HQ building. According to Medina's campaign expense reports, his campaign paid the rent on the party building and the utilities.[105]

Medina's mayoral campaign was a flop. Local Democrats were not impressed. He flip-flopped. He comingled personal, party, and campaign funds. He courted both progressives and conservatives. He signed onto a conservative anti-gay platform and then touted an endorsement from a LGBTQ group that local gay activists said didn't exist.

He made promises that he didn't keep. He was too glib, too facile. He had an answer for everything, and yet made nothing clear. For instance, when party officials asked him about running his mayoral campaign from party headquarters, he answered that he had leased the building under his own name. "Questions?" he parried. "Sound familiar?[106]

When Democrats were trying to raise a defense against Republican president Donald J. Trump, the local Democratic party chairman was focusing almost exclusively on his personal ambition to become mayor of San Antonio.

"Our party was non-existent (under Medina)," BCDP executive committee member Rose Marie DeHoyos told Texas Public Radio.[107]

Medina's decision to run for mayor turned out to be a costly strategic mistake. It gave San Antonians a clearer, more intimate look at the gregarious Democratic county chairman – and citizens clearly did not like what they saw. Monica Alcántara, a mostly unknown paralegal, ran against him for the position of party chair. She walloped him by a 2 to 1 margin. At election's end, Alcántara had captured 67 percent of the vote to Medina's meager 33 percent. After six years as the leader of the local Democratic Party, Medina was out. For the first time in a long time, someone other than Medina and his cronies would be looking into the party's financial accounts.

Medina immediately went into attack mode, unleashing a campaign of chaos on the new leader that almost brought the Bexar County Democratic Party to its knees.

The Naughty Table

Despite graciously conceding his loss to Alcántara in the media, Medina did not go quietly into that good night. He locked the party out of the headquarters he said he leased under his own name and, with the help of the local executive committee's secretary and treasurer, blocked the new chairwoman from accessing local party documents, including financial records.

On December 11, 2018, I learned that the Bexar County Democratic Party, now operating without a physical headquarters, would be holding its executive meeting at a local Luby's restaurant.

About 200 people, mostly precinct chairs, crammed into the cafeteria's private banquet hall. Rodney Kidd, Manuel Medina's communication person who hosted my bizarre visit to the old HQ and then refused to return my calls, sidled up beside me in an overfriendly, fake way. I knew he had been sent over by someone.

"Step away from me, sir," I murmured tightly. I didn't have time for his gaslighting. He feigned surprise. I repeated myself. He shrugged and with that familiar smirk moved about a foot away. I ignored him.

I described the meeting in the *Lamp*:

> A disruptive faction continued to wreak havoc on the Bexar County Democratic Party, disrupting an executive committee meeting December 11 before storming out en masse in an apparently staged exodus.
>
> The unseemly display came as BCDP treasurer Stephanie Carrillo and secretary Garret Mormando continue to withhold crucial party financial records. Both Mormando and Carrillo joined the walkout just minutes before Carrillo was supposed to present her treasurer's report. The BCDP bank account has a balance of just under $740.
>
> The meeting, held at the Luby's on Main Street, was defined by constant hullabaloo, mostly coming from a single table. Faction cronies yelled out insults, booed attempts to gain order, talked in loud asides during presentations, and huddled in roving groups.

Known as *manuelistas* for their loyalty to former chairman Manuel Medina, the group comprised about 40 precinct chairs and a handful of handlers.

Current chairwoman Monica Alcántara calmly soldiered on through the disruptions. She managed to swear in 15 new precinct chairs and six precinct coordinators.

By the time of the meeting, party members were well aware of Alcántara's repeated request for party records and how she learned the documents had been removed from the premises without her knowledge or permission. Alcántara, who beat Medina in the primaries, has been the brunt of numerous attempts to sabotage her chairmanship since her win. Still, she appeared confident and assertive throughout the raucous executive committee meeting.

But at every single turn, the disrupting faction tried to derail the process. At one point, the *manuelistas* tried to replace the approved agenda for one with attachments critical of Alcántara. The body handily defeated that motion, but only after the ensuing ruckus forced everyone to get out of their seats and move to the front to be counted. The *manuelistas* clamored for a recount twice.

Manual Medina was not present, but his thuggish henchman Adrian Flores stalked the room, berating Alcántara from the floor and terrorizing party members.

At one point, Flores assaulted a young male member. Towering over him, Flores placed his face within a hair's breadth of the cowering man's face and shouted, "What are you going to do about it? I'm a man! I'm a man!" Security guards finally escorted Flores from the building.

San Antonio Express-News columnist Brian Chasnoff characterized the meeting as party members being "at each other's throats." He noted that Carrillo and Mormando have ignored repeated request by the chairwoman to present financial and other party records.

Both Mormando and Carrillo have refused to allow Alcántara access to bank statements, lease agreements, tax filings and other records, Chasnoff wrote.

"Inside their offices, Alcántara found these documents missing. In the treasurer's office, she found an empty safe," Chasnoff reported.

He also reported that for some odd reason, neither the officers nor the landlord would provide Alcántara a copy of the party headquarters' property lease – despite repeated requests.

But Chasnoff failed to mention two developments that put all of the commotion in a much clearer – and disturbing – light.

First, precinct chair Anthony Blasi announced that only one of two local fundraising accounts connected to the state online donation website actually paid into Bexar County Democratic coffers.

This striking revelation places the onus on Medina and his cronies to explain how party funds were spent before he was ousted in the primaries. And it makes Mormando's and Carrillo's removals of party records look suspiciously like criminal activity.

Second, Chasnoff made no mention of a letter the *manuelistas* attached to their failed substitute agenda. In the letter, attorney Robert W. Wilson informed Alcántara that Carrillo and Mormando had retained him "regarding the claims you made".

Even though Alcántara had not publically spoken of a lawsuit, Wilson stated that she had "no right to any legal remedies" and insisted that the removal of party records was a matter for the party, not a court of law.

"The claims made by you do not allow a court of law to exercise jurisdiction," Wilson wrote.

"You are causing an embarrassment to the Bexar County Democratic Party," he added. "These issues are to be resolved by the Party and not by you acting personally and without authorization."

That letter puts a terrible light on the disruptive antics of the *manuelistas*. The strategy seems clear: keep the controversy as the business of the party, and then make sure the party cannot conduct business.

The Lamp could not reach Alcántara, but in a letter to precinct chairs after the meeting, she characterized Wilson's letter as a "contest to my right to access (party) documents" and reported that she had hired a lawyer in response.

"History has shown us the importance of transparency and fiscal integrity within our party," she stated, "which is why I am insisting these documents be made available."

She also announced the formation of an ad hoc committee, the Bexar County Democratic Party Transparency and Financial Integrity Commission. The commission will review procedures, financial documents, and other records and make periodic reports to the executive committee.

A second new ad hoc committee, the special projects committee, will put together fundraisers and other special projects for the party.
[108]

Despite the commotion, Alcántara calmly plodded forward with the meeting. I didn't know her, but watching her on that stage steadily doing the party's business while Medina's followers ran amok, I felt a surge of admiration. This chick is tough, I thought. It gave me hope.

Express-News columnist Brian Chasnoff, who had consistently painted the discord as a mere factional dispute, stood near a wall and watched the chaos, entertained.

I found his smirk so infuriating I approached him and snapped a close-up photo, enjoying his surprise and sudden discomfort. I later used the photo in a *Lamp* article I titled "The Naughty Table" that outlined the discord and the obvious reasons behind it. The photo cutline read, "*Express-News* columnist Brian Chasnoff reported on the story – but left out a few important details".[109]

When precinct chair Anthony Blasi told the rapidly dwindling crowd about party funds apparently being diverted, I looked to see where Chasnoff was. He was standing outside the door, talking indulgently to Medina aide Deborah Spence. It's a firing offense for a journalist to ignore the financial report of a political group under such conflict while present at a meeting he was assigned to cover. A day after the meeting, the paper made no mention of the fund diversion.

Brian Chasnoff had buried the nut.

After the raucous meeting, a group of *manuelistas* approached me and began insulting Alcántara. "She's homophobic and she is racist," said one of the *manuelistas*. The others nodded vigorously.

"I don't think so," I said doubtfully. I had, just weeks before, watched Alcántara pay loving tribute to her lesbian daughter from her inauguration ceremony stage. I asked the women why they thought she was racist. "You need to talk to Deborah Spence," one woman told me. "She won't even open a campaign office on the Eastside." I dismissed that as well. I had already spoken to Spence about her desire for a campaign office on the Eastside at a secretive Joe Gonzales/Nico LaHood district attorney debate in the Claude Black Community Center basement that had invited no Eastsiders. I left that conversation thinking that it sounded like just another Eastside expense account with little oversight. I would have declined the request, too, if I were Monica Alcántara. But what was clear was that Medina's minions were on a campaign to defame the new chairwoman to anyone who would listen.

WANTING TO GET A CLOSER look at the BCDP, I joined the Bexar County Election Integrity and Voter Protection Committee but with the exception of one zombie, the organization under Alcántara was running like a well-oiled machine.

I knew that being on the committee was a waste of my time. I needed to be concentrating on getting the book finished, so I resigned. Besides, I thought with relief, Alcántara, her staff, and the legitimate precinct chairs had everything well in hand, going about the party's business with alacrity and resolve. I admired them. I viewed them as the front line.

It took months, but the BCDP finally managed to get an audit of the financial operations under Medina. They found unexplained payments to party insiders and folks outside of the party. According to Alcántara, the financial records showed evidence of not just financial malfeasance, but forgery and money laundering.[110] More than $300,000 was unaccounted for, Alcántara said.[111]

"We are unable to discover any supporting documentation to substantiate the expenditure of hundreds of thousands of dollars," Alcántara told broadcast journalist Jim Lefko in March 2019.

On Wednesday, March 12, 2019, Alcántara called for the immediate resignation of party treasurer Stephanie Carrillo and party secretary Garrett Marmondo. Alcántara said former chair Manuel Medina was also heavily involved in the chaos. Alcántara said she felt compelled to share what she had learned after a local party commission found evidence of money laundering, forgery, theft, fraud, and conspiracy.

Alcántara took the information to both the district attorney and the county sheriff. They encouraged her to go to the FBI.

Medina remained mostly silent.

But while public radio news stations dutifully reported on at least some of Medina's misdeeds and financial shenanigans, other news outlets inexplicably framed the issue as a mere factional dispute. Indeed, newspaper reporters largely ignored or downplayed Medina's refusal to peacefully transfer power or release financial records.[112] Instead, *Express-News* journalists began referring to two local Democratic Parties using a narrative that bestowed de facto legitimacy on Medina's illegitimate campaign to keep control of party power after having been voted out. The newspaper referred to the *manuelistas*, as a "rival group".[113]

The *manuelistas* not only disrupted party meetings. They would call their own meetings, and then send out emails that the real party meeting had been canceled. They once improperly endorsed three charter amendments from the local firefighter's union, two of which eventually passed.

Even though they refused her authority and hid financial records, Mormando and Carrillo sued Alcántara to continue in their roles as secretary and treasurer.[114] They lost their lawsuit. The executive committee finally removed them from their positions as secretary and treasurer, respectively. Mormando was removed for, among other things, "intercepting mail, abandoning his position during meetings, making a major expenditure without proper authorization," and representing the executive committee without authorization. Carrillo had forged checks and committed other financial misconduct, according to Alcántara.[115]

After "The Naughty Table" article ran, Mormando approached a mutual friend.

"Garrett Mormando wants to speak to you," Barbara Renaud Gonzalez told me. We were meeting to discuss the launch of her book, *Dear San Antonio, I'm Gone but Not Lost* that Auris Books Press was publishing. It was a well written, inventive look at the life of San Antonio voting rights hero Willie Velasquez. Barbara had known Mormando for years. When he saw that she had written a column in the *Lamp*, he called her to complain about the article. He wanted to set the record straight. Yes, I told her, I'd be glad to talk to Garrett Mormando.

"He says you're not a real reporter," Renaud Gonzalez told me. I laughed.

But before I could call, Mormando and I stumbled into each other outside the Claude Black Community Center during the District 2 runoff election. Deborah Spence, Medina's Eastside aide, stood in the gaggle of campaign workers set up in the parking lot. She recognized me and approached. After a brief discussion where I declined her suggestion to vote for her candidate, I walked inside and voted for Jada Sullivan-Smith.

On my way back to my car, I saw Spence gesture to a thin, middle-aged white man, who quickly made his way towards me as I was putting something in my trunk. It was Mormando, the former BCDP treasurer. Anxious and wary, he told me that he didn't think the article I had written in the *Lamp* about the Luby's meeting was fair.

"You don't know the whole story," he told me. I asked him to tell me what I had gotten wrong, but he was short on specifics. The more we talked the more relaxed he became. The more relaxed he became, the more he talked. He seemed like a nice guy.

Mormando shared a little of his experience as secretary of the BCDP. He had been volunteering at the BCDP headquarters when Medina handpicked him to become the secretary, he shared. Medina called him into his office, told him he had potential, and asked him if he wanted the position. It was, Mormando said, one of the proudest days of his life. But as he spoke, he again grew anxious, insisting that he had done nothing wrong and that he was confident that Medina and his cronies would stand by him through his present ordeal. "I know where the bodies are buried," he said.

We chatted amiably for a few minutes. A man that neither of us knew walked away from the crowd of campaign workers and inserted himself in our conversation.

"You look like the actor Idris Elba," I told him. He thanked me and babbled on about nothing in particular, dominating the conversation. Losing interest, Mormando ambled off. The man abruptly ended his monologue and followed Mormando back to the gaggle of campaign workers.

I was getting a good look at the forces undermining the local Democratic Party. It was not a pretty sight. It was obvious to me that Manuel Medina, the former county chair, was behind the rancor. The disruption seemed calculated to undermine the current chair's ability to determine what Medina and his cronies had done with party funds. To that aim, Medina worked hand-in-hand with local attorney Robert Woodridge "Woody" Wilson.

Wilson sued Alcántara to keep Mormando and Carrillo in their party positions and to reinstate several precinct chairs that Alcántara had dismissed. Effectively blocking the new chair from accessing key financial records, Wilson would alternate between accusing Alcántara of being divisive and calling for party unity.

"We're all Democrats," Wilson would proclaim at a news conference after civil judge Stryker declined to reinstate Mormando and Carrillo. "We are not divided. We should be together."

Reporting on the Luby's fiasco for the *Lamp*, I called to interview Wilson at his law office. The lawyer who confidently handled questions at press conferences with shallow talking points seemed unusually nervous as he spoke to me on the phone. I asked him about a letter he had written Alcántara, rejecting her efforts to get party records. I could hear the trepidation and uncertainty in his voice over the phone line. Wilson explained that the courts had no jurisdiction over party affairs (that was before he unsuccessfully sued Alcántara in district court on Mormando's and Carrillo's behalf) and that the disputes roiling the party needed to be handled internally.

I thought it was all bullshit.

It wasn't the first time Wilson was at the head of a pack disrupting an important civic institution in San Antonio.

For several years, he was front and center in a raucous dispute challenging leadership in the august organization League of United Latin American Citizens. His antics challenging the leadership in LULAC was so disruptive that police physically removed him from a 2013 convention. And here he was again, front and center of a bizarre power struggle, this time involving allegations of fraud, forgery, and other crimes.

I thanked Wilson for his statement and signaled the end of the interview. I could hear the relief in his voice as we signed off. I knew exactly why he was nervous. At the time, I did not know about Alcántara's allegations of forgery against Medina and enablers like Wilson.

But I knew about other forgeries.

And I had in my possession documents that showed Robert Woodridge "Woody" Wilson front and center in those crimes.

The Quitclaim Deeds and Woody Wilson

When "practicing attorney" Kristina Combs, her father Roger Combs, notary Ofelia Lisa Hernandez, and her husband Erik Hernandez broke into the Auris Project information center at 1614 Martin Luther King Drive, they had every expectation that the police, lawyers, and judges could quickly cover up the crime.

Once I was summarily ejected, they could go about the process of falsifying the documents necessary to take control of the property.

Many victims of title fraud on the Eastside may not know how to search deed records or have the resources to pay a court certified forensic document examiner to inspect fraudulent documents. Corrupt conspirators count on that.

But I was a trained investigative journalist. Unexpectedly, I went digging for the documents they filed in the deeds office and with the help of a certified forensic examiner proved them to be false. It never occurred to the co-conspirators that I would find the fraudulent documents, much less have the wherewithal to test them for authenticity.

But I did. And this is what I learned:

To successfully transfer property in disenfranchised neighborhoods, one only needs access to four corrupt entities willing to falsify documents: a title company, a lawyer, a phantom buyer, and a notary. That is what the theft of the information center at 1614 Martin Luther King exposed.

Records show that notaries Ofelia Lisa Hernandez, Meagan Hollis, and Monica Arrellano forged signatures on bogus quitclaim deeds. Kristina Combs pretended to represent phantom buyer Michael Kissler. Alamo Title, a franchise run through former county commissioner Tommy Adkisson's firm on Goliad Street, ratified the bogus notarized quitclaim deeds by providing a title commitment.

And the law office of Gale, Wilson & Sanchez gave all of that criminality the sheen of legitimacy: [116]

> Prepared in the office of and after recording return to:
> Gale, Wilson and Sanchez, PPLC[117]
> 115 E. Travis, Suite 1900
> San Antonio, Texas 78205
> 210-222-8899

The records showed that Robert "Woody" Wilson's law firm not only prepared the obviously forged quitclaim deeds after the burglary of 1614 Martin Luther King Drive, but filed them in the county deeds office.

After learning of Wilson's participation in the attacks on LULAC and the Bexar County Democratic Party, there is no doubt in my mind that not only did he help facilitate the theft of 1614 Martin Luther King Drive, he was a mastermind. It looked like I had identified another cockroach. The conspiracy was starting to come full circle. But I had already learned that my proof didn't mean shit in Bexar County.

In November 2021, I sent Woody Wilson an interview request through his website and the state bar online portal. He did not respond.

The District 2 town hall

Sometime after the district attorney dropped the malicious prosecution against me, then-District 2 city councilman Cruz Shaw organized a town hall during election primaries. Emily Angulo, the assistant district attorney who supervised the malicious assault prosecution against me, and other prosecutors attended. Joe Gonzales, the billboard attorney who served me up to DA Nicholas LaHood's monkey prosecutors, was now running against LaHood.

LaHood sent Angulo and the others to show the Eastside that the district attorney's office cared about the Eastside. They all were coming out of the woodwork, I thought, begging for votes from the very people they had ignored for years.

I stood up and in front of everyone, asked Angulo why the DA's office had continued the bogus assault prosecution with all the evidence it had in its possession. She was aware of the case, she said. She would be glad to talk to me about it after the meeting. When the meeting closed, I made a beeline for her.

Angulo told me that Judge Scott Roberts would not allow the district attorney's office to close the case. My continued prosecution was what the judge wanted, she said.

Not realizing it, Angulo had revealed something important. The prosecutors had not made a motion to dismiss charges until after my habeas corpus hearing. If the judge had told the prosecutors to continue the prosecution, then he did so outside of court in a meeting I was not invited to. In other words, she revealed another Bexar County judge engaging in prohibited ex-parte communications, this time in a conspiracy to cover up crimes of fraud, theft, and assault.

And plus, the district attorney did not need the judge's approval to dismiss my case. It was more proof of collusion, as far as I was concerned.

During that town hall, the city councilman lamented the fact that there were no community newspapers providing real news to the Eastside. A few years later, when I showed him editions of the *Lamp* that produced real investigative stories, he and other black leaders flooded the hack tabloid *The Observer*, which contained no news, with advertising. And without notice, he abruptly quit his post as District 2 city councilman to take an appointment as a district judge.

19 | AUTHENTICITY

The descendent

IN 2019, I GOT A suspicious email. It was from someone claiming to be the descendant of Lorenzo de Zavala, one of the main historical characters in my history book *Making Myth of Emily*.

Zavala, a progressive, 19th century Mexican politician who played a pivotal role in Mexico's independence from Spain, ended up as interim vice president of Texas during the Texas Revolution. Although the book focused primarily on evidence exploring the African-American racial identity of his wife Emily, it spent considerable time exploring the life and work of Lorenzo, who turned out to be a fascinating man.

And now, someone was emailing me, claiming to be a descendent of this illustrious historical figure. The writer introduced himself as Wilbert Fernando Zavala Urtecho and he was a lawyer and businessman in Mérida, Yucatan, where his ancestor grew up and where some members of the prominent Zavala family still resided. The man claiming to be Wilbert Zavala wanted to know if I would be interested in sharing some of my historical research on Lorenzo de Zavala with him and other scholars in the Yucatan. My research into Lorenzo's experiences in Texas brought fresh insights into this important historical figure, he said. He invited me to Mérida as his guest.

I was highly suspicious. It wouldn't be the first or last time an Allstate imposter would try to tried to weasel his way into a position to gaslight me.

At first I was brusque with him, but as we talked I could tell he was exactly who he said he was. He was cultured, frank, highly intelligent, and knowledgeable. Goons and zombies tended to be somewhat coarse, not particularly bright, and deceptive. Then I saw a photo of Wilbert standing next to a portrait of his illustrious great-great-great grandfather. His resemblance to Lorenzo de Zavala was undeniable.

I accepted his invitation. I offered my historical research papers to the Universidad Autónoma de Yucatan and agreed to eventually make it down to the peninsula to gift the collection to the university's library.[118]

On January 26th, 2020, I finally made my trip to Mérida to donate the historical research papers from *Making Myth of Emily* to the Yucatan University. My youngest brother Johnny agreed to come with me. It would be our first visit to the Yucatan Peninsula. I was excited to experience Lorenzo de Zavala's homeland and meet his descendants. In the 10 years that I investigated the race of his second wife Emily West de Zavala, I had come to admire this important historical figure. I felt like I knew him.

Wilbert Zavala and his girlfriend, Wendy Angelina Duarte Méndez, met us at the airport and took us to one of Mérida's main downtown plazas for dinner. Teeming with a heady mix of Mayan and Spanish culture, the city of Mérida was prosperous and well ordered, steeped in Old World charm. John, Wendy, Wilbert, and I sat at an outdoor table and watched a group of folkloric dancers entertain the bustling night crowd. It felt good to be back in Mexico again. I drank up the sights, smells, and sounds as I mentally journeyed into speaking again in Spanish.

Zavala was the perfect host. Extremely smart, mild-mannered, and urbane, he treated me with enormous respect. We bonded over a shared love of Texas and Mexico history. He was a great storyteller. I would sit enraptured as he regaled me with historical tales of the Yucatan Peninsula from the Spanish Conquest to the present. The stories were "juicy," to say the least, and I wondered how it was that I did not know them. Duarte was a devoted teacher in a tiny Mayan village on the outskirts of Mérida. A former ballerina, she was beautiful and strong-willed, with a nurturing energy that I instantly responded to. I felt safe, appreciated. I knew that I had made good friends.

The press conference and the presentation at the Yucatan University's law school went well. I was surprised at the number of people who attended the event. Many Lorenzo de Zavala descendants visited from different parts of Mexico to hear about their ancestor's experiences during the Texas Revolution. A line of media cameras and journalists gathered at the back wall. Yucatan scholars interested in that era of Mexico's history attended, looking for insights.

The Denise McVea Collection of Lorenzo de Zavala's historical research paper now rests in the University of Yucatan library. Scholars and students in his homeland could now get a solid view of Lorenzo de Zavala's experiences in Texas during the Texas Revolution. I was proud.

The experience invigorated me. It reminded me that people in the U.S. would benefit from what I could tell them about corruption in San Antonio. Wilbert de Zavala and the *yucatecos* had reminded me that the written word could positively impact lives centuries after the fact. I was determined to get the story of Allstate on paper, no matter how long it took.

After a magical experience in a remarkable place, John and I headed home to San Antonio. While I had prepared for the conference in our shared apartment in Mérida, John had kept me up on U.S. news.

"This is interesting," he had said just a few days before our departure. "They are saying there is a pandemic. Something called the coronavirus."

When I got home, the author Barbara Renaud Gonzalez asked me to join a *Literaria Dignidad* panel at the Esperanza Center for Peace and Justice. The panelists, mostly authors and publishers, shared their perspectives on the state of publishing in America in the wake of the *American Dirt* controversy.

The book was a bestseller and enthusiastically promoted by Oprah Winfrey. But the author identified as white and real Mexican writers found the book derivative. Why, LatinX writers wanted to know, was the publishing industry and Oprah not publishing real Mexican authors telling authentic Mexican stories? It was a fair question. I joined the panel. My message was that the publishing industry was moribund, and that we needed to start building our own platforms and distribution channels.

Allstate goons glared at me from the audience.

A hard "no" on jury duty

On April 30, 2019, I got a jury summons in the mail.

I had no intentions of serving on a Bexar County jury. I had seen too much.

And it wasn't just what I had witnessed in the Allstate jury. Several unrelated instances of bizarre Bexar County jury outcomes had been making local news, which only solidified my suspicions about what I had witnessed in 2013. Plus, I couldn't help but wonder if the jury summons was just another distraction cooked up by my persecutors to distract me. They had demonstrated more than once that they could control any number of government systems.

I knew that I had an easy out this time. Tedi was still recovering from giving birth to our beautiful twins and I was her primary caretaker. But I also wanted to serve notice that even if I didn't qualify for the caretaker exemption, I was morally and legally obligated to decline a Bexar County jury summons.

I wrote the chief jury bailiff, Julieta Rabago Schulze, declining the jury summons based on the caretaker exemption. I also declined on ethical grounds.

"I am ethically and morally required to reject any request(s) to serve on a Bexar County jury," I wrote. "I am aware of ample and convincing evidence that the Bexar County jury system and other elements of the local judiciary have been substantially corrupted by organized criminal networks. These forces have degraded the integrity of our judicial system to such a degree that serving on a Bexar County jury knowing what I know is tantamount to collusion."

I asked her to remove my name from the jury list until the FBI task force announced it had completed its investigation into corruption. I copied the letter to the civil courts staff attorney Dinah Gaines and the administrative judge at the time, David Peeples.

Schulze wrote me a terse letter back, informing me that no "integrity exemption" for jury service existed. She let me know she would be summoning me for jury service again as soon as the caretaker waiver expired. And she did.

I refused that one, too. I wrote:

> As I have stated previously, I must respectfully decline to serve on a jury in any Bexar County civil or criminal court until the Federal Bureau of Investigation task force has publicly concluded its corruption investigation of the Bexar County Courts. As an involved witness, I am aware of evidence that the integrity of the Bexar County jury system and other local judicial systems have been compromised by organized criminal networks. As such, it would be morally irresponsible of me to knowingly participate in a jury trial whose outcomes may have already been prescribed. Texas law prohibits knowingly (or unknowingly, for that matter) participating in criminal activity. The potential for any Bexar County jury to enable obstruction of justice is real and probable.
>
> In the past, Bexar County jurors have been routinely approached by criminal actors and offered bribes, criminal associates have been placed on juries with instructions to deliver a certain outcome, and honest jurors are coerced into outcomes favorable to organized criminal actors. Last July, a Bexar County jury refused to convict a capital murder suspect who had recently escaped from the Bexar County Detention Center. Luis Antonio Arroyo has documented ties to organized criminal networks. The jury failed to convict him despite Arroyo being known to the surviving victim and despite that victim identifying him to authorities during the murders. Because the

jury hung, the judge declared a mistrial. According to the *San Antonio Express-News*, even the killer's defense attorneys displayed shock at that outcome. I myself documented derogation of the jury system firsthand when curated jury members refused to release a jury in my civil personal injury case against Allstate Insurance Company until the other members buckled to their will - despite overwhelming evidence against the eventual verdict. It is my contention that these debacles expose the extent to which organized criminal networks have negatively impacted our judicial system. There is more, of course, and more to come without serious judicial reform in the local courthouse.

Further, Bexar County continues to violate crucial state public information laws so it is virtually impossible for a concerned citizen to ascertain what steps, if any, the local courts may have taken to protect the integrity of the judicial process. For these reasons, I regretfully cannot currently serve on a Bexar County jury. If I can be of service in any other way, please be assured I am willing to do whatever I can to help. I realize the stakes are high.

Sincerely,
Denise McVea

I copied the letter to Judge Rosie Alvarado, the judge I was instructed to report to, and Sid Harle, the new administrative judge that had replaced Judge Peeples.

There was growing evidence of my claims, and it wasn't all mayhem and murder. Other disturbing jury verdicts had come out in Bexar County Courts.

One was an odd 2019 civil case where local car dealer Ahmad Zabihian sued the transnational automaker Hyundai for breach of contract. According to court records, Hyundai had given Zabihian first refusal for any new Hyundai dealerships in the San Antonio market. But the automaker awarded the dealership to one of Zabihian's competitors. Despite Hyundai admitting it had given Zabihian right of first refusal, the Bexar County jury found unanimously in favor of Hyundai Motor America.[119]

After the trial, however, a few jurors approached Alvarado, the same judge I was to report to as a juror, complaining that some jurors had forced the verdict. The controlling jurors pressured the others, they told the judge, and would not agree to anything except a certain verdict. The other jury members, wanting it all to end, finally acquiesced. That was similar to the scenario I complained about in the Allstate case.

"What they told me was that it wasn't their decision and that they felt pressured," the judge told *Express-News* reporter Patrick Danner. "They felt that they had to decide now."

Alvarado said she really didn't know what to do about this allegation of audacious jury misconduct. She would have to research whether that behavior amounted to misconduct, she said with a straight face.

"It's never happened to me before," she said.[120]

Schulze stopped sending me jury summons.

I kept fighting. I wasn't exactly racking up wins, but I was still standing. The carefully constructed criminal conspiracy was not crumbling by any stretch of the imagination. But I could see chips. Minuscule and hardly noticeable, but chips nonetheless.

Other people were starting to notice, too. For years, the attacks were so stealthy, so well-executed, I was often the only one who could see them. But by 2020, as operatives' and corrupt officials' desperation grew, what used to be quick and stealthy jabs had become wild haymakers that were consistently failing to connect. Enough mistakes were being made that other people had started wondering: what in the world was going on in San Antonio?

Despite COVID and frequent car wrecks, donkeys continued their daily circling of my home with IMSI catchers and signal extenders. Hackers continued intercepting my phone calls and emails. I continued tapping away on the book. I had come up with a name for the title. I decided to call the book *Evil Corp*, homage to the surreal dystopian television series *Mr. Robot*. But I kept the title to myself. The less Allstate's operatives knew about my intentions, the better.

On February 10, 2021, I called Mount Zion Baptist Church where the NAACP Jubilee festivities are held. I had run into Judge Mery at the celebration before the pandemic hit, but that wasn't the reason for my call. I wanted to know the name of the singer who had transported and healed me that day. I wanted to honor her by putting her name in my book. Mary, the church's office manager, took my number down. She said she would ask around. If she found out anything, she would call. At the same time, she was fielding calls from church members about where they could get the COVID vaccine. She accidently gave them my number. I got a few calls from a few elderly folks asking about COVID. I explained the mix up to the callers and, out of courtesy, gave them the numbers I had gathered about vaccine availability. But call the church if you have more questions, I said. I called Mary back and told her about the mix up. She apologized profusely, mortified by the mistake. It wasn't a big deal, I told her. I just wanted to let her know so she could have the right number.

"I see too much craziness to get upset over an honest mistake like this," I told her. I told her not to give it another thought.

She was grateful for my attitude. She promised to call folks she had given my number to, to correct the mistake. It was just a few people, she said. "You shouldn't be getting any more calls," she said.

But I did get more calls. I could immediately tell that they were zombies. They wanted know if I had gotten the vaccine. They were friendly and inquisitive and I made sure not to give them any accurate information. I called Mary back. I knew they would be listening. People keep calling asking for info, I told her.

"They shouldn't be," she said. "We haven't given out your number."

"I thought it was strange," I told her. "I get hacked a lot."

"That's not the only strange thing," she said. A man with a Middle Eastern accent had called the church and began asking her a series of bizarre questions. Was she a vegetarian? Did she have diabetes? Was her name Mary?

She found the call disturbing. She said she gave him no information.

You handled it perfectly, I said.

I never found out the name of the incredible singer who transported me that day. In my world, if the singer was identified and someone from the church called to give me her name, the call would not go through.

Out of the blue, Google contacted me and offered to enroll me in the company's Enhanced Protection Program for targeted individuals. I jumped at the chance. I had been slowly locking out the criminal network's aggressive hacking program, but it was a slow, sluggish and often reversible effort. Two steps forward, one step back. It was better than before, which was essentially one step forward, three steps back.

And certainly better than the beginning, which had been four steps back and then four more steps back.

Like Google Scholar years before, Google's Enhanced Protection Program improved my quality of life tremendously.

The urgent case of the service dog

I continued to complain to the Hackberry post office supervisor Victor Duncan about the postal service employee misconduct. In one letter, I carefully detailed my complaints over the years, the stolen mail, the delayed mail, the opened mail, and reminded him that he had an obligation to report my complaints to the proper authorities. Nothing ever came of it.

I visited the Hackberry office again to file a complaint in person against its mail carriers. Duncan came out. His employees were still harassing me, I told him. They were being bribed, I told him. My mail was constantly delayed, they threw my mail on the ground, and, they parked outside my home diddling with a personal cell phone while my network stalled and disconnected.

He looked at me disinterestedly, as though he had heard it all before, which of course, he had.

"Oh," he said.

"I'd like to file a formal complaint," I said.

"You can do that online," he said.

This was the part I hated. Online forms were notoriously vulnerable to cyberattacks. And because no law enforcement mechanism existed to protect citizens from man-in-the-middle attacks, online forms were the attackers' bread and butter. Easy to exploit, they were the least likely mechanism for reaching the proper authorities. In fact, I had used forms to file complaints with the Postal Service, the DEA, the FBI, the ACLU, other federal agencies, the attorney general's office, several journalism outlets, and countless law firms. Only twice was I certain I had gotten through. Mostly, I received no reply.

I sensed that Duncan knew about the cyberattacks and that's why he was directing me online. Otherwise, why would he stand there, unmoved, uncaring, unwilling to look into what amounted to allegations of serious federal crimes that quite literally impacted national security? I told him I didn't have access to the internet, which was essentially true. He shrugged. Oh, well. How unfortunate for me. He made no move to take a report, ask additional questions, or indicate that the serious misconduct and criminality I was alleging against postal workers would be investigated in any way.

A small, grey-haired woman walked by. She was holding a Chihuahua.

"Ma'am, you can't bring that dog in here," he told her forcefully.

"I already told you it's a service dog," she replied angrily.

The dog was wearing a vest that said "Service Dog."

The old lady and the young man glared at each other. This was apparently an ongoing issue. They disliked each other intensely.

He told her she would need to show the proper paperwork if she was going to bring in a service dog. She replied that she had already done that, twice, and that she wasn't going to do it again. They began to argue. He threatened to call the police.

"Call the police!" she challenged him.

I took an ironic interest in the exchange.

"Excuse me," Duncan told me, and marched into the back of the post office to call the authorities on a cranky old lady and her tiny dog.

"He's always harassing me," she told me bitterly.

"I can see that the vest says 'service dog,'" I sympathized. Of course, I was on her side.

I listened to her complaints until Duncan returned.

"The police are on their way," he told the lady.

"Good! I'll be here," she said defiantly, and went about her post office business. The dog seemed unaware he had caused a kerfuffle.

"Where were we?" Duncan said wearily.

"Oh," I said, "you were being forced to listen to credible allegations of serious federal crimes committed by post office employees under your supervision before you dashed off to call police on an old lady and her service dog."

The dig was not lost on him. He muttered something vague about looking into it, online complaint forms, and the postal inspector. The police arrived and he rushed out to brief them. I finished my business and jumped in my car to leave. I started the engine but sat there for a minute processing the image before me. Outside the post office, two burly SAPD cops and Duncan towered over the little old lady, intently discussing her service dog. She held her own, but it was clear they were all against her.

I shook my head, took a deep breath, and drove away.

What's going on at the U.S. Post Office?

Workers at the Hackberry Street post office continued to harass me. Postal carriers' behavior grew more brazen. One day, I watched as a postal worker parked the post office van next door. A familiar goon in a baseball cap and sunglasses pulled up behind him, blocking my neighbor's driveway. I watched as he approached the postal carrier who remained seated in the van. They greeted each other as the carrier handed the man a letter. There was no further discussion. The man jumped back into his car and drove away. Too many times to count, I would look out my window when my network began malfunctioning to see a postal carrier sitting in the post office van, punching at his personal phone. To aggravate me, postal carriers would throw mail over the fence during a downpour. When I complained to Duncan, nothing ever came of it.

The late and disappearing mail was one thing, but there were other strange goings-on. On several occasions, I saw goons passing Visa gift cards to grinning clerks without saying a word or engaging in any other transaction. And once, I stood by confusedly while a Hackberry post office clerk read the address on my letter out loud as a goon stood behind me holding his phone in that now-familiar recording pose. It was obvious to me that certain local postal service employees were enthusiastically working with private operatives, but evidence was also mounting that the United States Postal Service itself could no longer be trusted. *The Washington Post*, I noticed, instructed whistleblowers to used random post offices that they had not used before to send in sensitive tips.

I would see other, deeply troubling signs that the postal service had been corrupted by nefarious forces. In 2017, during a time of great hostility towards immigrants, Deferred Action for Childhood Arrivals applications sent certified mail to the U.S. Citizenship and Immigration Service inexplicably stalled in, of all places, Chicago.

In what journalists described as a "mysterious holding pattern," an immigration application packet arrived in Chicago on September 17th and was "in transit to destination" until September 19th. Then it suddenly, mysteriously, disappeared.

Two weeks later, it surfaced again. It arrived in the USIS processing warehouse on Oct. 6, a day *after* the application deadline. The federal government rejected dozens of DACA recipients because the U.S. Postal Service in Chicago inexplicably delayed their applications.[121]

Federal authorities had no explanation for that strange and troubling postal phenomenon. I saw it as a successful experiment.

As far as I was concerned, the U.S. Post Office was a co-opted agency that had no fear, not even of Congress.

In 2020, the U.S. Postal Service post office in San Antonio brazenly duped U.S. Congressman Joaquin Castro by hiding more than 150,000 pieces of mail during the lawmaker's inspection of operations in San Antonio.[122] Castro pledged to get to the bottom of that brazen crime, but his congressional office did not return an email asking for updates.

In 2021, I finally managed to break through Allstate's internet blockade, and successfully filed an online complaint with the U.S. Postal Inspector against the Hackberry post office for a variety of crimes and misdemeanors, including my allegations that local postal service employees were accepting bribes to interfere with the mail and invade postal customers' privacy. The inspector assigned Victor Duncan, the dog-hating Hackberry supervisor, to address my concerns. Duncan called, and left a message nervously expressing an interest in helping me resolve my concerns. But I could never get a hold of him. He avoided me like the plague.

In the summer of 2021, I mentioned to my sister during an unencrypted phone call that I had to go drop some mail off at the Hackberry post office. I purposely arrived after hours, with no intention of dropping my mail in the mail boxes. When I arrived, I saw that the post office was closed, but a goon stood waiting at the counter in the locked post office. Duncan stood nearby. They were waiting for something. When they saw me, Duncan retreated to the back. I hung around for about 15 minutes. The man stood there, discomfited. Duncan never reappeared.

I took pictures of the goon and his license plate and filed them away.

20 | ATTENDANCE

The next DA and the restaurateur

CANDIDATES FLOCKED TO THE EASTSIDE in 2018 in search of votes. Officials who had ignored and undermined the black community from their positions of power were showing up in black churches and community centers all over the Eastside, pretending to be allies to a downtrodden community in dire need of friends in high places.

One Sunday, driving down Hackberry in my old white pickup truck, I glanced to my left as I passed Tony G's restaurant. The parking lot was full. I did a double take. To my surprise, Joe Gonzales, the billboard lawyer who stole my money and then served me up to County Court 12 judge Scott Roberts was standing in the parking lot.

Despite irregular operating hours, Tony G's had become a popular spot on the Eastside, enjoying development grants and other financial incentives. The owner, Tony Gradney, a native of Houston, had quickly become a "black leader" in San Antonio. He served on several boards, including that of the local chapter of the NAACP. I had refused to set foot in Tony' G's after connecting Gradney to the drug complex at 315 S. Olive and the suspicious hacking group at the hotel.

Gonzales, now running a well-funded campaign for district attorney, was apparently making a campaign stop at Tony G's. In the rear view mirror, I could see that he was on the phone.

It made sense to me that Gradney would support Gonzales. The parking lot was full. My blood boiled. Both men were busy enjoying bounty paid at my expense, I thought. Tony Gradney was now the proprietor of a host of cash companies and becoming a respected and influential businessman on the Eastside. Gonzales was well on his way to becoming the most powerful government lawyer in the county.

I made a calculated decision. It wouldn't hurt to let them know I was still in the fight. It was Sunday so the street was empty except for me and my old truck. I screeched to a halt, put the truck in reverse, sped backwards, and pulled into the restaurant's parking lot to heckle Joe Gonzales.

"Where's my money, Joe?" I yelled.

Joe waved and smiled at me as though we were old friends. "Oh, hey!" he sputtered nervously, pointing at his phone.

"You know you owe me money, right?" I continued. "You robbed me, Joe."

This went on for about a minute, me yelling at an embarrassed and discomfited Joe Gonzales as he covered the microphone on his phone.

"I'll get in touch with you," he lied.

"You should be ashamed of yourself!" I yelled before driving off. It wasn't much in the way of empowerment. Still, it felt good.

I resolved that when I encountered some of the actors in the corruption probe, I would face them down directly. I had another such opportunity when I encountered Michael Mery, the abusive judge in the Greyhound and Allstate cases, at a black history event at the Mount Zion Missionary Baptist Church. One of the most influential black churches in San Antonio, Mount Zion had a long history of civil rights activism on the Eastside. Judges often made routine campaign stops through African American churches to get name recognition and to suggest that they were friends of the black community.

I joked to myself that black churches should have some type of visitation requirement card. If your card showed you had not visited at least 12 times prior to launching an election campaign, you could not gain admittance during elections.

Mery and other judges were attending the annual NAACP jubilee. It was a lovely ceremony, with a visiting pastor giving a stirring speech and a choir soloist singing in a voice that truly came from the heavens.

And there he was, sitting in the front row dressed in his black robe, smiling indulgently.

After the ceremony, I approached him. He turned slightly away from me, enabling the possibility that we could cross paths without having to acknowledge each other.

"Hello, Judge Mery," I said.

He turned to face me. "Oh, hey!" he exclaimed. I could tell that he was surprised that I had approached him. "How have you been?" he sputtered.

"I'm fine," I said, and handed him a *Lamp* newspaper.

"Oh, great, great," he enthused. "Well, take care of yourself!"

"You, too," I said. We parted ways.

On October 11, 2018, I attended the monthly meeting of the local NAACP chapter. The National Association for the Advancement of Colored People had a storied history in San Antonio. It had been instrumental in integrating major department stores, advocated for diversity in the new media, and represented minority workers in employment discrimination disputes. The first thing that struck me was the gentle, honest faces of the local members. The second was the dedication with which the officers took to their administrative tasks. The NAACP was also in the middle of an election. Tony Gradney, the restaurateur connected to the criminal enterprise at 315 S. Olive, was running for vice president of the local chapter of the esteemed civil rights organization. During the election, a rash of new members signed up. Tony Gradney won.

I took a few dozen editions of the *Lamp* newspapers to the next NAACP meeting a month later. Most people flipped through the pages with avid interest. But two men chatting with Gradney would point at the paper and visibly shake their heads in rejection. It was a typical effort to provoke me, part of the gaslighting campaign to make me doubt I could accomplish anything while Allstate's covert campaign worked diligently to make sure I didn't accomplish anything. I ignored them. Gradney, now an NAACP officer, frequently glanced my way from the dais.

At one point the panel of newly elected officers invited comments from attending members. I rose to speak. I introduced the *Lamp* and explained that while the newspaper was a pilot program, I hoped to build it into a resource for the community. I complimented the people there, thanked them for their efforts on behalf of the black community, and expressed a desire to help in any way that I could. "The people need to see you," I said.

I sat down. A woman in the back stood up and gave a full-throated defense of the restaurateur Tony Gradney, whom I had not mentioned.

"He does so much for the community," she said.

Allstate goons interfered with every aspect of the newspaper, including intercepting sales calls and disrupting my communications with distributors and printers. I knew that nothing would change until the book was out. I suspended the *Lamp* indefinitely.

Staff Attorney's Office Part II

Meanwhile, I was still trying to get a divorce from my college sweetheart so I could finally marry the love of my life.

Yes, I had successfully filed my petition for divorce from a man I had not spoken to in more than 20 years. Yes, the staff attorney's office had reviewed the petition and found it legally sound and procedurally sufficient to present to a judge. But the staff attorney's office policy was to hold petitions for three months if they were filed by people without lawyers, the assistant staff attorney informed me. If I wanted to see a judge right away, she said I would have to hire a lawyer. Otherwise, it's three months.

"That makes no sense," I argued.

I asked her to cite the statute or rule that allowed this court-sanctioned extortion attempt. She looked around in panic.

Brett Vangheluwe came running out. I had not spoken to him since he helped Judge Mery cover up the Greyhound assault and false arrest. I wondered how he had known to enter the room at that precise moment.

I asked Vangheluwe why he was holding pro se litigants' petitions for three months but not holding petitions filed by lawyers. It's policy, he repeated. Under what authority? I asked.

Ma'am, I don't have to answer your questions, he responded.

What authority gives you the right to delay access to justice, I asked.

Court rules, he said.

Nope, I replied. You can't make court rules that violate the constitution. Plus, I never saw it published. Show me where it says that.

We went around and around like that. He wavered between self-conscious arrogance and uncertainty.

His left hand rested on the counter between us. Trying to connect on a human level, I patted it.

He recoiled in disgust, grabbed his hand to his chest, and fell back into a chair. His face went ghostly white, then grey. "Don't...you...touch...me," he muttered. "If you...touch me again, I will call the police." He looked like he was about to vomit. This was not an act.

You fucking psychopath, I thought.

"Are you insane?" I asked.

"No," he gasped, struggling to gain control of himself.

"Oh my God," I said contemptuously. "Pull yourself together, man."

The young female lawyer sat quietly to his left, head down, shuffling papers.

By and by, Vangheluwe pulled himself together. "You can talk to Dinah," he began, wanting for it all to be over.

Just then, two deputy bailiffs walked past the door. He interrupted himself to call out to them.

They entered the room. Both were stocky, white, and bald.

Vangheluwe pointed at me. This woman is being difficult and will not leave, he told them.

"He's not answering my questions," I told them. We went over the issue again.

"I am asking what gives your office the legal authority to delay litigants' access to justice by 90 days just because they don't pay a lawyer," I repeated.

The deputies stayed neutral, watching the dispute attentively. At one point, as our exchange descended into bickering, one deputy loudly shouted us down. "One at a time!" he bellowed. People in the hallway peeked in.

Vangheluwe tossed a sheet of paper at me. It was the extremely restrictive list of understaffed, underfunded legal aid centers too overwhelmed to help virtually anyone handed the sheet. It was utterly useless.

"I don't want this crap," I said, and tossed it back. For some reason, this impressed the deputies. They settled in. I would leave when I had gotten the answer to my question.

I explained to the deputies that Vangheluwe couldn't explain why his office was sitting on pro se litigants' petitions in violation of the constitutional right to equal access. As I spoke, I gave the deputy nearest me a friendly pat on the arm.

Vangheluwe snorted.

"She likes to touch people," he said derisively.

The deputies looked at him strangely. There was a tense silence. The deputies had seen something in Vangheluwe that they did not like.

"I don't know what is wrong with this guy," I told the deputies.

Vangheluwe, seeing he wouldn't have the satisfaction of seeing me hauled out by burly guards, relinquished control. He called his boss, staff attorney Dinah Gaines.

"It turned out to be advantageous that you called in law enforcement," I gibed. "Suddenly, you have to do your job."

"Ms. McVea has some questions for you," he said into the phone. For the first time, after more than a decade of knowing him, I could finally see what Brett Vangheluwe looked like when he was acting professional. He chastely hung up the phone. "She's expecting you," he said, and explained how to reach her office, which was located on a higher floor.

The deputies moved from the doorway to let me pass. "All good?" they asked me.

"Yes, thank you," I responded. "I appreciate your professionalism."

"No problem," they said.

They were polite, almost gentle with me, as I turned to leave.

"Take care of yourself," they said.

When I reached Gaines's offices, she greeted me nervously. She had just a few moments, she said in a rush. She was late for a doctor's appointment. I repeated my question. What legal authority permits the court attorney to arbitrarily delay unrepresented litigants from accessing the courts? I asked. She mumbled something about the issue being settled by the courts for some time now. Where? I asked. When? Head down, she mumbled something about precedent. At least tell me the rationale, I said.

I really have to go, she told me, and headed out the door. I had no choice but to follow. We stood awkwardly waiting for the elevator. I tried to joke with her. She would not look at me. When the elevator arrived, we both stepped on. A young couple with an adorable little boy moved closer to each other to make room for us. Gaines squeezed into an opposite side of the elevator, as far away from me as she could reach. She looked upset.

These were the moments I enjoyed, the looks on the co-conspirators' faces when I popped back up asking the same access to justice questions I had asked years before. They had expected that they would commit their deeds and that would be the last of me, like so many others. But here I stood, asking the same questions with the same resolve as though no time had passed. Of course she was upset. What the Bexar county courts were doing – delaying and hampering unrepresented people from accessing judges – was not only morally wrong, but constitutionally illegal, a gross abuse of power. It was a pattern of abuse that had been ongoing for decades. And it was in danger of being exposed.

I considered filing a writ of mandamus to ask the higher courts to stop Bexar County practices that denied or delayed poor people access to the courts. Tedi begged me not to do that, just to get a divorce so that we could get married and go on with our lives. She was exhausted, she said, and she just wanted to move on. I understood. As my partner, she had been through a lot. She deserved peace. Hell, I did, too, although I saw no immediate path to obtain it.

Plus, with the way the courts were being administered in Texas, there was no guarantee that the law or constitutional protections, despite being entirely on my side, would make a lick of difference in the judgment that would eventually come down.

I paid a lawyer $1200. She walked into the courthouse and filed the petition I wrote. The lawyer had made no edits. Soon, I was standing in front of a judge and in less than 20 minutes I was divorced.

We stood before the clerk window to get a certified copy of the order. A courtroom administrator stood by, glaring at me. When my lawyer caught his eye, his face changed. He smiled and greeted her. Smiling back, she returned his greeting. When she turned away from him to manage her papers, his hostile glare returned. Apparently, his only purpose for being there was to give me dirty looks.

Catching cockroaches

The Allstate-sponsored stalking continued unabated and even under Allstate's crazy zero sum madness, became increasingly absurd. In 2018, a black sports car screeched to a halt in front of my house and my network immediately began to malfunction. The Trans Am had parked against traffic, a parking violation, so I called police. Even if the cops tried to ignore the hacking, they couldn't ignore the parking violation. But the officer who arrived, Yvonne Mauricio, refused to take a report. There's no crime, she said rudely. I gently pointed out that he was parked against traffic and so at the least he should be ticketed. "I'm not going to do that," she barked.

She was just like all the rest. "Get out of San Antonio," I told her as she walked back to her squad car, ignoring the illegally parked vehicle. "We are sick of you corrupt cops." In the months that followed she would make several public relations appearances on television with a single message: SAPD cares about the community.

Once, a white truck circling my house slammed into a work struck on the corner of Hackberry and Wyoming. It was a serious wreck, totaling both vehicles and injuring the stalker in the white truck. An ambulance, fire truck and police squad cars littered the scene. Paramedics were tending to the driver of the stalking truck. Inattentive to the road, my stalkers often got into wrecks. The accidents were great opportunities to build up my cockroach database. I went downstairs to take a photo of the scene. I knew goons would descend on the scene to remove backpacks from the disabled truck. I was not disappointed. Unexpectedly, another gawker struck up a conversation. "I know that guy," he told me. "He's an FBI agent."

"Really?" I asked, "What's he doing here?"

"Working," the man said. "You live around here?"

I pointed to my house. "I live there," I said.

Suddenly uncomfortable, he mumbled something and walked away.

I got pictures of the wrecked truck's license plate and the license plate of the goon who came to the scene to retrieve the stalker's backpack.

In one case, I tracked cyberattacks to the tiny mother-in-law unit behind my next door neighbor's house. I watched as goons drove down the alley to drop off devices and telephones to the young man occupying the unit.

Once I spoke to him from a distance as he walked his dog out to the alley to pee.

Me: Where are you from?
Him: Uh...Texas.
Me: Where in Texas?
(Long Pause)
Me: Texas is a big state. What town in Texas are you from?
(Another pause.)
Him: Syracuse, New York. I'm from Syracuse, New York.
Me: What's your name?
Him: Zachary McCollister.
Me: Stop interfering with my network, Zachary McCollister.
Him: I'm not hacking into your network, Denise. You're crazy.

His name really *was* Zachary McCollister, I soon confirmed, but he wasn't from the town of Texas *or* Syracuse. He was from North Carolina where he had engaged in petty crime before abruptly landing in the alley behind 1010 Wyoming Street in San Antonio, Texas. Tellingly, he had used the shady drug complex at 315 S. Olive as his address to buy a car when he showed up in San Antonio and began allegedly hacking me from the house next door.

That explained why the drug complex had more mailboxes than apartment units, I realized. In addition to being a hub for all sorts of street crime, it apparently served as a convenient mail drop. When I compiled a dossier on him and presented it to police alleging hacking, he abruptly moved down the street to another house that sometimes showed up on my phone screen as a cell tower.

After outing the petty criminal Zachary McCollister, I began looking to expose the street managers of Allstate's oppression campaign. McCollister was a zero, a petty criminal doing illegal work in exchange for money. I wanted to know the identities of more cockroaches. I made the decision to ignore the zeros and start looking for the cockroaches. There were, I knew, private investigators, but also operatives from private intelligence firms.

I had seen the goons from the private intelligence firms many times, usually directing the zeroes from luxury vehicles parked a block or two away. They managed the operation, but were always careful to put the zeros between them and me. It worked like a charm in the beginning because I hadn't known what was happening. Now, I had a better understanding of the illicit operation and the roles played by the people involved. I had also largely stopped talking to people about what I was learning.

When driving away from my house, I would drive aimlessly around corners – a left here, another left here, now suddenly a right. I kept an eye out for the folks managing the operation. But I had to be careful. While my gang stalkers were constantly getting into fender benders and more serious car wrecks, I had so far managed to avoid wrecking my vehicle. Even when zeros would deliberately swerve in my direction or suddenly brake in front of me on the highway, I maintained defensive driving principles. That meant that I would often catch glimpses of the cockroaches down side roads but be unable to safely get close enough to make a positive ID. For more than a week, a silver Infiniti SUV followed me from a distance.

Then, one day, I caught a break. I had been returning home after running errands, driving south on Walters towards E. Houston Street. As I passed the intersection a residential street, I saw it. It was the silver Infiniti SUV that had been flanking me for a few days. It had always kept a distance and I could not safely memorize the full license plate. But here it was now, parked on a side street with the driver inside, intently working on his phone. I pulled slowly past the SUV and looked inside. A middle-aged Latino man looked at me sheepishly.

I pulled past and parked in front of him, got out of the driver's door, and walked to the passenger side of his window. He seemed agitated, at one point looking forward out the windshield on a side street where nothing was going on as if there was no one standing outside his passenger window trying to get his attention. Finally, he looked my way. He looked ghostly, panicked.

I gestured for him to roll his window down. He blinked, hesitated, then reluctantly complied.

"Hi!" I said jovially, "Do you live here?"

"No," he croaked.

"Oh," I giggled. "I had a question."

"That's right," he responded incongruently.

"Thanks, anyway," I said. I smiled, walked around the SUV nonchalantly, and took a picture of his license plate. I had my private investigator run his plates. I put him in the database of cockroaches I was building for the FBI.

If I saw a stalker twice, I would nonchalantly take his photo. And I used cell tower apps to track my cellphone signal to people sitting in cars spoofing cell towers. I would take a photo of the person managing my phone signal and a photo of their license plate. The database was growing.

This new approach was paying off. The stalking campaign became less brazen as zeroes began to worry that their activity was being recorded. They would turn abruptly to hide their faces. One woman parked in front of my house literally covered her face with her arms Hollywood-style when she saw me approach with a phone in my hand. I never saw her again. Eventually, the stalkers stopped sitting in cars in front of my house altogether. They would drive up, two to a car, and pick up my phone signal before zipping away. Once I watched my phone's screen in disbelief as my phone's signal traveled to various locations on a cell tower locator app's graphical map. I watched in real time as my phone's signal entered homes I had long suspected were involved in the official oppression. I recorded the movement on my other phone.

Each time I got in my car, I started each trip by scouring the blocks around my house before ultimately heading toward my destination. Invariably, familiar vehicles sat in wait. I would slow down and take a picture of the license plate. Most of the surveillance cars had illegal dark-tinted windows. Sometimes, depending on my mood, I would peer through the surveillance car's windshield and wave. Sometimes, I would gesture for the stalkers to roll down their windows and then ask for the time. Sometimes, I would snap a picture of the stalker with my cell phone. These people were lowlifes who didn't have the first idea of what they were involved in. Someone offered them money and they took it. They probably didn't even know the full (or real) name of the person who handed them the cash.

I was getting compelling, irrefutable evidence of a sophisticated, covert harassment campaign.

Over time, I had a large database of cockroaches, goons, and zombies. I was making important, revealing connections between conspirators.

By 2020, I had learned a lot about Allstate goons' tactics. I had, at long last, secured my networks and devices. Hackers no longer had unfettered access to my operating systems and I became very good at hiding on the internet. Still, even one slip up, a single open port, or a careless click could cost me a day or two of rescuing my computer systems from hacks. The cybercriminals continued trying to hack my phone. Even now that the police had credible proof that stalkers were using **IMSI** catchers to spoof cell towers, mules still sometimes trudge around my house.

The gangstalking continued, but the taunting smirks had given way to hooded glances on tense faces. The zeros stalking me looked for the first time like they were engaged in serious work, not a game.

I made a point to approach my stalkers. If I saw someone twice in two separate locations, I would approach them and start a banal conversation. I enjoyed their surprise and discomfort. I asked what time it was, while recording them with my cell phone.

"My phone is broken," I would lie, even as they looked at it working just fine. It became clear that none of them were prepared to have a conversation with their target. They stuttered, muttered, and seemed to have problems concentrating. They invariably would look out and away, as though seeking guidance from an unseen guide. I could tell that turnover was increasing.

I soon realized that I could spend an eternity focusing on the endless supply of zeroes and goons stalking me, and really not get anywhere. While it was costing Allstate's contractors money to constantly have to replace people, it was also keeping me from telling the story of the people these goons were trying to protect. And besides, the money Allstate was spending to terrorize me was other people's money. Don't forget that, I told myself.

The zeroes and zombies would keep on coming as long as there was a chance they could keep the story from coming out.

On August 29, 2020, more than 200 anonymous viewers signed on to watch a history presentation I performed on Zoom.[123]

Jumping from one Allstate-induced calamity to another, I didn't have time to promote the event. Normally, it is would be considered a success if the Facebook Zoom presentation had gotten a dozen viewers. But more than silently signed on to watch my presentation about an obscure aspect of Texas history. I imagined a few of them were covert conspirators who wanted to assess me. Under a perfectly played zero sum game, I was supposed to be completely anxious, paranoid, traumatized.

It must have been disappointing to see me not just calm and confident, but coolly discussing a complex topic in clear and concise language. Millions of dollars had been spent. I was supposed to be babbling incoherently by now.

Still, the unrelenting stress was taking a toll. My marriage was becoming strained beyond repair. It seemed that Tedi and I were constantly at odds. She was angry; I was angry. We were both exhausted, traumatized. She had been loyal through years of unrelenting abuse from Allstate and its San Antonio conspirators. I knew that one part of her wanted out, to live a normal life and to be able to grow her family and career without constant stress and need for recovery. But she loved me. She couldn't bring herself to leave. She would stick it out.

Tedi's dissociative response to trauma was incompatible with my fight response. She needed to pretend it wasn't happening. I needed to anticipate and respond quickly to the constant barrage of assaults Allstate was throwing my way. The pressure to live normally almost always backfired. The minute I let my guard down, Allstate operatives would attack. My life wasn't normal, and I couldn't pretend that it was. The conspirators' ability to negatively impact my life was infinite.

I was stuck in a classic catch-22. I knew that I could not save my marriage if I did not complete this project and expose the participants who had been attacking my family with impunity for years. I also knew that I would probably not be able to do the staggering amount of work needed to complete the project and provide a safe and healthy environment for my family at the same time.

It was a toxic environment that could leave lasting scars on our children, despite our best efforts to shield them. I couldn't ask them to go through this anymore.

Tedi and the kids deserved a normal life. I had made up my mind. I knew what I needed to do. I looked at my beautiful partner of nearly 15 years.

"I want a divorce," I said.

21 | IMMUNITY

The ghost of Bobby Joe Phillips

ONCE, I SPOKE TO A real good cop. She was a detective in SAPD's Internal Affairs department. She treated me respectfully, investigated my complaint honestly, and recommended disciplinary actions for a San Antonio cop who had chummed with drug dealers behind my house and then falsified a police report. But that was more than a decade ago and at the time, she was already in the process of retiring from the force. She'd had just a few weeks left. I asked her what she would be doing once she retired. Her answer summed up the stark reality confronting the city of San Antonio:

"I know one thing," the retiring SAPD detective had told me, "I won't be calling the police."

San Antonio had a severe cop problem, but then so did the rest of America.

On May 25, 2020, the world watched in horror as Minneapolis police officer Derek Chauvin coldly murdered 46-year-old George Floyd. Video showed Chauvin deliberately kneeling on Floyd's neck, constricting his breathing until he died. Floyd was handcuffed at the time, lying prone on his stomach. While he could still breathe, the victim begged for his life and called for his mother. Increasingly frantic onlookers begged the cops for mercy. The camera captured Chauvin casually staring back with the indifferent gaze of a psychopath. He could not be persuaded to spare the victim's life. He had learned that he didn't have to.

Three other cops helped Chauvin by holding down the dying man and keeping the traumatized witnesses at bay while Chauvin coolly murdered. The video-recorded murder of George Floyd was a flashpoint for the country. Americans saw with their own eyes that the justice system had absolved bad cops' criminal behavior for so long that one of them thought nothing of callously snuffing a man on camera, in the middle of the day, for the entire world to see.

Protests rocked the nation, shining an unflinching light on the American government's complicity in the state-sanctioned murders of its own citizens. It was as if the benign mask of America's democratic image had slipped off to reveal something unexpectedly grotesque.

Russian president Vladimir Putin, long denounced by American politicians as a vicious, anti-democracy despot who assassinates his critics in cold blood, suddenly became more visible. He granted several high profile interviews with international journalists. It looked a lot like a victory lap.

Na-na-na-na boo-boo, that sort of thing.

The police murder of George Floyd had drastically altered the world's view of the United States, and Putin knew it. In a broadcast interview with NBC News, he countered questions about his alleged assassinations with commentary on police killings of black Americans. Putin, internationally condemned for multiple poison attacks of critics home and abroad, mocked American media's outrage at the idea of state-sanctioned murder. *Glass houses*, he seemed to be saying. *The pot calling the kettle black.*[124]

Meanwhile, the San Antonio Police Department was showing it couldn't reform itself. A collective bargaining agreement negotiated in 1974 had ensured that the SAPD would continue to provide a safe haven for bad cops. The false arrests, fictional police reports, and routine absolution by local, state, and federal authorities I documented revealed a terrible reality: *Nothing existed to stop a corrupt cop from turning his badge into a tool for criminal networks.*

The SAPD chugged along, a time bomb, as far as I was concerned. James Flavin, the SAPD captain who watched quietly as city attorneys taunted and abused me during depositions, had been promoted to assistant chief, charged with repairing the department's reputation for being infamously homophobic.

Phelan, the detective who helped "practicing attorney" Kristina Combs steal the Auris Project's information center assets, had retired from the SAPD. So had Michael Helle, the police union president so skilled at thwarting police accountability. I suspected that both former SAPD officers now worked for private intelligence firms, but couldn't figure out a way to prove my suspicions. The photogenic Flavin, I wagered, would one day be chief of police.

Still, the SAPD was experiencing a reckoning, of sorts.

In San Antonio, the Black Lives Matter movement coalesced in powerful ways. Protests started small, with a few dozen young activists marching against police brutality in downtown San Antonio. Before long, their ranks grew. The young protesters soon teamed up with veteran activists who had been protesting for police reform since the civil rights movement.

It turned out to be a powerful partnership. The young activists brought boundless energy and internet savvy. The longtime activists brought crucial historical knowledge and a deep understanding of local systems and people. The collaboration quickly grew into a powerful movement for police reform. Several generations of local activists working on a variety of social justice issues formed the San Antonio Coalition for Police Accountability, or SACPA.

Soon, San Antonians had approved the inclusion of a measure on the ballot that could ensure police accountability. Called Proposition B, it sought to remove the city's collective bargaining agreement with the police union, which severely limits the police chief's ability to discipline and permanently remove bad cops.

The union and its supporters responded aggressively to this unexpectedly sophisticated push to hold cops responsible. Poll watchers complained that cops in uniform accosted voters on their way to the polls, offering them pizza and water. Other activists accused goons supporting the police union of pulling down signs, intimidating voters, and otherwise harassing people as they walked up to voting centers. "I personally witnessed all sorts of violations of voting code," said Ananda Sunshine Thomas, president of ACT4SA, a leading organization in the local police reform movement.

And in a disquieting revelation, several reform activists reported being followed by men in baseball caps and sunglasses.

Prop B lost by a slim, two-point margin. But police reform advocates were upbeat after the loss. The accountability measure had performed better than most people had expected, and the coalition had gained crucial knowledge about how to rid the city of bad cops, said Thomas. The fight continued, but certain participants began fomenting discord. Collaborations that started out so promising began to fall apart. No one knew whom to trust.

THE MOVEMENT REVEALED ANOTHER STARK reality: before the Black Lives Matter movement, SAPD cops had received the message that the only limits to their conduct are the ones they impose on themselves.

Not much had changed in police accountability in San Antonio since the 1968 SAPD gang murder of Bobby Joe Phillips.

A black construction worker who had fled the scene of a bar brawl, Phillips would die a horrific death. Police pursued Phillips, caught him on South New Braunfels Avenue in front of the city graveyards, and savagely brutalized him until he was dead.

What the cops didn't know was that others had followed the pursuit from the bar and hid in the darkness of the city graveyard, where they had full view of the murder. The witnesses could see everything. They would later testify that they watched in horror as the cops viciously beat the victim with billy clubs, batons, and the butts of their guns. In a frenzy of bloodlust, cops jumped on the prone, unmoving man's head as it lay bloodied on the curb. The medical examiner ruled Phillip's death a homicide.

And yet, the killers of Bobby Joe Phillips were found not guilty by a three-judge civil service commission panel. In what would become a disturbing, systematized pattern of mutual absolution in local San Antonio politics, the district attorney, relying on the civil service commission decision, declined to prosecute the cops - despite eyewitness testimony, the medical examiner's report, and the overwhelming evidence that confirmed that the cops had committed cold-blooded murder.

The system of impunity for police officers is today an intractable element of police culture, a canker sore that has eroded public trust and provided cover for organized crime.

Many cops are emotionally, mentally, psychically, spiritually, and environmentally able to stop themselves from engaging in gross abuses and injustice. They were raised in good homes, encouraged to develop strong characters, avoided indoctrination into racism or homophobia, and entered the police force because they sincerely wanted to protect and serve their communities. We are predisposed to think of these folks as heroes, and in many ways they are. Of course they are welcomed into the police force.

But so are the racists, the misogynists, the homophobes, the narcissists, the cons, and yes, the psychopaths. It is, according to a growing mountain of evidence, a corrosive mingling of good with evil. Good cops, the ones who want to be heroes, are stuck in a morass of corruption, unfairly judged by the deeds of the worst among them.

The systematic betrayal of good cops has become rooted in police culture. No wonder so many are killing themselves.

The FBI, part III: a new reality

The federal government is supposed to step up when citizens cannot reliably depend on local authorities for justice. But by 2021, the San Antonio FBI had ensnared only two people in its much-publicized, high profile anti-corruption probe into the Bexar County, Texas courthouse: the bigmouthed lawyer Al Acevedo, and Angus McGinty, the sniveling judge whose car Acevedo had fixed in return for judicial favors.

The FBI had intercepted hundreds of phone calls in and around the courthouse for months in 2013. Eight years later, no additional charges had been filed against anyone else. Why? Was it because of the sheer immensity of the corruption that has bedeviled San Antonians? Or, was it something else, something far more disturbing? Had the local FBI quietly closed the investigation without telling the public? I just didn't know.

At the end of the day, ample evidence exists for charging many people with a multitude of federal corruption, constitutional, and racketeering crimes.

There's also plenty of evidence that the local district attorney's office and the police department use taxpayer funds to routinely protect corrupt public officials in San Antonio engaging in obstruction of justice, fraud, bribery, racketeering, corruption, battery, larceny, conspiracy, forgery, money laundering, and much more.

There is irrefutable evidence that Bexar County District Attorney Joe Gonzales knowingly assisted a malicious prosecution against a crime victim when he was still a billboard attorney; and that former DA Nico LaHood knowingly maintained a malicious prosecution. The record shows that Bexar County judges Antonio Arteaga, Barbara Nellermoe, Karen Pozza, Scott Roberts, Michael Mery and others covered up forgeries and theft of more than $100,000 in assets, and contributed to the destruction of a much-needed community information center during a time of rampant title fraud. Court records show that federal judges Robert L. Pittman, John W. Primomo, and David Ezra used the power of the federal courts to cover up assaults, thefts, and illegal detentions meant to silence an American citizen exercising her constitutionally protected rights. The conspirators committed these crimes confidently, coolly, without remorse. They were at all times empowered and protected by failed or co-opted public oversight systems. They committed these crimes under color of law, and they did it while the FBI was supposedly investigating local government.

They are just a few of the perpetrators, and I am just one of many victims.

If enough evidence exists for the feds to corroborate these allegations, why haven't they yet? Had the FBI missed the boat? Had it devolved so thoroughly under McKinsey's so-called engagement that it needs a whole new re-organization to be effective in this complicated new world?

It would not be the first time the FBI had to reinvent itself. It did so in the 1970s when it took on the Italian mafia. By that time, local law enforcement had ceded control of New York City to five mafia crime families. The Bonanno, Colombo, Gambino, Genovese, and Luchese clans were freely engaging in extortion, bank robbery, prostitution, drug dealing, loansharking, gambling, and murder. In a single month, 137 banks in the city were robbed while law enforcement stood by. The mafia controlled unions, judges, and cops. They had their hands in everything.

Good cops were powerless. They managed to arrest some mafia members, but those arrests made no difference to the city's crime rate. The mob bosses, the criminals directing all of the chaos, remained out of reach. The Italian Mafia organizational structure made it virtually impossible for investigators to link the masterminds to their crimes. The criminal organizations raked in money unfettered. The mafia's collective revenue totaled more than $50 billion a year, the feds estimated. The U.S. government stood humiliated.

"It was the golden era of the mob," former mobster Michael Franzese said in the riveting Netflix documentary series *Fear City*. "The FBI couldn't keep up with us. There was no way."[125]

The mafia's domination of law enforcement was so complete, the city so lawless, citizens started forming groups for self-protection.[126]

It turned out that the FBI actually had the perfect tool for fighting organized crime: the Racketeer Influenced and Corrupt Organizations Act, or RICO. A federal statute signed into law by President Richard Nixon in 1970, the RICO statute allowed the government to prosecute crimes committed by criminal organizations rather than just individuals. If the government could show you were a participating member of the organization committing the felonies, you could go down whether you were at the scene of the crime or not.

It was a powerful law. The problem? The FBI wasn't using it.

Robert Blakey, the Cornell Law School professor who drafted the law, began conducting RICO training camps at Cornell for somewhat dubious FBI agents. Soon, the FBI began using wiretaps, covert surveillance, and financial sleuthing to connect mob bosses to the actions on the street. Before long, the Justice Department began bringing down a host of organized criminal actors, including "organized crime members, corrupt political figures, and faithless union officials."[127] Criminals pulling the strings from a distance started doing real time.

The Justice Department convicted the San Antonio judge McGinty and lawyer Al Acevedo using some of the same investigative techniques that brought down the Italian Mafia. They tapped phones, conducted surveillance, used informants, and followed the money trail.

But the crime fighting tools that snagged McGinty and Acevedo are virtually useless against many organized criminal actors today.

As this book shows, the criminal networks running roughshod over American justice today are supported by experts in wiretapping, cyberhacking, covert surveillance, and financial wizardry. In many ways, they are more sophisticated than the government agencies who are supposed to be pursuing them.

These new criminal networks focus almost exclusively on quietly exploiting the frailties in the American protective systems from within. If you control judges, cops, and government administrators, you can commit almost any crime with impunity. If you want to "control your environment" as a criminal mastermind in America, you must build a network of "informants" across the political and social spectrum: lawyers, officials, postal workers, Apple "geniuses," garbage men, reporters, policemen, mailmen, store clerks, and delivery drivers.

While the feds focus on careless public officials, intelligence firms are busy bribing everyday citizens on a daily basis. Anyone bribable is brought into the fold as "informants," lavished with praise, and gifted money and unearned resources until the moment they are called to earn their place. That's apparently how Scientologists beat the government back in the 1970s and that is apparently how the networks used by Allstate and other powerful entities are preying on citizens in the New Millennium. The motive for the church was tax-free status; the motive for Allstate was 100 percent victory in the courts.

Only folks with billions of dollars of other people's money can expect to achieve something so ambitious.

So far, the FBI, indeed, the entire U.S. intelligence and law enforcement community, has failed to keep up with the threats. And while American law enforcement and intelligence agencies are floundering against systematic attacks, efforts are underway to infiltrate and control them, too.

American law enforcement are behind organizations like McKinsey & Company, Scientology, and Allstate, who have already mastered the ability to build robust systems of information gathering and public participation.

"The importance of integrated, all-source analysis cannot be overstated," the national commission on terrorist attacks asserted. "Without it, it is not possible to 'connect the dots.'"[128]

Which brings us back to the cops on the Eastside who spent years flooding police records with false reports.

I documented as SAPD police officers spent ten years scrubbing countless law enforcement records of brazen, destructive criminal activity. The names of people who committed fraud, theft, assault, and a host of other crimes are nowhere to be found in SAPD police reports. Meanwhile, local, state, and federal authorities routinely absolved cops of crimes ranging from fraud to murder by collective bargaining agreements, police unions, grand juries, police brass, and district attorneys. And not just in San Antonio.

If cops are the frontline of information gathering, and San Antonio police officers are examples of policing across the nation, then we can see why the government intelligence apparatus in the United States is floundering against the sophisticated criminal networks and domestic terrorists now threatening the United States. Routine falsification of police reports will continue to have a negative, potentially devastating impact on our government's ability to protect us. That's another reason why black lives matter.

Recent national news events reveal a country at severe risk.

In October 2021, the U.S. Central Intelligence Agency, also a former client of McKinsey & Company, acknowledged that dozens of its informants around the world had been compromised, arrested, or killed in what appeared to be a systematic attack on the American spy apparatus.[129]

The American intelligence community had experienced yet another devastating, mortifying example of its inability to understand the world it was confronting.

And therein lies the rub:

The question isn't whether SAPD officers systematically victimized Denise McVea, assisted in vast criminal conspiracies implicating a major corporation, or helped a shadowy network hound Kirsten Kloppe to death.

The question is: what's to stop them?

Under Color of Law

Like the RICO laws in the 1970s, the Justice Department today has a powerful law at its disposal to combat the corruption and official abuse that is threatening American society: Section 242 of Title 18, otherwise known as the "deprivation of rights under color of law" statute.

And much like the game changing federal RICO racketeering law in the 1970s, the Justice Department isn't using it.

Section 242 of Title 18 makes it a crime for a person acting under color of any law to deprive a person of a right or privilege protected by the Constitution or laws of the United States.

Since at least directly after the Civil War, or because of it, lawmakers recognized that government officials who used their official positions to abuse the rights of Americans were a threat to society.

Color of law violations include unlawful acts committed by federal, state, or local officials both inside and outside of the official's lawful authority. For instance, if a police officer illegally arrests someone, and a judge then misuses the law to absolve that cop of responsibility for the unlawful arrest, then both the officer and the judge have violated the federal color of law statute. All federal prosecutors have to do is show that the cop used his position to victimize the unlawfully arrested victim and the judge misrepresented law to cover up the unlawful arrest.

In other words, according to a 2004 report from Syracuse University, the statute provides penalties for officials who committed abusive acts "within their lawful authority, but also acts done beyond the bounds of that official's lawful authority, if the acts are done while the official is purporting to or pretending to act in the performance of his/her official duties."

Police officers, prisons guards, and other law enforcement officials can be subject to severe penalties for violating the act. Judges, public healthcare providers, and others who are acting as public officials can face charges for committing crimes under color of law. Unlike civil rights laws, perpetrators don't have to be motivated by prejudice against any protected group. The victim doesn't need to check a race, color, religion, sex, handicap, familial status or national origin in order to be theoretically protected by this law.

Theoretically, punishment for committing crimes under color of law range from a fine, one year in prison, or up to a life sentence. In particularly heinous cases, say, like the wanton George Floyd murder by Minneapolis police, penalties can theoretically include a death sentence.

The law reads:

> TITLE 18, U.S.C., SECTION 242
> Whoever, under color of any law, statute, ordinance, regulation, or custom, willfully subjects any person in any State, Territory, Commonwealth, Possession, or District to the deprivation of any rights, privileges, or immunities secured or protected by the Constitution or laws of the United States...shall be fined under this title or imprisoned not more than one year, or both; and if bodily injury results from the acts committed in violation of this section or if such acts include the use, attempted use, or threatened use of a dangerous weapon, explosives, or fire, shall be fined under this title or imprisoned not more than ten years, or both; and if death results from the acts committed in violation of this section or if such acts include kidnapping or an attempt to kidnap, aggravated sexual abuse, or an attempt to commit aggravated sexual abuse, or an attempt to kill, shall be fined under this title, or imprisoned for any term of years or for life, or both, or may be sentenced to death.

It is a powerful law designed to hold public officials, especially those in law enforcement and justice, accountable for abusing their authority.

According to Syracuse University study, however, federal prosecutors refused to prosecute color of law violations against American citizens 98.7 percent of the time.[130]

In contrast, the DOJ declined only seven percent of cases where a person was charged with attempting to reenter the United States.

Between 1986 and 2003, U.S. investigative agencies charged 43,331 public officials with violating the federal color of law statute.

The U.S. Attorney's Office prosecuted only 690.

The U.S. Attorney's Office in San Antonio, who had to recluse itself from the McGinty and Acevedo corruption trials for conflict of interest, declined *99 percent* of the color of law cases referred. So did the other thee judicial districts in Texas. All this while touting the law as crucial to the protection of democracy on DOJ websites.

Judicial districts in Manhattan, San Juan, Puerto Rico, Brooklyn, and Ashville, N.C. performed better, but only slightly.

"As the data make very clear," stated the report, "the role of the federal government as the court of last resort when it comes to dealing with abusive government officials has long been spotty, with almost all of the matters recommended for prosecution by the FBI being declined by the assistant U.S. Attorneys."

The DOJ's Civil Rights Division floated a number of excuses to explain why it refused to protect Americans' civil rights. The racism and elitism embedded in one excuse is eye-opening.

"The victims of most official misconduct cases tend to be unsympathetic while the defendants often are well respected members of the community," the division explained.[131]

As the Black Lives Matter's movement has demonstrated, most of the victims of the police and judicial abuse are law-abiding, contributing members of society. And as this book illustrates, many of the targets of official abuse are victimized solely because they do not have the financial resources to fight back.

Federal civil rights prosecutors used a number of rubber stamp reasons to decline the thousands of color of law cases: lack of evidence of criminal intent; minimal federal interest; no federal offense evident; or weak or insufficient admissible evidence. The rest, about 22 percent, were rejected at "agency request" or "per instructions from the Department of Justice."

In other words, it is U.S. Department of Justice policy to reject color of law cases.

The advent of social media has exposed police and judges' routine abuse of law-abiding Americans. The public now largely rejects the suggestion that accusers come from society's underbelly, even if that *was* an acceptable excuse, which, of course, it is not.

In the wake of the Black Lives Matter movement, the United Nations called for member states to end impunity enjoyed by police officers who violate the human rights of black people. The UN commissioned a global investigation, which found that police rarely are held accountable for violating the human rights of black people. The current and historical climate of systemic racism and impunity is "untenable," said U.N. High Commissioner Michelle Bachelet.[132]

She's right. History has shown that a cop who can turn against one segment of the population can just as quickly turn against the rest of his country.

For instance, when Nazis invaded Austria just prior to World War II, Vienna citizens were expecting to see violent clashes in the city's streets. Local police had sworn oaths to protect Austria as an independent state and had often cracked down on illegal Nazi activity, but when Nazi soldiers arrived in Vienna in March 1938, city police officers quickly pledged fealty to the invaders.[133] A citizen watched in disbelief as Viennese police officers lining the street reached in their pockets and slipped Nazi swastika armbands on their arms.[134]

In the following weeks, Austrian police stood silently by as Nazis began assaulting, kidnapping, robbing, and killing Austrian Jews and other citizens deemed enemies of the German state.

Some police officers participated in the violence.

22 | REVELATION

A new era

BY 2021, THE UNITED STATES WAS IN CRISIS. In January, most Americans remained quarantined against the coronavirus. On January 6, Trump supporters stormed the U.S. Capitol in a frantic bid to keep lawmakers from certifying the U.S. elections that ousted Donald Trump. Several people died as a result of the mob attack, including a capitol police officer. A few capitol officers committed suicide soon after, and Republican lawmakers strived to paint the violent event as just another capitol tour. Criminal and enemy state-sponsored hackers were successfully attacking U.S. government cyber networks at will. Conservative Republicans continued to foment lies about the 2020 presidential election but stopped scoffing at scientific evidence of climate change as whole swaths of the country burned, flooded, or whipped around in the wind. In Texas, more than 50 people died and roughly 4.5 million homes or businesses lost power in an unprecedented winter vortex. Mass shootings continued to plague the country.

I was trying to finish my book. And 12 years after the wreck on the corner of Hildebrand and Blanco, I was still ensnared in Allstate's zero sum game.

I had everything I needed to complete the book in terms of evidence. Tedi and the kids were safely ensconced in a small yellow bungalow in an old, quiet neighborhood on the Southeast side. But my life was in shambles. I was now twice-divorce, my house was falling down around me, and I remained under 24-hour surveillance.

My ability to make a living had been thoroughly degraded. The platforms I had created to support Auris Books Press sat partially constructed and wasting away. Over the years, I had spent thousands of dollars to build platforms and processes that I could not use due to incessant hacking. I could not develop or update my own organizations' websites because hackers continued to launch round-the-clock denial of service attacks against my network.

On January 19, Tedi filed for divorce. I divided my time between writing the book and trying to get the city to hold GL Hunt and their rubber stamp engineering companies accountable for helping Ruhd and Lopez destroy my historic home. I practiced meditation. I would occasionally jump on Facebook or Zoom to chat with close friends, but for the most part my only face-to-face contacts were with my children.

I installed extra security in my home, and I took other measures that I felt would keep me safe. I had secured my network and devices. Surveillance and attempts to hack into my systems continued, but I had learned my persecutors' tactics very well. I remained self-reliant. I had closed most of the internet attack vectors that Allstate's operatives had exploited for so many years, essentially protecting my files from attack. I had a harder time fighting man-in-the-middle, IMSI catcher, and denial of service attacks, but I was also making it hard for hackers.

I stayed vigilant. One misstep, I knew, and I could be back to square one.

My last trip to the FBI

On March 1, 2021, I went to visit the FBI. I wanted to hand over evidence of the open use of IMSI catchers in San Antonio. I didn't get past the perimeter.

Due to the Covid-19 pandemic, the guard informed me, the FBI was not accepting walk-ins. Aren't you all precious, I thought. The guard gave me a card with the FBI tip line on it. You have to make an appointment, he said. I decided to call while I sat in the FBI parking lot. I dialed the number on the card. A young man with dreads walked past my windshield. He was carrying a backpack and looking at his phone.

"FBI tip line," a woman answered.

I told her I wanted to provide an agent with information about the organized use of gang stalking and the use of IMSI catchers in San Antonio. That is not a matter for the FBI, she said. I told her I also wanted to make an appointment to provide the FBI with information about a murder. Call the local police, she said coldly, that is not a matter for the FBI.

'The local police cannot be trusted," I said.

"I'm going to release the line now," she said. She hung up.

I called back.

"FBI tip line," a woman answered.

I told her I wanted to make an appointment to speak to an agent.

"What is this regarding?" she asked.

I told her I had information about the identity of a private intelligence firm using cyber hacking and other illegal activity to cover up public corruption.

"How do you know this?" she blurted.

"Someone who worked for them told me."

"How do you know he worked for them?" she asked abruptly. I could hear the tension in her voice. Panic, even. I wasn't talking to the FBI.

"They paid him," I said.

"Do you know the name of the company?" she asked tightly.

"I don't feel comfortable saying over the phone."

"Well, the FBI is not doing in-person meetings because of COVID."

"Maybe I can drop the information off."

"No! Uh, you can mail it."

"Why can't I just drop it off? At the perimeter?"

"I suggest you mail it."

She hung up. I would not be using the U.S. Mail to send anything to the FBI.

The next day, a white man wearing a heavy orange backpack trekked up and down Hackberry on the side of the house each time I reset my virtual private network. I opened the window and yelled at nothing in particular, using my best Shrek impression: "Donkey! Donkey!"

He shot me the finger.

I laughed.

The killing of Kirsten Kloppe

On May 21, 2020, I wrote one last time to SAPD Chief William McManus, imploring him to do something about the constant hacking and stalking. I was determined that he could never say he was unaware of what was being done to me and my family, so I included numerous examples of the types of attacks I had been complaining about for years.

"The last time I called SAPD to file a complaint," I wrote, "the dispatcher asked if I had any evidence. Because I have provided evidence to SAPD officers in the past, I am copying this evidence to you."

The letter contained screenshots of all sorts of attacks reported by my cybersecurity apps, including account spoofing, network downgrade attacks, cross-site scripting attacks, fake security certificate attacks, and fake cell tower attacks. These were actual, verifiable reports from well-known cyber-security companies. I also showed evidence of illegal phone intrusion and surveillance. These are a fraction of the attacks I have endured, I wrote. With sense of utter futility, I asked the chief of police to once again to intervene.

He never responded.

On May 29, 2020, hackers instigated an all-out attack on my network. Frustrated, I called the police. I told dispatch that I wanted to make a report of the attacks. Twenty minutes later, two SUV squad cars pulled up in front of the house. I met a young officer at my gate. My five-year-old son Dax, who wanted to be a police officer, ran to put on his police uniform to greet the officer.

But the cop was stiff and cold when I greeted him. For the 100th time, I explained what was happening. Two cops sat in the other squad glaring at me. I waved at them. The cop in the passenger seat gave the tiniest unsmiling nod. The cop in the driver's seat didn't return my greeting. He just stared, ominously.

The responding cop looked at me coldly as I explained. He cut me off.

"Do you have any proof?" he asked abruptly.

"I'm glad you asked," I said. I held out the letter I had written to McManus, and explained that there was plenty of proof in it. He tried to ignore it. I explained that I had been instructed to provide it to police officers who came to my house. He took it reluctantly, but did not look at it. Dax ran out and stood proudly before the cop in his spiffy cop uniform. The cop ignored him. He was busy gearing up to refuse to make a report. The two cops in the squad car looked on. None of them acknowledged the little boy standing proudly in his cop uniform. It made me sick. Dax's five-year-old face fell.

I told him he looked great, and sent the crestfallen boy back into the house. I did not want my son around these people, anyway.

The cop was holding the letter at my gate but still hadn't looked at it. He said something about no suspects being identified or laws being broken so he couldn't make a report. He tried to hand the letter back to me, but I kept my hands down.

"The chief said I was to give that letter to the responding officer the next time it happened." I bluffed. "He said it needed to be recorded on the street level."

A look of concern flashed across his face. For the first time, the cop looked at the letter. His face changed. He perused the letter quickly. Yes, it was addressed to Chief McManus. He flashed a look at the cops in the other squad car, who now seemed more animated. His demeanor changed completely. In a warmer, friendlier tone, he asked if he could take the letter.

"That's why I brought it down," I told him sardonically. "Everything you need is there." He quickly filled out a report sheet and gave me the report number. He returned to his squad car and I walked back upstairs. Dax had taken off his police uniform. I went back to my desk. From my upstairs window, I could see that the monitoring SUV had pulled up next to the responding officer's squad car so that the cops could talk through the windows. When they didn't leave after a few minutes, I returned downstairs to get their badge numbers. The responding officer had given the other two cops the proof letter and left. They were reading it intently. When they saw me, they greeted me with forced joviality. You fake bastards, I thought.

"I'm just down to get your badge numbers," I said, matching their friendly tone. "It's no big deal. I was told to do that for every police visit."

They complied quickly, smiling pleasantly.

The letter had worked. Their Allstate mission had been to answer the call but avoid making a report. They wouldn't be able to do that now, I thought.

Weeks later, Dax and I would encounter a San Antonio cop while playing on the empty, expansive plaza at the Alamodome. I greeted the cop, but Dax turned away.

"You used to like to talk to officers," I told him. "Do you not like cops anymore?"

"No," he said decidedly.

"Why?" I asked.

"I don't know," he mumbled.

I remembered the cop who had dissed him at our gate. Even at the time I could see that the rejection had impacted my son deeply.

And then they wonder, I thought.

At the same time, we *were* living in the age of George Floyd, the poor man Minneapolis cops callously murdered in broad daylight on May 25, 2020. There was no telling what my beautiful boy had heard. I said something about there being many good cops out there, but my heart just wasn't in it.

I changed the subject.

"Let's play with our shadows!" I suggested. That did the trick.

Crooked cops quickly forgotten, Dax spread his arms wide, located his shadow on the Alamodome plaza pavement, and broke into a wild little dance.

LATER, I WOULD COME ACROSS the audio recording I made of the May 2020 encounter with the cops who dissed my five-year-old son and tried to avoid taking the letter showing screenshots of the cyberattacks on my network and devices.

I realized that I hadn't seen the police report from that day so I made a public information act request. It came fairly rapidly. I read it.

It was frightening.

According to incident report SAPD-2020-0647507, dispatcher Derek Bjerke was the first SAPD employee that day to characterize me as mentally ill.

Officer Irving Gonzalez was the officer who met me at my gate. He was the cop who tried to avoid taking the letter of proof before dutifully giving it to Levon Harrison and Christian Valadez, the two cops who glared so threateningly from their squad car and who I later surprised intently reading the letter that showed proof of systemic cyberattacks. Despite hungrily reading the letter, they omitted it completely from the police report. The report stated:

> POSS PSYCHE...BELIEVES SHE IS BEING "CYBER ATTACKED"...WHEN ASKED FOR SPECIFICS, WOULD ONLY STATE THAT ITS (sic) HER INTERNET AND THAT THERE ARE THOUSANDS OF OCCURRENCES...
>
> IS A PSYCHE BUT NOT A DANGER TO HERSELF OR OTHERS. (MCVEA) EXPLAINED TO ME THERE IS (sic) PEOPLE IN HER BACKYARD HACKING HER ACCOUNTS AND SENDING HER MESSAGES TO NO(t) PUBLISH ANY OF HER WORK REGARDING THE CORRUPTION OF THE CITY. WANTED ME TO GIVE HER A CFS# AND DOCUMENT THIS INCIDENT. NO FURTHER ACTION TAKEN. THOUSANDS OF OCCURRENCES...[135]

The cops had generated another false police report. There was no mention of the proof letter I had provided. Instead, they continued to characterize me as "psyche," while suppressing proof of my claims. But that wasn't the most frightening part. This time, there was another word included that I had never seen before. It rested on page 2, in the section where SAPD officer Levon Harrison recorded his reason for being there:

Cover, it said.

Cover? He was there to protect Gonzalez from me, the word seemed to imply. The letter to McManus had certainly thrown a wrench in the cops' plan, but what were their plans exactly?

I knew that Allstate co-conspirators were panicking. Allstate had spent millions to provoke, terrorize and agitate me precisely so that I would act out and thereby confirm the false claims of mental instability flooding court and police records. I had seen what happened when people fell into that trap. There was, for instance, California personal injury lawyer Christopher Hook who almost lost his law license when he blew up, called Allstate lawyers crooks, and told them to "eat a bowl of dicks."[136] There were also John Foddrill and Michael Cuellar, two local whistleblowers banned by San Antonio city officials from city hall after the men complained in separate cases about fraud, waste, and corruption in city departments. Police chief McManus and city attorneys repeatedly insinuated that the whistleblowers posed unspecified threats. City officials pointed to angry letters that the provoked men dashed off as proof that they were erratic.

I took those cautionary tales to heart. Despite the constant attacks, I continued to show remarkable restraint. I leaned heavily on my journalism training to keep my letters factual, professional, and objective. That had to suck for Allstate.

The cops' hiding of the proof letter in May of 2020 shook me. I felt like I had dodged a bullet. I knew firsthand how skilled SAPD cops were at escalating situations. I also knew that I wouldn't be the first person killed by cops who would later justify the killing by saying things had just gotten out of control.

Allstate had spent millions to drive me crazy, make me desperate. By this time, I was supposed to be a husk of my former self, a person so anxious and paranoid that I would be easily dismissed and discounted. I had, through spiritual fitness and determination, avoided that fate. But the police record said something different. The false police reports dating back years would certainly exonerate Harrison if he had to step in and protect Gonzalez in a confrontation with someone that multiple police reports had declared was "psyche." Someone unpredictable, paranoid, violently delusional.

Someone clearly responsible for her own death.

Someone like Kirsten Kloppe.

On Saturday, January 27, 2018, San Antonio resident Kirsten Kloppe called the San Antonio Police Department to report that someone was stalking her and interfering with her computers.

According to SAPD police chief William McManus, the three responding officers found Kloppe locked inside an upstairs room. McManus told reporters that officers asked through the door if she had a weapon and Kloppe said no. Cops broke down the door and, according to the police narrative, found the 43-year-old woman holding a gun to her own head.

The officers tackled her, police said, and tried to disarm her. In the struggle that ensued, according to police, the gun allegedly began "making its way" toward an officer's head. SAPD officer Crystal Estrada stepped back and shot one bullet into Kloppe's abdomen, killing her.[137]

McManus quickly told the press that Kloppe had a history of mental illness.

Wait a minute, I thought. The killing had just happened. *He must have gotten that from police reports.*

The cops' story changed several times. Follow-up news reports indicated that the officer who shot Kloppe later admitted seeing a gun magazine in a room before sending an unarmed recruit into the bedroom to disarm the victim. She was suspended for a few days for that. But overall, details were scarce.

Reporters did speak to a couple of people who said they knew Kloppe. Just a handful of comments made it into print, but they added troubling nuance to McManus' public declaration that Kloppe suffered from mental illness.

According to at least one friend, she had been under duress for some time, and had become "paranoid." She became increasingly isolated. One friend said Kloppe had been the victim of longtime domestic abuse, something the police seemed to overlook entirely as they constructed the narrative surrounding her killing. Her friends recounted that she would surface on Facebook for a time, things would seem normal, and then Kloppe would suddenly disappear from social media altogether. It sounded very familiar.

"She had a heart of gold," said one friend, "and was troubled due to things that happened to her."[138] The news reporter did not elaborate.

I read news accounts of the Kloppe killing several times. We had a lot in common, I noticed with dread. We both were characterized by the police as paranoid and delusional because we kept saying people were stalking us and hacking into our computers. Like me, Kloppe had pointed to certain neighbors as being involved in the criminal stalking and harassing activity targeting her. And like me, the police department dismissed her claims as fantastic and unfounded without even a cursory investigation.

And now, one of us was dead, killed by a cop who paid a weeklong suspension for the killing. Estrada, the cop who killed her, had received a month-long suspension but because of collective bargaining, her suspension was reduced to seven days.[139] At the time of Kloppe's death, the chief of police stood before reporters and quickly exonerated the cops of the killing.

"They did everything right," McManus said, although we would later learn that wasn't true. The American news media quickly reduced homicide victim Kirsten Kloppe for all eternity as "mentally ill." (The only news outlet I came across to resist that urge wasn't American: the United Kingdom's *Daily Mail*.[140]

The SAPD summarily closed the Kloppe case.

There had apparently been no investigation of her stalking and harassment complaints and no comparison between what she actually told cops and what they wrote in police reports prior to the killing. For the public, thanks to San Antonio police and local news media, the Kirsten Kloppe case started only after Kloppe allegedly pointed a gun at her own head. And now she was dead, forever remembered as little more than mentally ill based primarily on the word of the police department that killed her.

Poor Kirsten, I thought.

There but for the grace of God go I.

23 | BIRDSEYE

The city attacks 1006 Wyoming

AT EVERY TURN, ALLSTATE'S EFFORTS to silence me would expose other organized criminal conspiracies that, at least on the face of it, had nothing to do with Allstate.

By the end of summer 2021, Allstate and its enablers knew that I remained determined to complete this book and that I had gathered some damaging evidence. By this point, they had a good idea of what I would be alleging: that local judges routinely obstructed justice, county courts and offices contain records known by officials to be fraudulent, the county jury system is tainted, cops routinely falsify reports to hide criminal activity, and key local government departments are under private control. And I had proof.

Corrupt officials could not expunge public record as long as key evidence existed outside of government offices. When Combs, Hernandez, and the other burglars broke into the information center at 1614 Martin Luther King, the first thing they did was pore through file cabinets. But, after the 2010 Danny Santos burglary, I had kept most of the key documents at home.

The conspirators knew what I had, because years before I had given copies of the evidence to property crimes detective Val Garcia only to later learn that he hid them from the public record.

I wondered to whom he gave those copies.

Ignoring the zeroes and goons surrounding me every day, I began focusing primarily on indexing and securing the thousands of pages of evidence I had accumulated over the years. The documents at 1006 Wyoming provided devastating proof of everything I was alleging. That, I knew, was a problem for Allstate and a host of compromised co-conspirators.

There was damaging evidence at 1006 Wyoming Street and the conspirators wanted inside. Cockroaches began a concentrated effort to get unfettered access to my house. They were happy to destroy the century-old historic home to do it.

Once again, they could call on a team of enablers, this time managers in the city's code enforcement department. Under city manager Sheryl Sculley, the city had installed new leadership to fight corruption in the Development Services Department. The effort failed.

By 2022, I had paid about $40,000 to crooked contractors fed to me by Allstate hackers. The house now had a failing foundation, severely cracked drywall, falling ceilings, windows popping out of their settings, lead paint peeling from siding, wood floors bowing and warping, plumbing cut, and walls separated from their moorings. Several hundred feet of valuable antique shiplap had been stolen. Roofing material had been installed over a gap where a cedar plank had been mysteriously removed. My historic 121-year-old farmhouse was now in substantially worse structural and cosmetic shape than before I spent tens of thousands of dollars to renovate it.

The ability to destroy the old home was a direct result of the San Antonio Police Department's refusal to stop the constant man-in-the-middle and **IMSI** catcher attacks that allowed criminal hackers to control my communications. When I made a search for someone to fix something in my house, the hackers fed me compromised contractors.

Unethical contractors were apparently lining up to participate in the schemes against homeowners in San Antonio. It was a no-brainer. One could take the homeowner's money and breach the contract without repercussions. Getting paid twice is a seductive option for unscrupulous contractors – so long as they were assured they would not get caught. The system of corruption permeating city and county offices offered an almost foolproof guarantee of impunity. City employees worked hand-in-hand with cockroaches to insulate participants from the consequences of their misconduct.

Back in 2018, long before I fully understood the extent of the city's corruption problem, I had complained to DSD director Michael Shannon about contractor John A. Bonillas and his company, Countywide Exteriors. We had hired Bonillas to restore and paint the siding and replace the roof. He degraded the siding, removed planks on the roof, and stole antique siding. After hemming and hawing, DSD said it suspended Bonillas, but Countywide never stopped working in San Antonio. I also filed a police report about the theft and the antique siding, but police refused to investigate. "It's a civil matter," Eastside cops said.

The cops omitted Bonillas's name from the police report.

A few years later, I hired GL Hunt Foundation Repair. The project manager, Dustin Ruhd, was charming and knowledgeable, but by the time he pulled his crew from the site, the foundation was so degraded I couldn't even get under the house. The problems were so profound, and GL Hunt's glee at my distress so evident, I complained again to the city. After much delay, the code enforcement department finally sent combination inspector Gregory Lehman, a plumber, to inspect the work. The ruined foundation was evident even to the casual eye:

> I am not an engineer but I have been in construction for over 30 years, the work on Ms. McVea's foundation was not done to industry standards. Just by walking into her home, right away visible to the naked eye there are substantial drops in elevations throughout the home. Exterior sole plates are actually separated from the subfloors, windows have large gaps, floor tiles are cracked, and even tongue and groove hardwood flooring is bulging and splitting apart from the stress.
>
> On my initial visit there was some cracking in the wall boards which would be consistent with the leveling process, but on my second visit more cracks have appeared and some of the original gaps have worsened. Through my personal observations, I do not believe an actual structural engineer or a qualified individual from their office ever visited this jobsite, there is no way they would have approved this work!
>
> - Email, DSD Inspector Gregory Lehman to supervisors Jeremy McDonald and Ramiro Carrillo, May 14, 2021

Code enforcement supervisors quickly reassigned Lehman.

Thus began a dizzying series of misleading, contradictory, defamatory, and evasive tactics by the contractor and the DSD team in charge of oversight. In a draft report I titled *Conspiracy Theater*,[141] I detailed how DSD Strike Team supervisors Jeremy McDonald, Ramiro Carrillo, Eloy Resendez, and Joseph Bernal brazenly collaborated with the contractors and engineers to cover up the destruction of the house's foundation and help the contractor and engineers escape accountability.[142] Records in DSD files show that engineering companies contracted by GL Hunt - Hollingsworth Pack and Crosstown Engineers - repeatedly minimized or outright omitted code violations and shoddy work in their reports, despite the engineer's reports contradicting DSD inspectors eyewitness accounts, photos of severely degraded piers, and damage documented in DSD Strike Team's own records.

Revealingly, DSD allowed Hollingsworth Pack, the engineer of record, to willfully withhold the required post-pour report created by its engineer Levi Gates, which documented at least some of the destructive work. Despite ample evidence that a post-pour inspection had occurred, the city permitted the contractor to pretend the post-pour inspection performed by Gates never occurred.

This allowed the contractors and engineers to feign ignorance about the obvious errors causing severe damage to the house's structural integrity. It also permitted DSD supervisors to close the homeowner's complaint as unsubstantiated. Many DSD efforts to close the homeowner's complaint occurred directly after private meetings with the contractor and engineers.

After months of pretending to "negotiate" with the company that maliciously destroyed my foundation and the engineers who falsified reports, the DSD supervisor Jeremy McDonald called me.

GL Hunt had finally agreed to come to the property and get to work, he told me. They would need full access to the interior, he said. He sounded stressed.

I started paying close attention.

The contractor only had one request, he said.

I checked to make sure I was recording. I was.

They requested that I, the homeowner and victim, not be present while the crew was inside my house.

I burst out laughing. I knew it was a Hail Mary attempt to get unfettered access to my trove of damning records.

I'm not going to agree to that, I said.

Not long after, McDonald called to inform me that there was nothing more the city could do for me. The city's strike team closed the case despite the overwhelming evidence of criminal malicious mischief, extortion, fraud, and severe code violations. When I made an open records act request to examine DSD's file of my complaint against GL Hunt and the engineers, the city originally sent me my own emails but not a single document between DSD supervisors and the criminal actors attacking my house.

I persisted. When the city manager's office finally turned over the records, it was clear that the city had in its files two obviously fake engineering reports that approved malicious and destructive structural work on a historical home on the Eastside. Months later, despite maliciously destroying the foundation of the 120-year-old historic home at Wyoming Street, city employees invited GL Hunt to give a presentation at the city's Historic Homeowner Fair.

Then the UT law school released a report that put DSD supervisors' bizarre conduct in the proper context.

In November 2021, the Entrepreneurship and Community Development Clinic of the University of Texas at Austin School of Law Released *Ousted: The City of San Antonio's Displacement of Residents through Code Enforcement Actions*. A damning study, it revealed that in a span of five years, San Antonio's DSD code enforcement managers had issued more than 600 orders to vacate and demolish single-family homes in poor black and brown neighborhoods.

By comparison, Houston, Dallas, Austin, and Fort Worth had issued about 16 such orders – combined.[143]

So that was the underlying criminal scheme, I realized. DSD's summary evictions were just another tactic – along with title fraud and arson – to wrest property away from unprotected San Antonians. City officials who knowingly accept falsified engineers' reports absolving code violations could also approve engineering reports that falsely stated a house should come down.

The DSD managers were so confident they could help destroy the house on Wyoming without any repercussions because they had been doing it for years. The scheme had become obvious: corrupt city employees were summarily evicting poor folk on the Eastside and Westside from some houses, while criminal actors were filing forged deeds on other houses. Efficiently, brazenly, they illegally transferred ownership from poor residents to all sorts of shady operators.

Coupled with the evictions and code enforcement frauds against homeowners, it was now clear that the fraud involving Auris's MLK information center was part of a widespread criminal conspiracy by corrupt city employees, lawyers, underwriters, judges, notaries, and others to systematically rob poor people who could not fight back. It looked like I had stepped into another scenario where corrupt government officials were helping private interests prey on the city's most vulnerable citizens. Every aspect of local government seemed compromised.

On February 28, 2023, Amin Tohmaz, the deputy director of the DSD code enforcement department, sat on a panel addressing a group of about 20 neighborhood leaders from across the city. I confronted him. I asked him about the DSD demolitions and evictions exposed in the UT Law report. He was far from truthful in his response. Despite ample evidence, he used the same talking points that he had been using for months: that the UT Law report was "inaccurate," and that the destruction of the house on Wyoming was a "civil matter."

He didn't realize it, but Tohmaz's rote responses revealed that DSD middle managers engaging in corrupt activity against poor residents were, at the very least, acting with tacit approval from Development Services Department leadership.

Months later, pipe under the house sprung a spontaneous leak. I called Big City Plumbing to fix it. The plumbers disconnected an unrelated pipe that carried hot water to my second story living quarters and then extorted $1200 to fix it. The city referred me to the state plumbing oversight agency, the Texas State Board of Plumbing Examiners. The state investigator, Sidney Lankford, diddled with the complaint for a few months before closing it without taking action.

A tale of two cities

San Antonio would not be the first American city to end up completely under the control of secretive private interests.

In 1975, Scientology bought a hotel in downtown Clearwater, a lovely beach town on Florida's Gulf Coast, and wrote up plans to take over the city.

Members slowly began buying properties close to the cult's headquarters.[144] In 2017, companies controlled by Scientologists began scooping up property at a frenetic pace. "They now own most commercial property on every block within walking distance of the waterfront, putting the church firmly in control of the area's future," wrote reporter Tracey McManus of the *Tampa Bay Times*. The newspaper's investigation revealed that many of the sales were for amounts double the properties' appraised values.

The purchases were done so quietly that even city leaders had no idea that downtown real estate now belonged to Scientology. Considered by Scientologists as the church's spiritual headquarters, the city's downtown area now resembles a pristine ghost town.

And then there was Kennebunk, Maine.

When I finally secured my internet, I stumbled across the Kennebunk prostitution case. It was a riveting tale that apparently titillated the country while I was isolated behind Allstate's 24-hour cyber wall.

A pretty young Zumba teacher in the picture-postcard town of Kennebunk had been arrested for using the backrooms of her Zumba studio for paid sex with local men. She entertained more than a hundred men in that studio, from an ex-mayor to a popular high school football coach.[145]

Alexis Wright, then 22, videotaped her transactional trysts and then sent them to her co-conspirator and lover, 57-year-old Mark Strong. A licensed private investigator, Strong ran his own insurance agency in the nearby town of Thomaston.

It was a bizarre arrangement that the authorities never quite figured out.

Wright would send video recordings of her having sex with local men to Strong, all without the johns having any idea someone was watching and recording.

Strong reportedly never took a cut of the more than $150,000 Wright is reported to have raked in from her prostitution business between October 2010 and February 2012. He wanted something else from the arrangement: personal information about the men who paid her for sex. Wright sent Strong a trove of data about her johns – including their license plates numbers – and he badgered her for more. She later told authorities Strong led her to believe she was working for a shadow network.

Could it have been an elaborate plot to corrupt influential and respected citizens of Kennebunk? Strong reportedly was intent on identifying the men having illicit sex on video. What exactly did he intend to do with the information?

The story baffled law enforcement and journalists alike. Journalists seemed to dismiss Strong's alleged references to shadow networks as a fantastical ploy to control a gullible girl. It doesn't appear that police or the press viewed those claims as worth pursuing.

Knowing what I know now, I recognized the prostitution scheme as the first stage of what very well could have ended up a city completely compromised by the secrets held by Strong and his shadowy network. It also wasn't surprising to learn that Strong was an insurance agent *and* a private eye.

The men and the city of Kennebunk should breathe a sigh of relief, I thought. Their arrests probably saved at least some of them from a lifetime of compromised integrity.

CONCLUSION

The zero sum game

THEY DON'T TEACH GAME THEORY in public school, but it is a favorite intellectual topic for economists, executives, and business consultants like those at McKinsey and Allstate. A popular game theory is the zero sum game.

In a zero sum game, one player's gain is another person's loss. Using this theory, game logicians calculate the best way to bring about the best outcome for a favored player.

No wealth is created in this situation.

Zero sum games can be played with two players or millions. It doesn't matter. The amount of money, once on the table, stays the same. Money just travels from one player to another. The question becomes: who will end up with it? You can see this played out every day in discussions of market share. There is a limited amount of revenue in the markets. Corporations compete to increase their share of that market. When one corporation's market share increases, another corporation's market share goes down.

So why am I talking about this?

Because its time the rest of us understood how the game is played:

There are two general types of zero sum games: those with perfect information and those without. In a game with perfect information, every player knows the results of all previous moves. A good example of a game with perfect information is Tic-Tac-Toe. You watch your opponent's moves and he watches yours. When it's their turn, the players move based on what they just saw. In games with imperfect information, the players do not know the previous move, because the players play at the same time. Rock, Paper, Scissors is an example of that.[146]

Actors like McKinsey, Scientology, Allstate, Purdue Pharma, Wells Fargo, *ad nauseum,* have created a cunning hybrid. In the zero sum games they play, they know all of the previous moves, because, well, they designed them. They can see their opponent's moves because, well, they designed those, too.

But the other players, the customers, employees, and general public, can't see previous moves.

The American elite have rigged the game so well that they now get to describe the move they just played, whether it's true or not, and the public has to rely on that information. That is why information is at such a premium. They have it, you don't, so the rules are what they say they are.

Some referees - the courts, law enforcement, and regulatory agencies - are so thoroughly controlled by the favored players, they call disputed plays in favor of the elite without even looking at the board. The zero sum game is played against ordinary Americans all day, every day. It is clever, cynical, and grotesquely lucrative. It's how the top *one percent* of Americans controls $34.2 trillion dollars in wealth while millions on the bottom *half* collectively controls a mere $2.1 trillion.[147]

"Business strategy is all about using uncertain information to make unalterable choices that best create and capture economic surplus," explained McKinsey strategist Yuval Atmonson. "A successful strategist must find and exploit opportunities that establish and protect a sustainable advantage."[148]

In other words, if you control all the information and lock the system in your favor, you'll get all the money and stay on top.

It's working marvelously. With all that stolen money, you can control systems, processes, and people. You can buy anyone and make them do anything. You can move people around like chess pieces. With all that money, you don't have to wonder if the courts or the regulators will rule in your favor. You can make sure they do. That is precisely how San Antonio, Texas became a thriving kleptocracy.[149]

Ironically, the most reliable funding for the defense of atrocious acts committed against U.S. citizens are the U.S. taxpayers themselves. We are excellent sources of funding for our own victimization. Orchestrators of shadow networks know this. That is why they spend so much time and effort trying to control government institutions.

After the takedown of the Italian Mafia, a NYC news anchor concluded: "for law enforcement officials, the questions tonight are, 'who will the next generation of bosses be and what kind of shadowy crime game will they play?'"[150]

And now we know.

You can call this the era of the White-Collar Mafia.

Consider it an upgrade, if you will, of the organized criminal networks exemplified by the Italian Mafia of past lore. These new bosses run their criminal schemes from behind corporate walls and government desks. They can now casually victimize the public using a ruthless hybrid of the fair game/zero sum game using blanket, unchecked corruption.

Less murder, more fraud.

So far.

Allstate strategizes its survival

BUT EVEN THE BEST LAID plans can go astray.

By 2021, Scientology was experiencing mounting headaches. Defections of members continued. The public was turning against it, with mounting calls for the government to revoke its tax exempt status for good. The organization had also unwisely made an enemy of the strong-willed actor Leah Remini, who turned out to be a formidable foe. Remini, a disillusioned, former high-ranking Scientologist, made it her mission to expose the church as a money-hungry cult that brainwashed members, savagely attacked critics, extorted billions from believers, and routinely broke up families.

In her unflinching television series, "Leah Remini: Scientology and the Aftermath," the actor interviewed dozens of former members and others alleging a host of criminal and unethical conduct by the church. Scientology, true to form, responded with blistering, derogatory attacks against Remini and her interviewees, further alienating the public. By early 2023, cult leader David Miscavige was actively dodging subpoenas.

Meanwhile, Allstate's McKinsey-inspired Boxing Gloves policies were proving to be hard to survive over the long term. For one thing, Allstate's stranglehold on the Texas judicial system seemed to be slipping. Savvy young law firms aggressively challenging the insurer were chipping away at the insurer's long-enjoyed impunity. A hail damage case out of San Antonio exposed Allstate's fading ability to command its environment.

A San Antonio couple had made a claim on their Allstate policy after a storm of hailstones larger than golf balls damaged the roof of their home. But, in a familiar scenario, Allstate denied the customer's roof damage claim, citing a cosmetic exclusion. That was news to the Reiningers, who had bought their policy after Allstate convinced them to switch from Liberty Mutual. The policy they ditched did not have a cosmetic exclusion and Allstate assured them that the policy they were switching to was "apples to apples" with their old policy.

Watching other insurance companies quickly fix their neighbors' roofs, and unable to sell or insure their home due to the roof damage, the Reiningers sued Allstate. There was plenty of evidence to show that Allstate had improperly denied the claim. For one thing, the company refused to get an engineer's inspection, apparently not wanting to hear anything about structural damage.

The couple's attorneys offered to settle with Allstate for $40,000. Allstate refused.

During the trial, the Reiningers alleged that Allstate had defrauded the couple by secretly slipping the cosmetic damage exclusion into the Reiningers's new policy *after* the couple paid the premium. The jury agreed, finding that Allstate committed fraud against the couple, breached its contract, and engaged in deceptive trade practices. The jury awarded the Reiningers $1.5 million, three times the value of the policy.

Allstate appealed to the Fourth Court of Appeals in San Antonio.

Despite Allstate's well-documented history of insurance law violations, the Fourth Court of Appeals in San Antonio, who summarily dismissed my Allstate appeal as conspirators robbed Auris Project assets, continued minimizing penalties for the insurer.

The appeals court couldn't deny the overwhelming evidence of Allstate's misconduct in the Reiningers' case and didn't try to. But it did reverse the jury's treble award, because, it opined, it didn't believe Allstate knew it had violated the Texas Insurance Code.[151]

I laughed long and hard when I read that.

The insurance company's reputation and stock values continued a slow slide. Allstate began making big changes. As part of a restructuring program histrionically dubbed the "transformative growth plan," Allstate sought to drastically reduce costs and quickly increase revenue. With customers fleeing in droves, the company needed new customers to survive. But to keep shareholders happy and encourage investors to invest in the company, it also needed to drastically reduce costs. The plan showed Allstate's need to survive its dwindling market share and at the same time revealed what a daunting task that would prove to be.

The plan called for the company to bring in new customers by offering better prices and spending more money on marketing and technology. At the same time, the plan called for the company to cut costs. So in 2020, Allstate laid off 3,800 employees, about eight percent of its workforce in 2020.

"Implementing this plan is difficult as we still deal with the impact of the pandemic but necessary to provide customers the best value," Allstate CEO Tom Wilson said in a news release rife with corporate-speak. "We have expanded transition support for impacted employees including prioritized internal hiring, extended medical coverage, expanded retraining support and help in employment searches."

In plain English, the firings were unavoidable but Allstate promised to help fired employees as they looked for new jobs. As always, Allstate struck just the right public relations tone.

Still, Allstate's carefully crafted public image was showing ample cracks. For one thing, the company could no longer dismiss complaints about its treatment of agents as grousing from a few disgruntled employees. In 2019, Allstate took an internal poll. Half of Allstate agents disapproved of the company, the poll found. In what business journalist Steve Daniels called a "dramatic drop," agent approval had slid nearly 30 percent – from 78 to 50 percent – in a year. In some regions, the approval rating had dipped as low as 36 percent. And that was *before* Allstate cut valuable agent commission.

Despite the terrible poll results, Allstate abruptly announced it would be skimming a percentage point from the 10 percent it paid agents in renewal commissions.[152]

According to *Crain's Chicago Business*, between 85-90 percent of agent earnings came from ten percent commissions paid when customers renew their existing policies. Now, agents were told, they would earn only nine percent. Agents could replace that revenue, the company told them in an internal memo, by signing *new* business. The company didn't share the baseline, the number of new clients an agent had to sign before it would see these new commissions. To make matters worse, Allstate was now also investing heavily in direct sales call centers, which would help the company compete for new business against its own agents.

It was a brazen money grab, and the agents knew it. In all, more than 10,700 "captive agents" (agents who can only sell Allstate products) would be affected. The sudden commission switcheroo would have a devastating effect on their bottom lines. For larger agency owners, it was an especially devastating blow. Many could not see how they could generate enough new customers to replace the revenue lost in renewal commissions from existing customers. Some large agencies stood to lose tens of thousands of dollars. Some could experience more than $100,000 in lost revenue because of the new scheme, observers estimated.

Meanwhile, Allstate CEO Thomas J. Wilson raked in more than $18 million dollars in 2020 compensation alone.[153]

Agents were furious. "Agents feel the company is reducing expenses at their expense," said Ted Paris, executive director of the National Association of Professional Allstate Agents, told *Crain's Chicago Business*.

Crain's contacted the insurer with questions, but the company did not respond. So the reporter listened intently for insights during Allstate's quarterly earnings call later that month. Allstate barely mentioned the change, and then only vaguely.

"It really is about shifting towards new business production," the company's president of personal lines told listeners. "You ultimately compensate agents...for going out and hunting and getting new business."[154]

Later, the company announced its payments for that new business: 17 percent commission on 12-month policies. But the baseline remained mysterious. It all depended on agency size, location, and market conditions, the company hedged.

Allstate was at a crucial survival moment. It needed to meet analysts' expectations, but the cuts were a desperate gamble almost certain to fail. Allstate had tried the same thing in 2012 and it backfired. After the 2012 commission cut, thousands of agents quit Allstate. The company never fully recovered. According to SEC records, Allstate reported 12,800 agencies in 2008. Directly after the 2012 commission cuts, that number had fallen to 9,300. The company rebounded somewhat, but not fully. By the time it was trying the cuts again in 2019, the company had only about 10,700 agencies. Why do it then?

Crain's explains the gamble this way (although the news outlet doesn't call it a gamble):

> There's big money in agent commissions. The company is on course this year to collect $32 billion in total premiums from its Allstate brand. It's paying 10 percent commissions on at least 75 percent of that revenue. Reducing that payout to 9 percent would save Allstate about $240 million.[155]

That looks good to investors. Stock market analysts were, if not bullish, still sufficiently positive about the company's stock value, but nearly everyone was still expecting to see the company's earnings grow. Allstate needed to keep its shareholders happy and investors confident. To do that, it needed to cut costs and get more customers. Its future depended on it.

Allstate kept hard at work trying to "transform" the company. The insurer spent 2021 buying and selling other corporations. In an effort to grow its personal lines insurance, the company bought National General for $4 billion dollars. That moved increased the company's market share by 1 percent.[156]

In a telling piece of analysis, Simply Wall Street reported that the company was still, at least on paper, growing and paying reliable dividends to its shareholders. But the analyst also pointed out that Allstate was trading significantly below the analysts' estimated market value. The analyst estimated Allstate shares at $303.98. However the shares were trading at $187.93, a difference of more than 30 percent. That in itself is a big red flag.

And not bolstered by a continued policy of acquisitions, the analysts expected the company's earnings to begin dropping.

Then Allstate insiders, including presidents, vice presidents and board members, began selling large chunks of their personal shares of Allstate. That is rarely a good sign. One of the biggest sellers was Allstate CEO Tom Wilson, who on May 8, 2020, sold 652,868 of his shares of the company, pocketing more than $66.2 million.[157]

More than one analyst flagged the activity as worth watching. If Allstate executives expected share values to rise then why were they selling?

By late October 2021, some hedge funds began dropping Allstate from their portfolios. The corporation did not make the list for the most popular hedge funds.[158]

Allstate was taking a lot of casualties, and the outcome was far from assured.

On September 28, 2021, I sent an email to Allstate's media department requesting to interview Allstate executives. If possible, I wrote, I would like to set up an interview with Richard C. Crist, Jr., an East Coast executive appointed field vice president of Allstate's Texas region in 2006.[159] By the time he took over Texas operations, Crist had been with the company for more than 30 years and almost certainly attended the Scientology "management by statistics" seminars. I wanted to know if he had also sat in on McKinsey's zero sum engagement.

When he took over the reins in Texas, Allstate was under investigation by the Texas Department of Insurance for overcharging its customers. Two years after Crist took the Texas helm, he led the region in a $70 million settlement with the Texas Department of Insurance for overcharging Texans.

In 2013, according to a Google search, the company appointed Larry Sedillo, a graduate of the University of Texas at El Paso, as senior field vice president of the Texas Region. I asked to interview him, too.

I also sent that email to Allstate's media office in Chicago.

The company did not respond.

McKinsey still calls the shots

MEANWHILE, AS ALLSTATE WRITHED AROUND INDECOROUSLY in its struggle for survival, its former consultant, McKinsey & Company, was busy managing its latest scandalous "engagement."

This time, McKinsey had advised the notorious pharmaceutical company Purdue Pharma for 15 years on how to sell billions of pills of its highly addictive painkiller OxyContin. At the end of that years-long collaboration, the pharmaceutical company was held most responsible for the U.S. opioid epidemic that addicted 1.5 million Americans. Insanely profitable, the marketing and distribution juggernaut designed by McKinsey helped kill more than 400,000 U.S. citizens – almost seven times the number of American soldiers killed in combat in Vietnam.

Despite whole communities being destroyed by opioid addiction, McKinsey advised strategies that would help Purdue Pharma "turbocharge" sales, including pushing higher doses for bigger profits.[160] McKinsey consultants also asserted that Purdue could boost sales by giving rebates to pharmacies for every customer who overdosed from opioids.[161]

In business terms, the campaign was wildly successful. "McKinsey was using its immense talents to help Purdue Pharma sell more pills, and it worked," North Carolina Attorney General told the *Washington Post* in early 2021. "The number of pills prescribed, Purdue's profits, and McKinsey's fees all skyrocketed, but so did the number of people addicted, the number of people overdosing, and the number of lives lost."

In a zero sum game, American deaths were meaningless. What mattered were profits. As overdoses soared, distribution executives mocked poor addicts dying in the Appalachians, derisively referring to them as "pillbillies."[162] What was important was that the money that formerly belonged to the pillbillies now belonged to the pharmaceutical companies and their partners.

For Big Pharma to win, others have to lose.

Eventually, McKinsey acknowledged its role in the national tragedy and agreed to pay a paltry $600 million to 49 states trying to recover from the opioid epidemic. The penalty amounted to about 60 percent of McKinsey's revenue for a single year. Despite the overwhelming, well-documented evidence of widespread drug trafficking, no arrests were made. How much McKinsey's engagements with Justice Department agencies impacted the department's refusal to bring criminal charges is unknown.

Once again, the notorious consulting giant McKinsey & Company had demonstrated its uncanny ability to spread its zero sum game philosophy to the corporate elite and to retain command of its environment in the shattering aftermath. At the same time it was showing opioid companies how to boost sales of addictive narcotics, it was also receiving healthy fees for advising U.S. government agencies and nonprofit organizations how to respond to the overwhelming number of overdoses and deaths.[163]

And, it was later revealed, McKinsey's hedge fund, MIO Partners, holds ample stakes in addiction treatment centers across the nation.[164]

In 2019, Jeff Skilling, the disgraced former Enron CEO and McKinsey consultant, exited prison after serving half his sentence for the fraud that collapsed Enron. Skilling immediately created an energy trading company called Veld Applied Analytics, which claims to help investors evaluate a product's potential returns. For help, he tapped two other former McKinsey consultants to help run the venture.

Reading about guys like Skilling, I always remember that poor addict in Denton, Texas when I was a journalism student at TWU. He had been sentenced to 60 years in prison for stealing T-tops off of Camaros. Skilling had stolen billions, shattered thousands of lives, and yet served a mere 12 years in prison.

Observers generally agree that Skilling's past fraud convictions would mean little to investors looking for hefty returns.

A criminal conspirator in one of the financial market's worst failures, the McKinsey alum could expect a bright future.

PERP WALK

THE FEDERAL ANTI-CORRUPTION TASK force made no more arrests after the federal prosecution of Angus McGinty and Al Acevedo in New Mexico.

It was almost as if someone had quietly closed the federal probe, counting on the public's short memory. In fact, when San Antonio FBI Special Agent-in-Charge Christopher Combs retired in 2022 to ply his intelligence skills in the lucrative private sector, he made no mention of the investigation.

Most of the people implicated in the criminal conspiracies discussed in this book simply went on with their lives, business as usual. Several popped up on my radar for a variety of reasons. Some merit a quick update:

Officer Christian Valadez

Valadez, the SAPD cop who inserted himself in a call for service, hid my letter showing proof of cyberattacks, and then falsified a police report by describing me as "psyche," performed a traffic stop of my vehicle on May 5, 2022 as I left the pharmacy. He had stopped me, he said, because I hadn't turned on my blinker when I turned left. We both looked down at my still-blinking blinker. Nearby, a second cop car and a familiar-looking sedan pulled over and idled. I told him he was in *Evil Corp* as a cop who falsified police reports. I recited his first name. "It's Christian, right?" I said. He blanched, and then quickly abandoned the traffic stop.

Attorney Elliot Cappuccio

Cappuccio, the abrasive lawyer who used his seat on a Texas Supreme Court committee to bring false unauthorized practice of law charges against me during the Allstate lawsuit, went on to represent the wife of a chief operator of Scientology's covert warfare program.

When Marty Rathbun, often described as Scientology's "chief enforcer" and "attack dog," fell out with the church, Scientology operatives began an attack campaign against him and his wife Monique, using the same tactics that Marty Rathbun had reportedly used against countless Scientology victims. Operatives rented houses near the Rathbuns' Ingleside on the Bay, TX home and set up cameras to keep the couple under 24-hour surveillance. They followed them around yelling insults. They even sent a sex toy to Monique Rathbun's work and wrote steamy letters to a female co-worker, signing Monique Rathbun's name. They spread rumors that she was secretly a man. When the couple moved to Bulverde, Texas, the harassment team reportedly followed.

The couple hired Cappuccio and San Antonio lawyers Ray Jeffrey and Marc Wiegand to sue the church for harassment, illegal surveillance, and intentional infliction of emotional distress.[165]

Cappuccio represented Monique Rathbun against the Church of Scientology for several years. He was humiliated when the couple abruptly fired him and his legal team and without explanation closed their lawsuit against the church.

Observers speculated that Marty Rathbun had reconciled with the church's controversial leader, David Miscavige, who had successfully dodged efforts to draw him to Texas to give sworn testimony.

Blindsided, Cappuccio was convinced that the church's alleged Fair Game master operator and his wife had reached a settlement with Scientology behind his back. Without filing a separate suit, Cappuccio requested a hearing with Karen Pozza, one of the Bexar County district judges who had helped facilitate the MLK property fraud and theft. He asked Pozza to order the Rathbuns to turn over confidential financial records. From what I can tell from court records, nothing ever came of it. Cappuccio, who had joined Allstate's zero sum game against me, had gotten bitten by one of Allstate's mentor's chief covert harassers. I found the whole sordid affair delicious.

Judge Michael Mery

Michael Mery, the judge who covered up the Greyhound bus station assault and illegally conspired with lawyer Albert Gutierrez in the Allstate case, lost his seat in the 37th civil district court to civil rights lawyer Nicole Garza.

In introducing Garza to his audience, video blogger Gabriel Lara described Mery thusly: "He is part of this upper echelon of elitists within this city that think that they can operate with impunity."[166]

After his decisive loss to Garza, Mery simply challenged Republican Melisa Skinner in the general election for her seat on the 144th district criminal court. He was a Democrat and she was a Republican in a staunchly Democratic city where voters are encouraged to vote down ballot. He beat Skinner in the 2020 general election with 56 percent of the vote.

Such was the absurd nature of Bexar County elections. Voters could dump an unpopular, harmful judge like Mery, who can then simply stroll down the courthouse hallway and quickly unseat another judge who, for all we know, might have been doing a decent job.

Judge John Primomo

Federal judge John Primomo, who brazenly covered up the phony "misdemeanor garage sale permit violation" arrest, continued to hear cases on the federal docket. While presiding over a 2016 immigration naturalization ceremony in San Antonio, Primomo began a disturbing rant.

As brand-new American citizens sat uncomfortably in the gallery, Primomo began haranguing them, raging that Donald Trump was their president and that "if you do not like that, you need to go to another country."[167]

He couldn't seem to stop himself. He fumed against peaceful protesters demanding democratic reforms of the Electoral College. He blasted black NFL football players who knelt during the national anthem to protest police brutality and racial injustice. They knelt!

"I detest that," he complained, tellingly.

The diatribe was so biased and venomous, the Mexican American Legal Defense and Educational Fund, or MALDEF, filed a complaint with a federal appeals court commission. Chief Judge Fred Biery, who had been so permissive of the judicial misconduct displayed in my federal civil rights case, suspended Primomo from conducting any more naturalization ceremonies but allowed him to continue hearing other federal cases – further proof that shining a light for all to see makes all the difference in the world.

After a deflecting non-apology where he said his words were taken out of context, the judge who officially absolved SAPD cops of civil rights abuses on MLK Drive on MLK Day during the MLK march finally retired from the federal judiciary.

Kristina Combs

Combs, the thuggish "practicing attorney" who spearheaded the MLK title fraud, battery, and theft got a free house out the criminal conspiracy to rob the Auris Project of its assets. If Combs thought that her contributions to the Allstate criminal conspiracy would translate into a lucrative job in a prominent local law firm, she would be disappointed. She landed pretty much where she'd been before she committed property title fraud, assault, theft, perjury, battery, burglary, forgery, obstruction of justice, wire fraud, conspiracy, and filing multiple false police reports.

By 2021, she was leasing pooled office space and offering dubious legal services to a trickle of unsuspecting clients. So far, she has not been charged for any of her long list of federal and state felonies.

Notary Ofelia Lisa Hernandez

Hernandez, the chief forger of the fraudulent quitclaim deeds who pretended to be an heir to the property at MLK Drive, eventually left Lipscomb & Loree. She is currently the public policy director and paralegal for the Maldonado Law Group. She has not been charged for the forgeries or her part in the felony frauds, breaking and entering, or thefts related to the information center on MLK Drive.

Attorney Martin Phipps

Goldman Pennebaker Phipps, Allstate's lead boxing gloves law firm in the *McVea v. Keller* case, disbanded soon after the improper Allstate jury verdict. Partner Larry Goldman moved further north of Loop 410 and continued quietly representing insurance companies against their customers. Douglas Pennebaker opened a law office where he claimed to represent folks against insurance companies. He knew insurers' secrets, he advertised.

Martin Phipps opened a swanky rooftop bar, Paramour, over his law office on the River Walk. He has been awash in legal troubles, including a November 2021, wrongful death suit. The lawsuit alleges that Phipps's bar continued serving alcohol to an obviously drunk New Braunfels man who killed three people in a fiery car crash after leaving the bar.[168] That lawsuit came seven months after Phipps's paralegal, Samantha Castillo, was charged with intoxication manslaughter after she plowed her black Mercedes Benz into a cyclist after leaving a bar. The family of the cyclist has filed a $209 million dollar wrongful death lawsuit against Castillo and

"Unknown Bar X". Paramour insists that Castillo hadn't been drinking there the night of the manslaughter, pointing to the police report filed that night, but journalists seemed to initially discount the SAPD police report almost entirely. Castillo would later name another bar as the culprit.[169]

Phipps's firm quickly began threatening Texas Public Radio with legal action, accusing the news outlet of making a fake account on the gay hookup app Grindr to elicit information from Phipps employees.[170]

In early 2021, Phipps was accused of sending junior lawyer Chase Hardy and an imposter into a store with false identification in a bizarre dispute over some "no-longer-used" clothes he had given his estranged ex-girlfriend Caroline Duesing to sell on consignment.[171] The imposter, pretending to be Duesing, requested to see financial records. Hardy and the imposter allegedly presented a photocopy of Duesing's valid identification card, but the imposter looked nothing like the I.D. photo. When store employees balked, Hardy reportedly began threatening to sue the store. Employees called the police but the two Phipps operatives reportedly fled the scene before police arrived. Phipps denied the encounter occurred. A related defamation suit against him is pending.

His troubles didn't end there. Police arrested and charged Phipps with telephonic harassment for allegedly terrorizing his estranged wife of 90 days, a Class B misdemeanor. By that time, Phipps was a lead attorney in Bexar County's potentially lucrative lawsuit against opioid companies.

But, even though Phipps' wife was so terrified of her husband she fled to Mexico, the criminal case against him stalled. Bexar County prosecutor Richard Guerra gave a weak explanation for the delay.

"Investigators may not have been able to access Phipps' phone without compromising protected work as an attorney," Guerra hemmed. "I was told that they were still conducting interviews and that is where we are right now."

The District Attorney's Office ultimately recused itself from prosecuting Allstate's former civil defense lawyer due to "entanglements between the DA's office and Phipps's current and former employees."

That's rich, I thought.

Michael McCrum, the white-collar criminal lawyer who foiled the FBI's tax evasion case against corrupt judge Angus McGinty's allegedly corrupt lawyer Alan Brown, represented Phipps. Eventually, all charges were dropped.

Phipps continued to represent Bexar County in its litigation against opioid manufacturers and distributors, but appointed lawyer Mikal Watts as lead attorney while he was under bond.

Looking for legal help a few years back, I had visited Watts' Dominion-based law firm after a web search identified him as a pro bono civil rights attorney. After a meeting in his offices where a junior lawyer and private investigator intently questioned me about my complaints against Allstate, its lawyers, and Judge Mery, the firm declined to represent me. The men did not disclose that Watts was working with Allstate's lawyer on a billion-dollar opioid settlement for Bexar County.

Sgt. Val Garcia

Val Garcia, the Eastside property crimes detective who finagled documented evidence from me by falsely leading me to believe he would help me press charges in the MLK theft and fraud case, soon retired from the SAPD. He became the front man and president of a bizarre new company: Trusted Driver Program.[172] The program, marketed as a convenience for motorists and police officers, allows cops (and, of course, others) to know when and where you are driving your vehicle and monitor your cellphone activity *in real time*. It is being tested by the suburb Windcrest and the notoriously corrupt Webb County. When I learned that, I finally understood how Allstate handlers were managing the vehicular gangstalking.

Judge Scott Roberts

Scott Roberts, the judge who was one of the forces behind the malicious criminal assault charge against me, lost his seat in Criminal County Court 12 to progressive attorney Yolanda Huff in 2018. Huff ran a barebones campaign against Roberts with virtually no financial support from Bexar County's entrenched political power structure. Still, she managed to unseat Roberts by a telling 14 percent margin.

Roberts immediately skipped down the hall and now works as an assistant DA for District Attorney Joe Gonzales, the former billboard lawyer who took my money and then refused to defend me in Roberts's court.

Former District Attorney Nico LaHood

LaHood, the district attorney who used a two-year malicious assault prosecution to help cover up the forged MLK quitclaim deeds, lost his re-election bid to Joe Gonzales, my deliberately useless defense attorney. After his ouster from the DA's office, LaHood went back to practicing private law. It wasn't until 2023 that I was able to put his refusal to release me from the malicious assault prosecution in the proper context.

It turns out that LaHood had close personal and professional ties to Jay Norton, one of the attorney's defending judge Angus McGinty against federal corruption charges and who McGinty would later allege was equally corrupt. When McGinty charged that Norton manipulated him during his federal prosecution into taking the fall for all the corruption going on in San Antonio, LaHood joined Norton in strenuously denying that Bexar County courts were a hotbed of corruption.[173]

But the record now shows a clear connection between Roberts, Gonzales, McGinty, LaHood, Norton, and Norton's former partner Alan Brown. The incestuous nature of the duplicitous relationships infesting San Antonio had become apparent. I now know why LaHood refused to stop the malicious assault prosecution in County Court 12 against me when he was district attorney. It was apparently a favor to a friend.

While serving as district attorney, LaHood hired Norton directly after Norton helped pack the hapless McGinty off to federal prison. Norton quickly rose to section chief in the DA's office.

When disappointed voters ousted LaHood from office, he and Norton founded the LaHood Norton Law Group, where they promise to "fearlessly defend the accused and protect their innocence."

Angus McGinty

Ex-judge McGinty, the self-described "whore for money," served his time in federal prison and returned to San Antonio, where he began making a living as a deliveryman. He apologized to the citizens of San Antonio for his crimes during a broadcast interview, but he was bitter. He was only doing what everyone else was doing, so why was he the only judge arrested?

During his federal prosecution, McGinty admitted to being under the corrupt influence of Jay Norton at the same time he convened a shadow court to prosecute a crime (garage sale permit misdemeanor) against me that did not exist. In late 2021, I made an open records act request. I wanted all the records associated with the malicious prosecution of the bogus misdemeanor garage sale charge.

"We are seeking case files for the prosecution of Denise McVea before Judge Angus McGinty regarding a criminal charge of holding a garage sale without a license," I wrote.

The city needed more information in order to meet the request, an information officer responded. I searched through my documents and found the criminal cause number.

When the county released the records, they were revealing.

They showed that I had been criminally charged with the non-existent "no garage sale permit misdemeanor AGAINST THE PEACE AND

DIGNITY OF THE STATE," and that the case had been scheduled for a jury trial when I refused to plea bargain.

The Municipal Court kept only a single page to record the February 2013 proceedings where I stood before McGinty in an empty courtroom and learned he would deny my request to dismiss the bogus charge against me.

The page had been scrubbed.

No judge's name or signature is present on that document.

All prosecutors are identified by initials.

EPILOGUE

The San Antonio Barbecue Murder

IN 2014, CANDIE DOMINGUEZ INVITED her cousin Jose Luis "Pee Wee" Menchaca to her house for a barbecue.

Pee Wee should not have gone. Prior to the invitation, Pee Wee had allegedly attacked Candie's ex-boyfriend Daniel Lopez with a knife during a drug deal gone bad. As Pee Wee headed toward Candie's north side San Antonio house, Daniel and his cousin, Gabriel Moreno, lied in wait.

Before the night was over, Pee Wee would be savagely beaten, suffocated, and dismembered in a bathtub, his remains roasted on a backyard barbecue pit.

The Bexar County Barbecue Murder Trial of 2018 was scandalous, featuring a motley crew of local underworld characters that included drug dealers, addicts, kidnappers, and Mexican Mafia members.

Also featured were other familiar faces.

Joe Gonzales, the billboard attorney who in 2013 extorted money from me in the malicious County Court 12 criminal assault case, was now Bexar County's district attorney-elect.

Matthew Ludowig, the assistant DA who helped maintain the two-year malicious criminal case against me, was now lead prosecutor in the barbecue murder trial.

Moreno's defense attorney was none other than Albert Gutierrez, the Allstate contract attorney who I reported to the state bar for tampering with the record, quoting false case law, and holding illegal ex-parte meetings with judges. For some reason, the criminal court had beckoned Gutierrez, Allstate's go-to guy in *McVea v. Keller, et al,* away from civil court to represent the Mexican Mafia associate Gabriel Moreno in this bizarre murder trial.

I couldn't believe it. I had accused all three men of wanton misconduct and obstruction of justice. To me, they were the poster boys of the corrupt lawyer class infesting San Antonio. Ludowig and Gonzales had helped cover up the use of forged quitclaim deeds to steal property on the Eastside, the unconstitutional dismissals of thousands of civil lawsuits, and civil rights abuses by cops and judges. I had watched Gutierrez engage in document tampering, violations of judicial procedure, and citing false case law, all while representing Allstate. I also recalled that it was Gutierrez's suspected private investigator that I witnessed cozying up to the jurors in the Allstate case in 2013.

This is going to be a shit show, I thought.

I was right.

The three lawyers would play major roles in one of the most shocking jury verdicts in recent San Antonio history.

Not long after Pee Wee arrived at Candie' house, he was beaten with an aluminum baseball bat and metal pipe. When the beating didn't kill him, he was suffocated. Several people were present during the murder. The eyewitnesses, terrified of the cousins and doing what they were told, helped end Pee Wee Menchaca's life and dispose of his body. By all accounts, it was a gruesome, ghastly, soul-shocking scene.

Lopez eventually received a life sentence but it was the Moreno prosecution that perfectly captured the contaminated nature of the Bexar County justice system.

In Moreno's first trial for the murder of Menchaca, 11 of the 12 jurors voted to convict him.

A single holdout forced a mistrial.

The jury in Moreno's second trial heard credible, eyewitness testimony that showed Moreno was a leading participant in the murder. A fearsome associate of the Mexican Mafia, he had already done time for violent crimes that included kidnapping, and was currently facing charges for possessing a deadly weapon in a penal facility. One eyewitness to Pee Wee's murder, security guard Dennis Austin, testified that out of fear for his own life, he helped hold Menchaca down as Moreno smothered him. Austin also helped bury the body. He kept silent about the murder, he said, because he was afraid he would end up like Menchaca.

In a plea bargain with prosecutors, Candie Dominguez admitted to helping Moreno chop up and burn her cousin's body. On the stand, she showed no emotion, no remorse. She got 30 years for her part in the murder.

Still, after deliberating for less than six hours over two days, the second jury acquitted Moreno. An *Express-News* photographer captured the defense table seconds after the verdict came down. In the photo, Moreno, his face covered with jailhouse tattoos, is leaning forward, flashing a satisfied smile at Gutierrez. The lawyer is looking forward, unsurprised.

Nearly everyone else was stunned. Ludowig, the lead prosecutor, spoke with jurors after the shocking verdict to try and make sense of it all, but reported after the conversation that he was still mystified as to how he had lost the case.

"Obviously, we believed he was guilty," a dumbfounded Ludowig told a local reporter. "I don't know what the problem was."

This had been a big case for Ludowig, who had spent much of his career with the Bexar County District Attorney's Office handling lowly misdemeanor cases. With the Moreno case, he could have made a name for himself.

Instead, karma tapped Matthew Ludowig. He had helped keep me under bond for two years knowing I was a crime victim. He had helped cover up judicial misconduct. To accomplish that, he had ignored statute, procedural rules, and constitutional protections.

And this was the thanks he got: he was now the public face of a mortifying, high-profile prosecutorial fiasco in what should have been a slam dunk case. He watched helplessly as a Bexar County jury freed a violent associate of a highly organized criminal organization that he had argued was a sadistic, cold-blooded killer.

District Attorney-elect Gonzales quickly turned against Ludowig. He promised "a full investigation" into the prosecutors' conduct during the botched case. Although it seemed to have little impact on the outcome, the incoming DA focused on prosecutors' impromptu decision to interview a subpoenaed defense witness they unexpectedly encountered in a courthouse hallway.

Defense attorney Gutierrez, who wasn't invited to the interview, had complained loudly about that meeting and unsuccessfully called for a second mistrial. He needn't have worried. According to a DA investigator, two of the witness's uncles, known Mexican Mafia members, waylaid the witness in the hallway after her meeting with prosecutors and told her to plead the fifth when she got on the stand. She did.

At any rate, it looked like Ludowig was on his way out.

After the shocking acquittal, I sent an open records act request to the district attorney's office, asking Ludowig for all internal records associated with *State of Texas v. Denise McVea*. Despite a ruling from the state attorney general deeming the documents public records, the DA has not provided the materials.

Soon after, no longer of much use to Bexar County courts, Matthew Ludowig quietly left the DA's office. He landed in Houston, working as a staff attorney for a pharmaceutical company. I thought about writing him a letter. Not to gloat, but to put what happened to him in the context of the awful choices he'd made. I would explain the difference between an operator and a pawn. I would explain how, by design, only a tiny fraction of participants in a criminal conspiracy can expect to come out on top.

I may get around to it someday.

Albert Gutierrez, on the other hand, had chalked up yet another improbable win. He stood portentously in the courthouse hallway, reveling in the toadying attention of the press and his colleagues. The Moreno case constituted another stepping stone on his path to local legal stardom; he was fast becoming known as the San Antonio lawyer who could win any case.

"After 24 years as an attorney, including civil work and as a prosecutor in Laredo, Gutierrez takes remarkable verdicts in stride," the *Express-News* fawned.

While Gutierrez basked in the limelight, the district attorney's office and the judge faced a shaken, incredulous public. The Bexar County officials struggled to explain the barbecue murder acquittal in light of the overwhelming evidence against the defendant.

For his part, Gonzales blustered in press conferences about the Brady Rule and the Michael Morton Act, two laws that require prosecutors to turn over favorable evidence to the defendant. I laughed derisively. Ludowig and Judge Roberts had ignored my motions mentioning those same two laws as they continued to withhold evidence in the state's malicious criminal assault case against me. I had paid Gonzales $3500 for pretrial representation in that case and he had never mentioned those rules to me no matter how many times I asked. I had to find them myself after I had fired him.

Listen to him now, I thought.

Judge Ron Rangel also took a stab at easing public disquiet over the shocking verdict. Juries were less trusting of police and prosecutors, Rangel publicly theorized. They are questioning the credibility of witnesses more, he opined. The Moreno jury probably wanted to see more hard evidence like fingerprints and bloody clothes, he supposed. Maybe the state should have brought more charges just in case the murder charge didn't stick, he offered.

Of course, neither the judge nor the DA mentioned the very real possibility that Moreno's jury had been tampered with. In my opinion, that was more plausible than the ideas they were floating. By this time, I had seen enough to know that I could never sit on a Bexar County jury. My conscious forbade it.

As Pee Wee's devastated family filed out of the courthouse, lawyer Amir Mamori tentatively approached a smug Gutierrez, who was still holding court in the courthouse hallway.

Mamori had attended the trial, heard all the testimony, and weighed all of the evidence. He couldn't believe what he had just witnessed. None of it made sense. He stared at Allstate's old Boxing Gloves lawyer, who I had futilely accused of document tampering, illegal back door conferencing, and numerous other violations of rule and law as far back as 2010.

"How can you explain this?" a shocked Mamori asked Gutierrez.
"How did this happen?"[174]

-30-

ABOUT THE AUTHOR

A SOCIAL JUSTICE ADVOCATE AND investigative journalist, Denise McVea writes to bring about social change for marginalized communities. She has confronted corruption and civil rights abuses for decades using the literature of exposure.

In 2003, she founded the Auris Project, Inc., a 501c3 non-profit organization dedicated to helping marginalized communities gain access to key rights and development information.

She is currently the executive editor of Auris Books Press, a nonprofit publisher dedicated to empowering communities. She is the author of *Power Plays: The Poor People's Guide to Fighting City Hall...and Other Maddening Bureaucracies*, and *Making Myth of Emily: Emily West De Zavala and the Yellow Rose of Texas Legend*.

Her nonfiction book *Evil Corp: Allstate Insurance, Shadow Networks, and the Corruption of a Major American City*, was researched and written at great personal sacrifice. She says she'd do it all again.

She has three beautiful children - Dax, Zuri, and Kenna - and lives in San Antonio, Texas.

INDEX

1614 Martin Luther King, 48, 80, 83, 92, 93, 95, 97, 99, 115, 138, 190, 191, 236
Academia Falcon, 33
Acevedo, Albert "Al", 107, 108, 109, 110, 111, 112, 113, 120, 161, 162, 220, 221, 225
Acevedo, Albert "Al", xvii
ACLU, 133, 200
Adams, Bill, 17
adjuster, 4, 13
Adkisson, Tommy, 96, 115, 174, 190
affidavit of inability, 40
Agent Orange, 27
agent, Allstate, 4
Alamo Heights, 49
Alamo, The, 36, 150, 190
Alamodome, 46, 72, 231
Alcántara, Monica, 182, 183, 184, 185, 186, 187, 189
Allstate, i, ii, xvii, xviii, xix, xx, xxi, xxii, xxiii, xxiv, xxv, 2, 3, 4, 5, 6, 7, 9, 10, 11, 12, 13, 14, 15, 17, 18, 21, 22, 23, 33, 35, 38, 39, 45, 49, 50, 51, 52, 53, 54, 55, 56, 57, 64, 65, 67, 69, 70, 71, 72, 73, 74, 75, 76, 77, 80, 84, 86, 90, 93, 94, 97,98, 100, 104, 110, 111, 114, 115, 116, 118, 123, 126, 128, 129, 133, 135, 138, 139, 140, 142, 143, 145, 146, 147, 148, 149, 150, 160, 161, 163, 166, 168, 170, 171, 172, 177, 178, 179, 193, 195, 197, 198, 202, 205, 206, 210, 211, 213, 214, 222, 227, 228, 231, 232, 233, 236, 237, 241, 243, 244, 245, 246, 247, 248, 249, 253, 255, 256, 257, 260, 261, 264, 265, See Allstate Insurance Company
Allstate Fire and Casualty Company, 50
Allstate insurance policy, 2

Altiplano Potosino, 34, 35, 139, 140
Alvarado, Rosie, 197, 198
American Airlines, 117, 149
anti-corruption resolution, 181
Arrellano, Monica, 91, 92, 95, 96, 190
Arroyo, Luis Antonio, xiv, 196
Arteaga, Antonia, 92, 96, 97, 115, 116, 117, 118, 173, 220
assault, xxiv, 57, 64, 65, 102, 184
Associated Press, 30
Atmonson, Yuval, 244
Auris Books Press, ii, 188, 227, 265
Auris bookstore, 99
Auris Project, ii, 34, 35, 45, 48, 57, 86, 94, 96, 97, 114, 115, 116, 128, 129, 131, 136, 140, 160, 178, 180, 190, 217, 265
Austin, Dennis, 261
Austin, TX, 240
Barbecue Murder Trial, 260
Barberena, Laura, 37
Barchas, Myles, 148, 149, 150
BCDP. See Bexar County Democratic Party, See Bexar County Democratic Party
Beacon Hill, 2
Bednarski, Richard Lee, 31
Beeville, TX, 109
Behar, Richard, 146, 147, 148, 149, 150
Berardinelli, David, xviii
Bernal, Joseph, 238
Bexar County, xiv, xv, xvi, xxii, xxiii, 9, 38, 39, 40, 42, 43, 44, 48, 53, 54, 56, 65, 67, 71, 72, 73, 79, 81, 82, 83, 92, 93, 95, 96, 97, 101, 103, 105, 107, 108, 109, 110, 111, 113, 114, 116, 127, 129, 131, 132, 133, 134, 138, 140, 141, 157, 158, 159, 162, 171, 176, 178, 179, 181, 182, 183, 184, 185, 186, 191, 195, 196, 197, 209,

220, 253, 254, 256, 257, 258, 260, 261, 262, 263
Bexar County Court 12, 104, 134, 138, 140, 180, 204, 257, 260
Bexar County Courthouse, 38, 92
Bexar County Democratic Party, 181, 182
Bexar County District Attorney, 262
Bexar County District Clerk, 96
Bexar County Election Integrity and Voter Protection Committee, 186
Bexar County jail, xiv, 79
Bezos, Jeff, 169
Big Pharma, 250
Biles, Simone, 165
Bill Miller's restaurant, 1
bills, medical, 4, 5, 53, 72
Black Cube, 169
Black Lives Matter, xxiv, 217, 225, 226
Blakey, Robert, 221
Blanco Road, xxii, 1, 70, 227
Bonillas, John A., 237
bookstore, online, 35
Bosch, Nicholas, xiii
Bower, Marvin, 18
Boxing Gloves program, xviii, xix, xxi, xxii, 6, 245, 264, 277
Brackenridge High School, 76, 85
Bradshaw, Audra, 65
Brady Rule, 263
bridge, international, 35, 139
Broadway, 49, 177
Broadway Street, 49
Brock Person Guerra Reyna, 49
Brockhouse, Greg, xv, xvi, 172
brokers, xvii
Brooke Army Medical Center, 27
Brown, Alan, 111, 112, 113, 256, 258
Butolph, Teresa, 4, 5, 38, 49, 50, 54, 55, 89, 126, 127
Buttigieg, Pete, 19, 20
California, 15, 22, 138, 182, 233
call log, 122, 124, 125
Canadians, 14
Canales, Kelly, 72, 76
Cappuccio, Elliot, 55, 56, 104, 178, 252, 253
Carlson report, 95, 128
Carlson Report, 94, 95
Carlson, Wendy, 94, 130

Carolina Treviño. *See* Treviño, Gustavo and Carolina
Carrillo, Ramiro, 238
Carrillo, Stephanie, 183, 187
Carroll, BJ, 73, 131
case law, 71, 74, 124, 125, 126, 161, 260, 261
Castillo, Samantha, 255
Castro, Joaquin, 202
Catholics, 25, 47
Catorce, SLP, Mexico, 34, 35, 116, 138, 139, 140
catorceño, 140
Central Intelligence Agency, 19, 223
cervix, 3
Chasnoff, Brian, 176, 184, 185, 186, 277
Chauvin, Derek, 162, 176, 216
Chicago, 13, 18, 19, 172, 202, 247, 249
Chicago World's Fair, 13
Church of Scientology, 17, 18, 21, 22, 253
Cibolo, Texas, 72
Citizen Band Potawatomi, 34
city desk, 31, 177
City Hall, 265
claimant, 5, 171
claims process, xix, 22
Clearwater, Florida, 145, 241
CNN, xix, 117, 277
cockroaches, 118, 140, 170, 172, 178, 210, 211, 212, 213
Cockroaches, 155, 170, 237
Coleman Street, 24
Colossus, xviii
Combs Family, 99
Combs, Christopher, 109, 252
Combs, Kristina, 80, 81, 82, 90, 92, 94, 96, 97, 99, 100, 102, 104, 105, 114, 115, 116, 131, 135, 136, 137, 138, 140, 141, 161, 190, 217, 236
Combs, Roger, 81, 82, 87, 99, 138
Comfort Inn, 151, 152, 154
conspirators, xix, xxiv, xxv, 86, 90, 109, 137, 144, 145, 166, 170, 190, 209, 213, 214, 220, 232, 237
constitutional protections, 209, 262
Consumer Federation of America, xxi, 277
consumers, xx, xxi, xxii, 6, 7, 12, 13, 147
Conterio, Theodore, 13
contractors, xxii, 14, 36, 46, 237

cop, 2, 61, 62, 63, 81, 82, 83, 84, 85, 88, 89, 102, 103, 126, 138, 148, 149, 153, 162, 165, 176, 216, 217, 224, 226, 230, 231, 232, 234
Coulter, Tim, 34
County Court 12, 258
County Court Precinct No. 4, 86
Countywide Exteriors, 237
Courthouse regulars, xvi, 92
courts, federal, 120, 220
Covarrubias, Chris, 116
COVID, 198, 229
Covid-19, 228
Crain's Chicago Business, 247
Crist, Richard C. Jr., 249
Cuellar, Michael, 233
Custer, SAPD sgt., 88, 89
cyber attacks
   denial of service, 228
   man-in-the-middle, xxv, 104, 200, 228
cyber security, xxv, 155, 178
D Magazine, 33
Dade County, 26
Daily Lasso, 31
Dallas Observer, 50
Dallas, Texas, 9, 30, 31, 33, 36, 50, 115, 117, 148, 150, 240
Daniels, Gary, 58
Daniels, Steve, 247
Danner, Patrick, 198
Danny Santos, 236
Davis, Len, 165, 166
Dear San Antonio, I'm Gone but Not Lost, 188
Deceptive Trade Practices Act, 6, 69
deeds
   quitclaim, 90, 91, 92, 94, 95, 96, 97, 114, 123, 128, 136, 137, 160, 161, 190, 255, 261
deeds office, 81, 84, 90, 94, 190
deeds, phantom, 90
default judgment, 42, 43, 44
DeHoyos, Rose Marie, 182
delay, deny, defend, xix
Deleon-Vargas, Ana Liz, 133
Democratic Party headquarters, 180
Democratic primaries, xiv
demolition, 46
denial of service attacks, 228
Denton, Texas, 30, 31, 251

Department of Defense, 19
Development Services Department, 237, 239, 240
Dianetics, 16
Diaz, Rene, 53
district attorney, xiv, xv, 129, 133, 136, 137, 173, 174, 180, 187, 191, 204, 219, 220, 257, 260, 262, 263
District Attorney, xv, 130, 132, 133, 137, 191, 256, 257, 258, 262
District Attorney's Office, 131, 138, 141, 256, 262
District Court Clerk's Office, 39
DOMINGUEZ, CANDIE, 260, 261
Don Inez, 139
donations, 34, 77
drug cartel, 139
Drug cartels, 139
DSD Strike Team, 238, 239
Duarte Méndez, Wendy Angelina, 194
Duesing, Caroline, 256
Duncan, Ellen, 4
Duncan, Victor, 4, 199, 200, 201, 202, 203
Duong, Tiffany, 40, 94, 117
E. Houston Street, 212
Eastside, xvii, 25, 34, 45, 46, 47, 48, 77, 78, 83, 86, 96, 98, 101, 102, 109, 115, 118, 150, 151, 155, 156, 157, 172, 174, 175, 176, 186, 188, 190, 191, 204, 205, 222, 239, 240, 257, 261
Eastsiders, 178, 186
Eastwood Village, 24
Eaton, Emilie, 174, 175, 176, 177, 178
Eckman, Aaron, 133
Editors, 31, 33, 175
Edwards, Al, 149
Elbel Lane, 25
Embezzlement, xviii
encryption, xxv
Enron, 20, 251
Erik Hernandez, 190
Esperanza Center for Peace and Justice, 195
Esperanza Peace and Justice Center, 133
Estrada, Crystal, 234
Ethics Follies, 92, 94
Evil Corp, ii, xxv, 198, 265
Executives, Allstate, xviii, 7, 18, 21, 23, 149
ExxonMobil, 117

Ezra, David A., 120, 122, 123, 124, 125, 220
Facebook Messenger, 138, 139
Fair Game, 16, 17, 22, 253
Fair Game., 16
Fallaci, Oriana, 30, 32
False arrest, 57, 99
FBI, xvi, xvii, 44, 56, 66, 67, 68, 107, 108, 109, 111, 112, 113, 121, 139, 143, 160, 161, 162, 163, 164, 165, 166, 171, 173, 174, 187, 200, 210, 212, 219, 220, 221, 222, 225, 228, 229, 256, *See* Federal Bureau of Investigations, *See* FBI Special Agent-in-Charge, 252
FBI, San Antonio, 252
Federal Bureau of Investigation. *See* FBI
Federal Bureau of Investigations. *See* FBI
Flavin, James, 121, 217
floods, xxi
Flores, Adrian, 180, 184
Floyd, George, 162, 176, 216, 217, 224, 231
Foddrill, John, 233
forensic document, 94, 131, 190
Fort Sam. *See* Fort Sam Houston Army base
Fort Sam Houston, 24, 25
Fort Worth, 180
Fort Worth, TX, 240
Fourth Amendment, 79, 120
Fourth Court of Appeals, 77, 114, 246
Fox News, 3
Franklin, Benjamin, 11
Franzese, Michael, 221
fraud, xxiv, 20, 36, 38, 71, 90, 96, 110, 115, 123, 128, 136, 150, 161, 171, 176, 180, 187, 189, 190, 191, 220, 222, 233, 239, 245, 246, 251, 253, 255
Freedom of Information, 45
Freeman, Randy, 153, 154
Freeman, Reginald, 83, 85, 88
Frost Bank, 91
Gaggy Award, 45
Gaines, Dinah, 40, 43, 44, 196, 208, 209
Galbreath, David, 58, 59, 60, 61, 63, 64, 125, 128
gangstalking, 97, 158, 162, 171
Garage sale misdemeanor, 79

Garcia, Ann, 34
Garcia, Cesar, 35, 69
Garcia, Val, 119, 236, 257
Garza, Nicole, 253
gatekeepers, xxiv
Gates, Levi, 239
Gazette, 11
gentrification, 47
Gill, Chuck, xxi
GL Hunt, 228, 238, 239
Goffney, Vivian, 40, 41
Goldman Pennebaker & Phipps, 50, 53, 54, 69
Goldman, Larry, 53, 101, 255
Gonzales. *See* Gonzales, Joe
Gonzales, Joe, xiv, xv, 97, 104, 105, 106, 132, 161, 171, 178, 180, 186, 191, 204, 205, 220, 257, 258, 260, 261, 262, 263, 277
Good Hands motto, xviii, xix, 13, 277
Google, 8, 38, 54, 71, 92, 133, 150, 199, 249
Google Enhanced Protection Program, 199
Google Scholar, 38
goons, 118, 142, 170, 172, 179, 181, 195, 201, 206, 210, 213, 214, 218, 236
GPS trackers, xxiv
Gradney, Tony, 153, 204, 206
greed, xx
Greyhound, 26, 57, 58, 59, 61, 63, 65, 89, 93, 125, 126, 128, 205, 207, 253
Groves, Kim, 165, 166
Guanajuato, 33
Guerra, Richard, 133, 256
Gupta, Rajat, 19, 20
Gutierrez Albert M., 49, 53, 70, 72, 73, 74, 101, 126, 161, 253, 260, 263
Gutierrez Wymer, 49
Gutierrez, Albert M, 55
Gutierrez, Albert M., 49, 53, 54, 56, 69, 71, 72, 73, 74, 75, 76, 77, 260, 261, 262, 263, 264
habeas corpus, 105, 133, 135, 191
Haber, Jon, xix
Hackberry Street, 46, 80, 89, 151, 157, 199, 201, 202, 204, 210, 229
hackers, 57, 90, 104, 128, 132, 133, 143, 151, 163, 170, 171, 178, 227, 228, 230, 237

Hackers, 123, 172, 198, 213
Halliburton, 117
Hampton, Jack, 31
harassment, 16, 55, 103, 128, 146, 147, 159, 171, 213, 235, 253, 256
Hardberger, Phil, 36
Hardy, Chase, 256
Harrington, Jim, 133
Harrison, Levon, 232
hedge funds, 249
Helle, Michael, xvi, 172, 217
Hernandez, Ofelia Lisa, 91, 92, 95, 190, 236
Hernandez, Tommy, 92
Hildebrand Avenue, xxii, 1, 49, 227
Hollingsworth Pack, 238, 239
Hollis, Meagan, 91, 160, 190
Houston, Kelly, 113
Houston, Texas, 20, 30, 40, 43, 57, 58, 62, 113, 117, 126, 240, 262
Hubbard, L. Ron, 15, 16, 17, 143, 144, 145, 146
Huff, Yolanda, 257
Hunter, J. Robert, xx, 277
Hurricane Katrina, xxi, 22
Hurston, Zora Neal, 28
Hyundai, 197
IET, 18, *See* International Executive Technology
IMSI catcher, 228
IMSI catchers, 169, 170, 179, 198, 213, 228
Indian Law Resource Center, 34
information center, 45, 46, 47, 48, 76, 77, 78, 79, 80, 84, 86, 92, 99, 103, 114, 128, 150, 190, 217, 220, 236, 255
Ingleside on the Bay, TX, 253
IntegriClaim, xviii
intelligence, American, 21, 174, 223
Internal Affairs, SAPD, 89, 216
Internal Revenue Service, 16, 143
International Executive Technology, 15
Interview with History, 30
invasion of privacy, 16
investigative journalism, xxv, 32, 33
investors, xvii, 246, 248, 251
Italian mafia, 220
Italian Mafia, 161, 221, 244, 245
Jackson, Tandylyn, xiv

jail, xiv, 64, 78, 79, 103, 117, 122, 133, 141
Jeffrey, Ray, 253
judges, federal, 120, 122, 125, 220
jurors, xv, 72, 73, 75, 76, 196, 197, 261, 262
Justice Department, 21, 112, 120, 221, 223, 250
Katz, Steve, 49
Kazen, Philip, xiv
Keller, James, 2, 4, 38, 49, 52, 53, 54, 69, 70, 72, 73, 74, 75, 77
Kemmy, Nicholas, 133
Kennebunk, Maine, 241, 242
Kidd, Rodney, 180, 183
Kissler, James Michael, 90, 91, 92, 93, 95, 96, 115, 190
Kloppe, Kirsten, 223, 229, 233, 234, 235
Korea, 24
Kosanovich, Mark, 120, 121, 122, 157
Kroll, 169
Krupa, Robert, 173
Kuwamura, Frank, 3, 4
LaHood Norton Law Group, 258
LaHood, Nico, xiv, 136, 141, 174, 186, 191, 220, 257, 258
Lamp, 183, 185, 186, 188, 189, 205, 206
Langeman, Michael, 163
Lankford, Sidney, 241
Lara, Gabriel, 254
Larkin, Richard, 147
League of United Latin American Citizens, 189
Leah Remini
    Scientology and the Aftermath, 16
Leary, Mike, 159, 176
Ledesma, Lilia, 116, 117, 118
Lee, Audrey, 177
Lehman, Gregory, 238
Lehnertz, William, 13
Leifer, Jack, 69, 70, 71, 72, 74
Lewis, Stephanie, 133
Liberty Mutual, 245
Linda Drive, 109
Linebarger Goggan Blair & Sampson, 48, 115, 116, 117
Lipscomb & Loree, 255
Littlejohn, Janet, 52, 72, 76, 77
local collaborators, xxiii
local judges, xxiii, 64, 236
Loomis, Gilbert J., 12

Lopez, Daniel, 260
Lopez, Rogelio, 178
Loree, Hernandez & Lipscomb, 91, 92
Los Zetas, 139, 140
lowball offers, xviii
Lowry, Robert L., 41
Ludowig, Matthew, 105, 129, 130, 133, 136, 260, 261, 262, 263
Madison Avenue, 28
MALDEF, 254
Maldonado Law Group, 255
malicious, 77, 105, 129, 132, 133, 134, 136, 139, 140, 141, 171, 178, 191, 220, 239, 257, 258, 260, 263
Mamori, Amir, 263, 264
manuelistas, 184, 185, 186, 187
Marmondo, Garrett, 187
Maroney, McKayla, 163, 164
Martin Luther King Drive, 45, 47, 48, 80, 92, 93, 95, 99, 190
Martin, Monica, 25
Martinez, Officer, 102
Marziani, Mimi, 157, 158, 159
Mason Street, 25
Massachusetts Institute of Technology MIT, 69
McCollister, Zachary, 211
McCombs, Red, 36
McCrum, Michael, 113, 256
McDonald, Jeremy, 238, 239
McDuffie, Arthur, 26
McGinty, Angus, xvii, 107, 108, 109, 110, 111, 112, 113, 120, 161, 162, 220, 221, 225, 252, 256, 258, 259
McGlothlin, John, 50, 51, 54
McKinney, Donna Kay, 40, 114
McKinsey & Company, xviii, xix, xx, xxi, 14, 18, 19, 20, 21, 22, 66, 163, 220, 222, 223, 243, 244, 245, 249, 250, 251
McKinsey, James O., 18
McKnight, Amelia, 92, 93, 95
McLane, David, 105
McManus, Tracey, 241
McManus, William, 155, 156, 174, 229, 230, 232, 233, 234
McVea v. Keller, 49, 72, 178, 255, 260
McVea, Dax, 230, 231, 265
McVea, Denise, ii, 38, 69, 91, 104, 127, 129, 135, 138, 141, 156, 157, 172, 181, 194, 197, 223, 258, 265

McVea, Jacquie, 10, 73, 74, 76
McVea, Kenna, 265
McVea, Robert C., 27
McVea, Tedi, 2, 46, 55, 58, 60, 61, 76, 77, 80, 81, 85, 87, 89, 100, 103, 110, 118, 134, 195, 209, 214, 215, 227, 228
McVea, Zuri, 265
mediation, 53
Medical Center, 118
Medina, Manuel, 180, 181, 182, 183, 184, 185, 186, 187, 188, 189
MedPay, 4, 5
Meerscheidt Street, 47
Menchaca, Jose Luis "Pee Wee", 260, 261, 263
Mendoza, Jesse, 84, 102, 103, 138
Mercedes Benz, xvi, 107, 255
Mérida, Yucatan, Mexico, 193, 194, 195
Mery, Michael, 71, 72, 74, 93, 126, 127, 128, 198, 205, 207, 220, 253, 254, 257
Mexican, 34, 35, 139, 140, 154, 193, 195, 254, 260, 261, 262
Mexican American Legal Defense and Educational Fund. *See* MALDEF
Mexican Army, 139, 140
Mexican Mafia, 260, 261, 262
Mexico, xxii, 33, 34, 35, 45, 47, 48, 116, 138, 139, 140, 150, 172, 182, 193, 194, 256, 265
Miami, 26, 27, 28
Michael Morton Act, 263
Michigan State University, 164
Midlothian, 31
Miscavige, David, 145, 253
misconduct, judicial, xxiii, xxiv, xxv, 8, 52, 56, 61, 62, 69, 79, 105, 111, 122, 134, 159, 161, 173, 176, 187, 198, 199, 200, 225, 246, 254, 261, 262
misdemeanor garage sale violation, 122
MLK. *See* Martin Luther King Drive
MLK Drive, 254, 255
Moreno, Gabriel, 260, 261, 263
Mormando, Garrett, 183, 184, 185, 187, 188, 189
Mt. Zion First Baptist Church, 198, 205
Mulberry Street, 2, 7
Municipal Court, 259
Muñoz, Robert, 61, 62, 63, 64
NAACP, 198, 205, 206

Nabokov, Vladimir, 28
NASA, 70
Nassar, Larry, 163, 164, 165
National Association of Professional Allstate Agents, 247
National Enquirer, 169
Nellermoe, Barbara, 54, 93, 94, 95, 96, 99, 120, 131, 220
Nesmith, Rodney, 26
New Black Panther Party, 33
New Mexico, xviii, 109, 120
New Millennium, 222
newspapers, xvi, 11, 17, 31, 32, 110, 159, 175, 176, 177, 178, 180, 187, 205, 206, 241
newsroom, 31, 50, 177
Nin, Anaïs, 28
Nissan, 1, 3, 4, 70
Norton, Jay, 111, 112, 113, 258
Obama, Barak, 45
obstruction of justice, xxiii, 56, 127, 144, 159, 196, 220, 261
Odell, Carl L., 12
Office of Inspector General, 164
officers, SAPD, xxv, 217, 229
Ogbu, Portia, 27
Operation Snow White, 142, 143, 144, 150
operatives, Allstate, xxv, 80, 168, 214
Operators, 170
opioid, 250, 256
Oregonian, The, 32, 33
organized criminal networks, 171, 196, 245
orthopedic, 3, 4
OxyContin, 250
Pacific Northwest, 31
Padilla, Gloria, 176
paramilitary, 168
Paris, Ted, 247
Pearson, Donald, 15
Pecker, David, 169
Peeples, David, 196
Peña, Erica, 133, 137
Peña, Juan, 117
penalty, 23, 31, 125, 250
Pennebaker, Douglas, 255
Pentagon, the, 27
Perez, Manuel, 155, 156
Petty, Keely, 174
Phelan, James, 81, 82, 83, 87, 153, 217

Philadelphia Contributionship, 11, 12
Phillips, Bobby Joe, 216, 218, 219
Phipps, Martin, 101, 255, 256
pillbillies, 250
Pinchback v. Hockless, 41
PIP, 4, 50
Pitman Sullivan Park, 82
Pittman, Robert L., 47, 124, 125, 220
Poker, 22
policyholder, 5, 7, 13
policyholders, xviii, xix, xxi, 7
Politico, 21
Port Arthur, Texas, 117
Portfolio Recovery Associates, 178
Portland, OR, 9, 32, 46
Portland, Oregon, 9
Pozza, Karen, 96, 114, 220, 253
Price, Richard, 53
Primomo, John, 122, 124, 125, 157, 220, 254
private intelligence firms, xxii, xxiii, 129, 168, 169, 170, 217
private investigators, 92, 118, 159, 212, 242, 257, 261
pro se, xx, 7, 9, 39, 52, 55, 71, 120, 123, 130, 133, 161, 176, 207, 208
Promise Zones, 45
Prop B, 218
propia persona. See pro se
Proposition B, 218
prosecutors, xvii, 62, 97, 109, 110, 112, 129, 130, 131, 132, 133, 134, 136, 137, 140, 141, 191, 224, 225, 259, 261, 262, 263
psyche designation, 142, 232
Purdue Pharma, 244, 250
Putin, Vladimir, 217
Pytel, Jack, 117
Quantico, 121
racial integration, 31
Racketeer Influenced and Corrupt Organizations Act, 221
Rangel, Ron, 263
Rathbun, Marty, 253
Rathbun, Monique, 253
Real de Catorce, SLP, Mexico, 140
Reem, Anthony, 109
Reiningers, the, 245, 246
Remini, Leah, 16, 245
   Scientology and the Aftermath, 245
Renaud Gonzalez, Barbara, 188, 195

Rene. *See* McVea, Rene
Republicans, 227
Resendez, Eloy, 238
Richards, Ann, 149, 150
RICO, 221, 223, *See* Racketeer Influenced and Corrupt Organizations Act
Rife Market Research, 27
Rio Grande River, 35
Rio Grande Valley, 109
Roberts, Scott, 96, 129, 130, 131, 132, 133, 136, 138, 140, 141, 178, 180, 191, 204, 220, 257, 263
Rock, Paper, Scissors, 243
Rossi, Lisa, 28
Ruhd, Dustin, 228, 238
Ruiz Street, 115
Saldaña, Gloria, 44
Sam Houston High School, 25, 26
San Antonians, xvi, xvii, xxiii, 36, 174, 182, 218, 220
San Antonio, ii, xiii, xiv, xv, xvi, xvii, xxi, xxii, xxiii, 1, 3, 6, 23, 28, 29, 30, 34, 35, 36, 37, 45, 48, 57, 65, 66, 73, 78, 80, 81, 83, 84, 93, 96, 98, 107, 111, 113, 114, 117, 119, 120, 128, 133, 139, 143, 150, 152, 153, 159, 160, 162, 163, 165, 166, 168, 169,170, 172, 173, 175, 177, 178, 182, 184, 188, 189, 190, 195, 197, 198, 202, 205, 206, 210, 211, 214, 216, 217, 218, 219, 220, 221, 223, 225, 228, 231, 233, 235, 237, 240, 244, 245, 246, 254, 258, 260, 261, 263, 265, 277
San Antonio Community College, 26
San Antonio Express-News, xvi, 107, 159, 172, 174, 175, 176, 178, 184, 185, 186, 187, 197, 198, 261, 263, 277
San Antonio Police Department, 233, *See* SAPD
San Francisco, 27
San Luis Potosí, 34, 139
San Marcos, Texas, 54
Sanchez, Lauren, 169
sanctions, 52, 69, 115, 116, 117, 121, 122, 125
Santos, Danny, 85, 138
SAPD, xvi, xxiv, 61, 62, 64, 65, 77, 82, 83, 89, 97, 121, 122, 126, 132, 137, 138, 141, 154, 156, 157, 165, 169, 174, 201, 210, 216, 217, 218, 222, 223, 229, 232, 233, 234, 235, 254, 256, *See* San Antonio Police Department, *See* San Antonio Police Department
Sartre, Jean-Paul, 28
Schaeffer, Tylden, 277
Schulze, Julieta Rabago, 196, 198
Scientologists, 15, 16, 17, 22, 56, 143, 144, 145, 146, 222, 241
Scientology, 14, 15, 16, 17, 18, 19, 21, 22, 143, 144, 145, 146, 147, 150, 222, 241, 244, 245, 249, 253
Scott, Daniel, 79, 122
Sculley, Sheryl, 36, 37
Sears, 12, 13, 14
Section 8, 46
security guard, xiii, 57, 58, 61, 63, 64, 65, 92, 126, 173, 261
Sedillo, Larry, 249
Seimer, Michael, 120, 121, 122, 157
Senate judiciary committee, xxi
Senate Judiciary Committee, 164
Serratorubio, Martin, 138
Shannon, Michael, 237
sicarios,, 140
Simpson, Nicole, 50
Simpson, O.J., 50
Skilling, Jeffrey, 20, 251
Skinner, Melisa, 254
slumlord, 33
Snell, John, 32
social fabric, xvii, 173, 181
Sonterra Boulevard, 91
Soros, George, xiv, 180
South New Braunfels Avenue, 219
South Texas, 173
Southwest Worker's Union, 133
Southwestern Bell, 26
Sparks, Mary, 30
Spence, Deborah, 186, 188
St. Patrick's Catholic School, 25, 28
St. Philip's Community College, 47
Staff Attorney's Office, District Court, 39, 40, 42, 43, 44, 94, 127, 196, 206, 207, 208, 262
State Farm, xxi, 7
State of Texas v. Denise McVea, 104, 129, 262
Statewide Patrol, xiii, 58, 64, 65

Steinbeck, John, 28
Stingrays. *See* IMSI catchers
Stone, Catherine, 114
Strong, Mark, 241
Studebaker, 13
Sullivan-Smith, Jada, 188
summary judgment, 52, 53, 54, 56, 72, 76, 122, 124, 125, 126
Supreme Court, 38, 40, 41, 252
Supreme Court of Texas, The, 40
surveillance, 16, 72, 111, 125, 126, 132, 142, 147, 148, 149, 162, 168, 172, 213, 221, 222, 227, 230, 253
Swan, Joseph, 78, 79
Tampa Bay Times, 241
Taylor, Ivy, 173
Texas, ii, xxi, xxii, xxiii, 6, 8, 9, 17, 25, 26, 28, 31, 33, 35, 36, 39, 41, 46, 51, 52, 55, 61, 65, 69, 70, 91, 92, 93, 95, 96, 101, 103, 104, 109, 114, 117, 122, 125, 129, 130, 131, 138, 140, 141, 148, 149, 150, 157, 158, 159, 161, 162, 170, 173, 178, 179, 181, 182, 190, 193, 194, 196, 209, 211, 214, 220, 225, 227, 245, 246, 249, 251, 252, 265
Texas Civil Rights Project, 133, 157, 158, 159, 173
Texas Department of Insurance, 148, 249
Texas Judicial Commission, 8
Texas Public Radio, 256
Texas Region
Allstate, 249
Texas Republic, 35
Texas Revolution, 193, 194
Texas State Board of Plumbing Examiners, 241
Texas Woman's University, 30
Tex-Mex, 36
the Claude Black Community Center, 186, 188
The Dallas Morning News, 31
the Electoral College, 254
The Naughty Table, 183, 186, 187
The Oregonian, 31
The Texas Department of Insurance, 23
The Washington Post, 202
Thetans, 15
Thomas, Ananda "Sunshine", 218
Thomas, Dave, 131
Thomaston, Maine, 242
Tic-Tac-Toe, 243
title company, 115
Tohmaz, Amin, 240
Tower of the Americas, 46
Treviño, Gustavo and Carolina, 47
Trial Lawyers Association, xx
Trinity University, 69
Trump administration, 20, 21
Trump, Donald, 67, 227, 254
Trusted Driver Program, 257
Tullis, James, 81, 83
tumor, 27
TWU. *See* Texas Woman's University
U.S. Attorney General, 166
U.S. Attorney's Office, 67, 225
U.S. Federal Bureau of Investigation, xvi, 66
U.S. Homeland Security, 139
unauthorized practice of law, 55, 56, 178, 252
United States, 7, 14, 21, 22, 23, 24, 27, 34, 36, 67, 125, 143, 145, 146, 165, 168, 169, 170, 171, 202, 217, 223, 224, 225, 227
United States., 14, 36, 67, 143, 169, 223, 225
University of Guanajuato, 33
University of Texas Health Science Center, 57
UPLC. *See* unauthorized practice of law
Urban Rehabilitation Standards Board, 9
Urban, Hugh B., 16
USA Gymnastics, 164
UTSA, 92
Uzomba, Grace, 176
Valadez, Christian, 232, 252
Valero gas station, 1
Vanessa. *See* Esbry, Vanessa
Vangheluwe, Brett, 40, 43, 44, 127, 207, 208
Velasquez, Willie, 188
Venezia, Cathy, 28
Vietnam, 24, 25, 27, 250
Vietnam jungles. *See* Vietnam
Volunteers, 34
Wall Street Journal, 15, 17
Washington, D.C., 171
Watts, Mikal, 256, 257
Weinstein, Harvey, xxiii, 169

Wells, Ida B., 32
Wendell, Ware, 178, 179
Westside, xvii, 115, 240
white male historian. *See* historians, white male
Whitley, Deanna L., 178
whore, 108, 110, 258
Wiegand, Marc, 253
Wilson, Robert W., 189
Wilson, Tom, 246, 249
Windcrest, TX, 257
Winfrey, Oprah, 195
wiretap, 165, 166, 177
wiretapping, 67, 72, 107, 113, 144, 222
Wood, Robert E., 12
Worst Insurance Companies in America, xx, 277
Wreck, 1
Wright, Alexis, 241, 242

Wymer, Matthew, 49, 50, 51, 52, 101
Wyoming Street, 152, 211, 237, 239
Young, Michael, 65
Yucatan University, 194
yucatecos, 195
Zabihian, Ahmad, 197
Zapata, Jaime, 139
Zavala Urtecho, Wilbert Fernando, 193, 194
Zavala, Lorenzo de, 193, 194
Zavala, Wilbert, 193, 195
zero sum game, xix, xxii, xxiii, 7, 21, 22, 23, 64, 67, 72, 80, 84, 97, 163, 168, 214, 227, 243, 244, 250, 253
Zero Sum Game, the, 243
zeroes, 142, 170, 171, 211, 212, 214, 236
zombies, 171, 193, 199, 213, 214
Zoom, 214, 228
Zumba, 241

NOTES

1. Tylden Schaeffer.
2. Chasnoff, Brian. "Gonzales recruited old colleagues to server under him." *San Antonio Express-News*, Jan. 5, 2019.
3. Zavala, Elizabeth. "DA won't prosecute San Antonio instigators in death of Madison High grad," *San Antonio Express-News*, July 12, 2019.
4. https://law.cornell.edu.
5. Berardinelli, David J. *From Good Hands to Boxing Gloves*, p.33. Trial Guides, 2008.
6. "Auto insurers play hardball in minor-crash claims," CNN, Feb. 9, 2007. Archived from the original on March 24, 2010.
7. "The Ten Worst Insurance Companies in America," American Association for Justice.
8. Testimony of J. Robert Hunter, Director of Insurance, Consumer Federation of America, Before the Committee on the U.S. Senate Judiciary regarding the McCarran-Ferguson Act: Implications of Repealing the Insurer's Anti-trust Exemption March 7, 2007.
9. The ability to deny involvement in illegal or unethical activities because there is no clear evidence to prove involvement. *Political Dictionary*.
10. Discovery is the legal process by which each party in a lawsuit can obtain evidence from the other party.
11. Testimonials, https://allstateinsurancesucks.com.
12. Source: Self-Represented Litigation Network.

13 Jordan, John W. "The Fellowship Fire Company of Philadelphia, Organized 1738," Also *The Pennsylvania Magazine of History and Biography*, Vol. 27, No. 4 (1903), pp. 472-481.
14 "The Ten Worst Insurance Companies in America," American Association for Justice, undated.
15 https://xenu- directory.net
16 "Allstate Acknowledges Scientology Training Program Was A Blunder," Associated Press, March 22, 1995.
17 Evans, Jim. "Scientology Inc." *Sacramento News & Review*, Aug. 23, 2001.
18 Saunders, John. "How Scientology's message came to Allstate," *Globe and Mail* (Canada), April 24, 1995.
19 Labaton, Stephen. "Scientologists granted tax exemption by the U.S." *The New York Times*. Oct. 14, 1993.
20 Labaton, Stephen.
21 Remini, Leah. "Leah Remini: Scientology and the Aftermath", the Intellectual Property Company, A&E, 2016.
22 Urban, Hugh B. "Fair Game: Secrecy, Security, and the Church of Scientology in Cold War America", *Journal of the American Academy of Religion*, Volume 74, Number 2, June 2006, pp. 356– 389. Oxford University Press. Also, Behar, Richard. "The Thriving Cult of Greed and Power," *Time*, May 6, 1991.
23 Wakefield, Margery. "Understanding Scientology," Chapter 11: Ethics – The Greatest Good for the Greatest Number of Dynamics. https://www.cs.cmu.edu/~dst/Library/Shelf/wakefield/us- 11.html8/
24 "Allstate Says Scientology Training Was Mistake," Associated Press, March 22, 1995.
25 Reprint of *Wall Street Journal* article, March 22, 1995. https://www.lermanet.org/scientologynews/allstate.html.
26 Raymond, Nate. "Ex-McKinsey Partner Arrested for Fraudulent Invoices, Expense." *Reuters*. Jan. 4, 2016, and "Former Partner in Global Consulting Firm Sentenced to Two Years in Federal Prison for Billing $586,000 in Bogus Consulting work and Travel Expenses," United States Attorney's Office, Northern District of Illinois, March 15, 2018.
27 McDougall, Ian. "McKinsey Called Our Story About Its ICE Contract False. It's not." ProPublica. Dec. 16, 2019.
28 Bertrand, Natasha and Daniel Lippman. "Spies fear a consulting firm helped hobble U.S. intelligence," Politico, July 2, 2019.

29 Bertrand, and Lippman.
30 MacDougall, Ian. "How McKinsey is Making $100 Million (and Counting) advising on the Government's Bumbling Coronavirus Response." *ProPublica*, July 15, 2020.
31 Berardinelli.
32 Schorey, Shannon Trosper. "Religion is Free, $cientology is Neither," Master's Thesis, Department of Religious Studies, University of Colorado, 2012.
33 Schorey.
34 "Ten Worst", AAJ, page 4.
35 Foster, Haley. "Agent Orange: It's affecting veterans and their kids," *State Veteran News*, North Dakota Department of Veteran Affairs, March 23, 2015
36 McVea, Denise. *Making Myth of Emily: Emily West de Zavala and the Yellow Rose of Texas Legend*, Auris Books Press, 2005.
37 Torralva, Krista. "Segregation still haunts S.A. schools," *San Antonio Express-News*. Aug. 2, 2020.
38 Garcia, Gilbert. "Scandal-plagued '90s councilman attempts a comeback." *San Antonio Express-News*, March 22, 2019.
39 Sculley, Sheryl. *Greedy Bastards*, Lioncrest Publishing, 2020.
40 Jefferson, Greg. "City Manager Sheryl Sculley Has Her Detractors. We Sort Out a Few of the Reasons." *San Antonio Current*, April 10, 2018.
41 *Goffney v. Lowry*, 554 SW 2d 157, Tex-Supreme Court 1977, Google Scholar.
42 *Pinchback v. Hockless*, 139 Tex. 536, 164S.W.2d 19 (Tex.Com.App. 1942)
43 "Bubble town" is former colleague's term for prosperous neighborhoods that incorporate their own municipality although surrounded by a larger, poorer city.
44 Summary judgment is a discretionary tool judges use to dismiss cases before evidence can be presented to a jury. It is ripe for judicial abuse and perhaps the greatest enemy of the poor seeking justice in Texas.
45 SAPD Officer Robert Munoz, San Antonio Police Department Offense Case # SAPD11046131, Feb. 23, 2011.
46 Italics added.
47 Special agents assigned on a daily basis to meet with complaining citizens and tipsters.
48 Leifer, Jack. "Leifer Report" Cause No. 2010-CI-11896, *McVea v. Keller*, et al. March 16, 2012.

49 Appellant/Defendant Denise McVea's Out-of-Time Motion for New Trial Based on Newly Discovered Evidence, Cause No. 2013-CI-14927 with Movant's Supporting Affidavit and Attachments. June 30, 2014.
50 Forced error: A mistake in play attributed to the skill or effort of one's opponent rather than one's own misjudgment. Lexico.com
51 Morris, Angela. "Judge texted, 'I'm a whore for money,' alleges bribery indictment," *Texas Lawyer*, June 20, 2014.
52 Venema, Paul. "Confessed killer gets 2 life sentences, leaves courtroom singing," KSAT.com, July 24, 2017.
53 *Sealed Appellant v. Sealed Appellant*, U.S. Court of Appeals, Fifth Circuit, Case No.17-50487, Doc. No. 00514605935, Aug.17, 2018.
54 *Sealed Appellant v. Sealed Appellant*.
55 Ibid.
56 Ibid.
57 Ibid.
58 *U.S. v. Search of Law Office*, Residence and Storage Unit of Alan Brown, Cause No. 02-51031, U.S. Court of Appeals, Fifth Circuit. July 31, 2003.
59 Bragman, Walker. "Americans are at least $27.6 Billion in Debt to Courts." *Jacobin*, June 23, 2021.
60 The firm also briefly collected taxes for the IRS, but that contract was short lived. Ellis, Blake and Melanie Hicken. "The story of Linebarger Goggan Blair and Sampson." CNN Money, Feb. 17, 2015.
61 Thomas, Mike W. "Prison sentences handed down in city hall corruption case." *San Antonio Business Journal*, March 31, 2005.
62 Rood, Lee. "County attorneys, courts spar over debt collector." *Des Moines Register*, July 23, 2015.
63 Ellis, Blake and Melanie Hicken. The debt collector that runs Texas, CNN Money, Feb. 17, 2015.
64 Anderson, Kristin M., RPR. "Transcript of Motion Hearing Proceedings before the Hon. David A. Ezra," *McVea v. Swan*. SA: 14-CV-00073-DAE, U.S. District Court-Western District of Texas, Dec. 16, 2014.
65 Pittman, Robert L. Order and Opinion, *McVea v. Swan*, 5:14-CV-073-RP, U.S. District Court-Western District of Texas, July 17, 2015.
66 Ibid.
67 Affidavit of Teresa Butolph, July 28, 2014.
68 Latin for "on the face of it," accepted as correct until proven otherwise.

69 Offense Case #SAPD13252834, San Antonio Police Department, San Antonio, Texas, Nov.16, 2013.
70 Wilkinson, Tracy. "U.S. agent killed, second wounded at Mexico drug gang blockade," *Los Angeles Times*, Feb. 16, 2011.
71 Urban, Hugh B. "Fair Game: Secrecy, Security, and the Church of Scientology in Cold War America,"*Journal of the American Academy of Religion*, Volume 74, Number 2, June 2006, pp. 356– 389. Oxford University Press. Also Behar, Richard. "The Thriving Cult of Greed and Power," *Time*, May 6, 1991.
72 Welkos, Robert W. and Joel Sappell. "Burglaries and Lies Paved a Path to Prison," *Los Angeles Times*, June 24, 1990.
73 *United States v. Mary Sue Hubbard et a*l., 493 F. Supp. 209 (D.D.C. 1979)
74 Morgan, Lucy. "Critics Public and Private Keep Pressure on Scientology//Abroad," *Tampa Bay Times*, July 6, 2006.
75 "List of Guardian's Office operations," Wikipedia.org.
76 Behar, Richard, Jane Furth and Tricia Welsh. "Stalked by Allstate: Being an agent for the insurer can be tough – even terrifying," *Fortune*, October 2, 1995.
77 Ibid.
78 Ibid.
79 Ibid.
80 Ibid.
81 Ibid.
82 Ibid.
83 Ibid.
84 Ibid.
85 Letter, Denise McVea to Mimi Marziani, Texas Civil Rights Project, Oct. 1, 2016.
86 Letter, Denise McVea to Kevin Levine, Sunset Advisory Commission, Oct. 6, 2016.
87 Fox, Ben. "U.S. cyber security agency warns of 'grave' threat to government from attack," Associated Press, Washington, D.C. Dec. 17, 2020.
88 Turton, William. "Hackers used obscure Texas vendor to attack U.S. agencies," *Bloomberg News*, Dec. 14, 2020.
89 Report. "Investigation and Review of the Federal Bureau of Investigation's Handling of Allegations of Sexual Abuse by Former USA Gymnastics Physician Lawrence Gerard Nassar," Office of the Inspector General, Department of Justice, 21-093, July 2021.

90 Video clip. "Watch: McKayla Maroney says FBI made up statements she never said to protect Larry Nassar." PBS NewsHour, https://www.youtube.com, Sept. 15, 2021.
91 Crane, Emily. "FBI agent fired for failing to properly investigate Larry Nassar," *New York Post*, Sept. 15, 2021.
92 Mustian, Jim. "A murder 20 years ago marked low point for NOPD," *The Advocate*, Oct. 15, 2014.
93 Ward, Marguerite. "The U.S. is going backward in terms of social progress, a global survey shows," *Inside*r, September 11, 2020.
94 Farrow, Ronan. "Harvey Weinstein's Army of Spies." *The New Yorker*, November 6, 2017.
87 Calberg, Sue. "'Really concerned': Five suicides in seven months, SAPD says."KENS-5, October 14, 2022
96 *Labella v. Fed. Bureau of Investigation*, 11-CV-0023 (nGG) (LB) (E.D.N.Y. Mar. 16, 2012).
97 Eaton, Emilie. "Numbers don't tell full story of crime." *San Antonio Express-News*, Oct.15, 2017.
98 Ibid.
99 Morris, Allie. "Eyes in sky for border often trained on S.A." Austin Bureau, *San Antonio Express-News*, Nov. 5, 2017.
100 Vega, Melissa. "FBI enlists public's help to continue to fight against corruption." Fox 29, March 28, 2017.
101 Padilla, Gloria. "Partisan sweeps chaos into these courts," *San Antonio-Express News*, March 3, 2020.
102 Abernathy, Penny. "The State of Local News," *Local News Initiative*, Northwestern University, June 29, 2022.
103 I would try again in 2022. Local organizers turned out the lights and declared the county convention over when I attempted to introduce the resolution to delegates. I have no idea what became of the anti-corruption resolution.
104 Guenther, Rocío. "Manuel Medina: From Mexico to County Democratic Chairman, *San Antonio Report*, Feb. 17, 2017.
105 Davies, David Martin. "Questions Rise About Manuel Medina's Many Roles in Bexar County Democratic Party," Texas Public Radio, TRP.org. May 12, 2017.
106 Davies, David Martin, "Questions Rise," TPR.
107 Ibid.

108 McVea, Denise. "The Naughty Table: A group loyal to former BCDP chairman Manuel Medina is wreaking havoc within the local parry. But what are they trying to hide?" *Lamp*, San Antonio, Winter 2019.
109 Ibid.
110 Lefko, Jim. "Local Democratic Party officials accused by chair of financial improprieties," News4SA, March 13, 2019.
111 Ibid.
112 Huddleston, Scott. "In San Antonio, the Democratic Party is still putting out factional fires." *San Antonio Express-News*, Jan. 14, 2020.
113 Ibid..
114 Velasquez, JJ. "Bexar Democrats Remain at Odds as Medina Loyalists Reinstated." *San Antonio Report*, May 16, 2019.
115 Ibid.
116 Doc# 20130188778, 09/09/2013, Official Public Records of Bexar County Gerard C. Rickoff, County Clerk.
117 Ibid.
118 "Catalogue of copies of historical research documents regarding Lorenzo de Zavala's experiences in the United States and Texas." Denise McVea Collection, Universidad Autónoma de Yucatan, 2020.
119 Danner, Patrick. "Trial ends with odd twist as jurors rule against San Antonio dealer who sued automaker," *San Antonio Express-News*, Aug. 30, 2019.
120 Ibid.
121 Robbins, Liz. "Post Office fails to deliver on time, and DACA applications get rejected," *The New York Times*, Nov. 10, 2017.
122 Oxner, Reese and Abby Livingston. "San Antonio postal office hid problems from Joaquin Castro," *Texas Tribune*, Aug. 20, 2020.
123 "The Untold Story of the Texas Revolution," East-West Series. Curator: Fabiola Ochoa Torralba, San Antonio, August 28, 2020.
124 Simmons, Keir, interviewer. "Exclusive: full interview with Russian President Vladimir Putin." NBC News, June 14, 2021.
125 "Fear City: New York v. the Mafia," directed by Sam Hobkinson, Raw Television and Brillstein Entertainment Partners, 2020.
126 The most famous of the groups, the Guardian Angels, gained nationwide attention for patrolling the subways and streets to protect citizens from random street crime.

127 Blakey, G. Robert. "RICO: The genesis of an idea." *Trends in Organized Crime.* Piscataway, New Jersey, Jan. 6, 2006.
128 Final Report of the National Commission on Terrorist Attacks Upon the United States, 401,408 (2004).)
129 Barnes, Julian E. and Adam Goldman. "Captured, Killed or Compromised: CIA admits to losing dozens of informants." *The New York Times,* Oct. 5, 2021.
130 Report: "Under Color of Law," Transactional Records Access Clearinghouse, Syracuse University, 2004.
131 https://trac.syr.edu/tracreports/civright/107/.
132 Mohdin, Aamna. "UN calls for end of "impunity" for police violence against black people," *The Guardian,* June 28, 2021.
133 https://perspectives.ushmm.org/item/film-of-austrian-police-during-the-german-annexation-of-austria, TRAC, Dec.1, 2004
134 Documentary: Garbus, Liz, director. "The Nazi Officer's Wife", based on the book by Edith Hahn. Narrated by Susan Sarandon, 2003.
135 Gonzalez, Irving and Levon Harrison. San Antonio Police Department Incident Report SAPD-2020-0647507, May 29, 2020.
136 Weiss, Debra Cassens. "Lawyer who told Big Law attorneys to 'eat a bowl of dicks' faces possible sanctions," *ABA Journal,* Dec. 11, 2019.
137 Sabawi, Fares. "Records: Officer who fatally shot mentally ill woman handed suspension for protocol breaches," MySA.com, Aug. 22, 2018
138 Downs, Caleb. "Friends remember mentally ill S.A. mom who was shot as loving, troubled," *San Antonio Express-News,* Feb. 1, 2918.
112 Sabawi, Fares. "Records: Officer who fatally shot mentally ill woman handed suspension for protocol breaches," MySA.com, Aug. 22, 2018.
140 Haney, Stephanie. "Texas woman who said she was being stalked is shot dead by the police responding to her call for help," *Daily Mail,* dailymail.co.uk, Jan. 29, 2018.
141 McVea, Denise. "Conspiracy Theater: Eastside Promise Zone, Westside become theaters for white-collar criminal conspiracies to drain wealth from unprotected SA communities," Auris Press, https://bit.ly/conspiracytheater, July 2022.
142 https://www.bit/ly/conspiracytheater.
143 Way, Heather. "Ousted: The City of San Antonio's Displacement of Residents through Code Enforcement Actions." The Entrepreneurship and Community Development Clinic, University of Texas at Austin School of Law, Nov. 23, 2021.

144 McManus, Tracey. "Clear Takeover" *Tampa Bay Times*, Oct. 20, 2019.
145 McClean, Bethany. "Town of Whispers", *Vanity Fair*, Feb. 2013.
146 Atmonson, Yuval. "To develop a winning strategy, know who you are fighting." *McKinsey Quarterly*. June 27, 2017.
147 Beers, Tommy. "Top 1% of U.S. Households Hold 15 Times More Wealth Than Bottom 50% Combined," *Forbes*, Oct. 8, 2020.
148 Atmonson, Yuval, "To develop a winning strategy, know who you are fighting." *McKinsey Quarterly*. June 27, 2017.
149 Literally meaning "the rule by thieves," kleptocracy is a form of political corruption in which the ruling government seeks personal gain and status at the expense of the governed, typically by misappropriating government funds.
150 Hobkinson, Sam. "Fear City: New York vs. the Mafia," Raw Television, Brillstein Entertainment Partners.
151 *Allstate Vehicle and Prop. Ins. Co. v. Reininger*, No. 04-19-00443-CV, 2020 WL 6928405 (Tex. App.-San Antonio Nov. 25, 2020).
152 Daniels, Steve. "Allstate angers agents with sudden pay cut," *Crain's Chicago Business*, Nov. 1, 2019.
153 Compensation Information for Thomas J. Wilson, Chair, President, and Chief Executive Officer of ALLSTATE CORP, Salary.com.
154 Daniels, Steve. "Allstate angers agents with sudden pay cut," *Crain's Chicago Business*, Nov. 1, 2019.
155 Ibid.
156 Press Release. "Allstate Corporation acquisition of National General Holdings Corp closes," https://www.liveinsurancenews.com/national- general- holdings- corp/8550569/2/5. Jan. 7, 2021.
157 "Allstate insider Trading history," MarketBeat, date of trade: May 8, 2020.
158 Husna, Asma Ul. "Is The Allstate Corporation (ALL) Going to Burn These Hedge Funds?" https://finance.yahoo.com, Oct. 18, 2021.
159 "Crist Appointed Field Vice President of Allstate's Texas Region." *Insurance Journal*, Feb. 10, 2006.
160 Whoriskey, Peter and Christopher Rowland. "McKinsey, advisor to businesses around the world, agrees to pay $573.9 million to settle charges for its role in opioid epidemic." *The Washington Post*, Feb. 4, 2021.
161 Hart, Benjamin and Andrew Rice. "What a Spectacularly Ill-Advised Idea Says About McKinsey." *Intelligencer*. Nov. 30, 2020.

162 McGreal, Chris. "Big pharma executives mocked 'pillbillies' in emails, West Virginia opioid trial hears." *The Guardian*, May 16, 2021.
163 Whoriskey, Peter and Christopher Rowland. "McKinsey, advisor to businesses around the world, agrees to pay $573.9 million to settle charges for its role in opioid epidemic." *The Washington Post*, Feb. 4, 2021.
164 Morgenson, Gretchen. "Consulting giant McKinsey allegedly fed the opioid crisis. Now an affiliate may profit from treating addicts." NBC News. Feb. 8, 2021.
165 Ortega, Tony. "Ray Jeffrey to Judge: Order Rathbun to Turn Over Financial Records and Testify," https://www.tonyortega.org, *Underground Bunker*, July 24, 2017.
166 Correspondent, The Carpenter's Apprentice video blog.
167 Contreras, Guillermo. "SA judge under fire for telling new citizens to accept Trump or 'go to another country.'" *Houston Chronicle*, November 21, 2016.
168 Danner, Patrick. "2 San Antonio bars, prominent attorneys, carmaker named in wrongful-death suit over 2019 crash." *San Antonio Express-News*, November 12, 2021.
169 Ibid.
170 Flahive, Paul. "Reporting on Deadly Collision Leads to Legal Threats against Journalist." Texas Public Radio, May 6, 2021.
171 Flahive, Paul. "Strange court saga for Martin Phipps takes a stranger turn," Texas Public Radio, July 20, 2021.
172 Cabrera, Kristen. "Former San Antonio police officer wants to 'save lives' with ticket-texting program," Texas Standard, TPR.org, Jan. 26, 2022.
173 Baucum, Emily. "How deep does courthouse corruption run?" NEWS 4 San Antonio, July 16, 2015.
174 Selcraig, Bruce. "New D.A. Gonzales wants to review acquittal in dismemberment case," *San Antonio Express-News*, Dec. 17, 2018.

Made in the USA
Monee, IL
29 July 2025